THE DESCENDANT OF DARKNESS

BY JUSTIN LANCASTER

authorHOUSE®

AuthorHouse™
1663 Liberty Drive
Bloomington, IN 47403
www.authorhouse.com
Phone: 1 (800) 839-8640

Published by AuthorHouse   07/06/2017

ISBN: 978-1-5246-9853-9 (sc)
ISBN: 978-1-5246-9851-5 (hc)
ISBN: 978-1-5246-9852-2 (e)

Library of Congress Control Number: 2017910273

Print information available on the last page.

Any people depicted in stock imagery provided by Thinkstock are models,
and such images are being used for illustrative purposes only.
Certain stock imagery © Thinkstock.

This book is printed on acid-free paper.

ACT I

NOVEMBER 24, 2015

This is the first entry in what I hope to be a lengthy and successful journal. At this point, I am uncertain as to the content of this journal in addition to the classifications of said content. I am unsure as to who will have unparalleled satisfaction or utter misery by reading this journal. In fact, I'm quite suspicious as to if anyone will ever read this journal. Either way, the hope of rejuvenating my desire to unveil imagination in the form of writing is undeniably a priority. However, this is a daunting task; the thought alone covers my poor beating heart in a cold blanket of fear. It is appropriate for this thought to bring my world into a catastrophic darkness, mainly due to the abnormal reasoning behind the creation of this journal. But I will not go into detail at the present. I voice my apologies, but another equally intriguing thought has entered my head.

My father always wanted me to write a journal. I just referred to my dad as "my father," and that confuses me. I don't call my dad "Father," nor have I ever called my mom "Mother." Does this make me a liar? Are my words no different from those of a compulsive liar? It's also possible I'm over analyzing my own thought, which results in self-criticism. It would be soothing to know I'm not the only person who thinks intensely about almost everything.

Anyway, my dad always wanted me to write a journal. I never really understood why he, of all people, wanted me to keep a record of my thoughts. He has never seemed to enjoy writing, although he is very scientific and philosophical. Those are two passions I hope he explores further in his life, maybe after retirement. My only theory is that my dad has or had a secret passion for literature. He enjoys reading books—I know this as a fact—but I have never seen him write. His dad, my grandpa, is an avid writer, as am I, so it would make sense if my dad were also a writer. I don't know, and I have no intentions of asking. Still, my dad wanted me to start a journal.

"You know, it'd be great if you wrote in a journal every day."

"Why?" I asked. I was slightly perplexed by the idea, but I didn't let on to it.

"You should really write down all the things that happen in your life so someday in the future you can look back on everything. Or maybe it would just be a good idea to record your thoughts. But it's not an eight-year-old girl's diary. It should be a little more sophisticated."

That's basically how that conversation went; at least, that's what I remember from it. I'm not sure why, but it has stuck with me for a long time. It has probably been over two years since that conversation, but right now, as I write these words, the memory resonates strongly in my head. Finally, I am writing in a journal. I hope this journal brings some peace of mind to either myself or someone else.

I haven't quite decided how I would like to organize this journal. Should I speak in proper format or should I speak informally? Should I use a combination of both to appease my audience? Who is my audience? What will I include in the content of this journal? Am I telling the story of myself, or am I writing a collective story of others based upon my unique perspective? Is that even possible? The answer to all of those questions is simple: I have no idea. I should note that the writing style will most likely vary throughout the journal, and for that I apologize. However, the variation of style grants an interesting read—that is, if anyone is reading this entry or any of the entries that will soon follow.

Reader, if you have read this far into the introduction of this journal, I hope you continue to do so. Why are you reading this? Where are you reading this? Most importantly, how are you reading this? Are you casually browsing this journal in the vague hope of discovering something you would actually like to read? I promise there will be enjoyable moments, although the extent of that joy I cannot and will not promise. I enjoy the thought of an audience, but I hope to strike a personal connection with each reader. I do not want to write words that only tell a story. Stories have endings. I am a living and breathing person; therefore, my story continues until I die. But my story does not end when I die. At least, I urge myself to think in that manner. These words do not die because words are not alive, although I will try my best to test the limits of imagination. These words should be more important than a story because this is more than a story to me. These words are my life.

I had an epiphany before I started this journal. The epiphany struck a chord with me, and I felt it was something of substance that I should share. For the longest time, I have struggled to produce a genuine and decent story. It bothered me to the point where I gave up writing as a whole, which bothered me further. Basically, I quit. I gave up. Forfeit. Game over. I used to write poetry, too, but I stopped doing that because I realized I wasn't very good at writing poetry.

Back to the epiphany. I struggled to write unique poems, but even more so I struggled to write stories. Every time I tried to write a story, I duly realized that my story was neither original nor good. I was angry because I do have an active imagination, and I can be insanely creative. Yet, to my dismay, I failed to complete even a simple short story. I was angry. I am not a famed writer. I am not J. D. Salinger or Ray Bradbury or Charles Dickens or John Steinbeck. If anything, I am nothing more than a lone character in the gloom-stricken pages of a story.

That is when I realized my worrying should be over, because the greatest classic of all time has yet to be written. My classic has been in front of my eyes for years, and yet it has somehow eluded my grasp. The greatest story is the story I am living, and that story is called *life*. I am the main character, and all the people in my life are the other characters. Never again shall I struggle to invent some worthless character with an equally fake name. Instead, I can pick one of the billions of unique people to include in my story. The possibilities are infinite, and I mean this figuratively because the number of humans is a finite number. Nonetheless, I have characters of complexity in my story. The plot could not be any simpler: my life and everything that happens in it. Is that not the most unique story of all time? There is only one of myself, and my story is special. However, this is not simply an autobiography. I am developing a story with each passing second, and it is my duty to record it. Perhaps I am writing a piece of history, and maybe my name will be remembered in the future. It is a pleasant thought.

That was my epiphany, which granted me the power to begin this story—although the "story" actually began a little over sixteen years ago. If you, reader, by some chance already know who I am, that is wonderful. However, if you do not know me, do not fret, for I will explain myself in time. I'm fairly interesting, or at least I'd like to think so.

It is with regret that I must close the first entry of my journal. It is late, and I really should get some sleep, even though the mysteries of the night are an excellent reason to continue writing. Nighttime produces crazy ideas. Anyway, my introduction is complete. I hope it was not too lengthy and boring. Good night.

NOVEMBER 25, 2015

Today my adventure truly begins. I woke up this morning feeling refreshed, and I was excited to start writing. Now, I could go through my entire morning routine by meticulously recording everything I do to get ready in the morning, but I've decided against that. It would be like the opening scene of a movie—I am most specifically thinking of the cult classic *Office Space*. That movie is one of my favorites, especially the opening scene.

Anyhow, I woke up this morning. I wasn't entirely sure what I was going to write about because, as you know, nothing interesting had happened. However, while brushing my teeth, I had a small predicament. I started to brush my tongue, and then it started bleeding everywhere! A decent amount of blood gushed out of my tongue. It hurt, too! My tongue was in so much pain. Of course, that is when I remembered how I carelessly burned my tongue yesterday on amazing chicken soup. Note to self: soup is dangerous and should be treated as such.

I am not sure if this journal should be free of vulgarity such as swearing. First of all, I swear. I am extremely respectful with my word choice around others; specifically, I am respectful of my family, teachers, and anyone else who may be offended by my words. To be honest, I think swearing is a good thing and should be encouraged. Seriously. When I was little, I recognized swears as bad words that should never be spoken. But as I got older, I learned there is absolutely nothing dangerous about swearing. Sure, it's a little rebellious, but it is perfectly fine as long as the words are not directed toward someone. But, hey, if I stub my toe on something, I should totally be allowed to express my frustration.

"Fuck! Matchbox cars hurt like shit!"

I usually only curse around my friends, but I curse most often when I'm upset. It's a good way to express emotions without actually causing problems. Some people get upset and they get physical, but that can be hazardous. I prefer swearing. Swearing is fucking amazing. Swearing is the shit. Swearing is so damn great.

I feel safe swearing freely in this journal, but it's odd. I'm not going to lie: my literary style is varied. Most people think it is crazy to have such a wide vocabulary—from fuck, shit, piss, and shit to the complexity of my literary dictionary—and those people are probably right. It's cool, honestly. I can talk like a prestigious college professor who uses equally prestigious words to describe a relatively simple concept, or I can talk like my IQ is Jay Cutler's quarterback rating. I'm a Chicago Bears fan, by the way. Fuck. That's depressing.

Today was a typical day. I was a little disappointed, but tomorrow is Thanksgiving. Thanksgiving is exciting, and I will undoubtedly have much more to write about tomorrow. As for today, I guess my journey starts with a few slow steps. I am willing to accept that. Besides, this journal is not a simple sprint; it is a marathon and should be treated as such.

I did do something interesting today, though. Since tomorrow will be busy, I decided to work out because I will not have the opportunity tomorrow. My workouts are simple. First, I run on the treadmill while listening to my favorite music. I stretch myself out after running, which works nicely to loosen my muscles. Then, I proceed to lift weights and dumbbells until I am exhausted. Finally, I do abdominal exercises to strengthen my abs. I have scoliosis, a curvature of the spine, so these exercises are crucial to my health. That is my workout regimen. Although it is not complex, it definitely keeps me in decent shape. Unfortunately, I'm as skinny as a rail, as the expression goes. Fuck genetics and Gregor Mendel, the Austrian monk who discovered genetics. Thank you for giving a reason to my slim body design. That last statement was sarcastic, obviously. I wouldn't thank that damn monk even if he was the only person who could save my life.

It is late. In fact, it is almost a new day. That is my cue to sleep. I'll write more tomorrow, if I even have the energy to write. Darkness, take me into a deep and luring sleep.

NOVEMBER 27, 2015

I have much to write about. I was so busy yesterday that I didn't have an opportunity to write until today. Yesterday was a hectic Thanksgiving, and I shall try my best to record important events and, as always, my own thoughts. I shall start from the beginning.

I woke up and looked around my dark, dungeon-like room. There is no light in the room, spare my alarm clock, because there are no windows. It is a struggle to wake for school. But today is Thanksgiving, and so I knew I had no time to lose. Quickly, I got out of bed, gathered the clothes I needed, and headed into the bathroom. Showering is essential to one's personal appearance and health.

After a refreshing shower, I helped my parents prepare our house for company: my grandparents. To be specific, the family lunatics. Darla and Charlie were coming over, but we call them Mama Dar and Papa Charlie, although Charlie has no relations to any of us. Those two are an interesting combination, and, quite honestly, I could write an entire story about them alone. But words alone cannot do justice to their characters; they are truly unique, and, therefore, perfect for my journal. Typically, a visit by them is not well received.

"Mama and Papa are coming over," my mom says.

"Okay, thanks for letting me know," I respond. But in my head, it's a different story.

"Mama and Papa are coming over," my mom says.

"What the fuck? They are annoying as shit. All they do is bitch and complain, or bicker and fight. It pisses me off. Plus, they are so damn old they have black and white memories. The next time I hear Papa say, 'Back in my day,' I'm going to light myself on fire and jump out the fucking window. This is not the 19-fucking-70s, so get with the program old timers. Technology is advancing. Also, quit telling me to 'don't do drugs' as you look for a beer to wash down your cigarette. Whoever thought it was a good idea to inhale smoke is a dumb sack of shit. Furthermore, elders should not be given automatic respect just because they are old as fuck. Earn my damn respect. You fought in Vietnam? You have my respect, of course. You are a lazy prick that drinks beer all day? Fuck you."

That is my rant against elderly people. But, don't worry, it will not be the last rant. I will also offer praise to many people, so please do not jump to conclusions; I am not a heartless person. And, one more thing, I guess this journal is not entirely appropriate. I'm an explicit person who believes life, although precious and innocent, should be unedited. I do not like censorship because it blocks the truth. The content of my journal may seem rude or hateful, but I base my content on years of observation. I look and listen rather than speak. I digest information, and then, sometimes over an extended amount of time, I evaluate all of my information. Some may call this just my opinion, and, in a sense, it is my opinion. However, I hope my opinions are fact, because, if not, then that means everything I think is wrong. That would be difficult to accept. But, thankfully, this is my journal. Nobody can tell me I am right or wrong. There is only my thinking being presented. For once in my life, it is my turn to speak.

Papa and Mama argue all the time. It is never-ending. That is really the only reason it is annoying when they come over. But, on the bright side, it is rather amusing. Specifically, Charlie is hilarious. He's quite the character.

They arrived at our house around noon. Darla walked in first. She is short and round, and age has crippled her. It is difficult for her to walk up and down stairs. In her younger years, she probably had striking features, but time is a critical enemy. Years of smoking disintegrated her once healthy skin—skin that is now destroyed by stress and bad decisions. As for her personality, she loves and cares for our family very much. However, she absolutely despises her, technically speaking, husband, Charlie.

Speaking of Charlie, he walked through the door next. He is practically the opposite of Mama Dar—he is tall, lanky, and frail. He is known for his white moustache, his humor, and his ability to misuse drugs. Years of alcohol abuse are evident in his skin. He quit smoking a year ago after being hospitalized—an oxygen mask over his face finally convinced him to quit smoking. His arm is in a cast because, a few weeks ago, he was drunk and he tripped and smashed his face on the concrete. And, a few months prior to that instance, he went to get the newspaper while drunk and ended up slipping on the plastic cover; he broke a few ribs and moaned on the ground for a while, but he lived. He's known in the family for his humor.

In fact, as soon as he walked in through the door he started talking. The Macy's Thanksgiving Day Parade was playing, and it didn't take long for Charlie to find a problem with that.

"What the hell is this? Get these purple-people-eaters off the damn stage! This is a parade, not a damn circus act! These people are on more than the payroll; I'll tell you that."

As usual, Mama assumed her natural role. They are both extremely loud.

"Charlie, would you shut the hell up? Give it a rest!"

"Darla, don't get involved in this. Make yourself useful and get a beer!"

"Charlie, you've had too many beers already, don't you think?" Charlie, of course, ignored her. Unfortunately, it never ends at that.

"Charlie?" Mama Dar scornfully asked. "Do you have a problem, Charlie?"

"Yes, Darla, I have a problem. You. I can't get rid of you either."

"You know what, Charlie? You can drive yourself home because I don't want to drive with you."

"Good! Then I won't have to listen to you bitch the whole damn time I'm driving!"

That is how they talk to each other. Great communication, right?

The majority of the day was spent watching football and listening to Charlie complain about things—mostly his arm.

"This damn cast," and he would hold it up in the air for me to see like it was a battle wound, "can't do anything with it on." Then he would lean in close to my ear and talk to me as if he were telling me a terrible secret. "This isn't a good way to live, Bud." Yeah, like I didn't already know that.

Thankfully, the highlight of the day was the splendid meal cooked by my mom and grandma. The gourmet display featured hot, steamy turkey, sugary sweet potatoes, warm mashed potatoes with a side of delicious gravy, green bean casserole, silky smooth, white rolls, and, to top it off, terrific stuffing—the kind that tastes wonderful sliding down your throat. It was truly beautiful, but, unfortunately, there is always a catch. We had to say grace before we ate. My dad, taking his throne at the end of the table, went ahead and said grace.

"Dear heavenly Father, thank You for this wonderful meal, and thank You to the two wonderful women who prepared it. We pray that You will watch over us and bless us. We pray that Mama and Papa arrive home safely. In Jesus' name we pray, amen." After this, we all began to eat.

I found this the most difficult time of the day: grace. It is not easy being an atheist. Yes, I am an atheist, and I am content. Atheism is simply the lack of belief in a deity or deities. That is all it is! I am not some abnormal freak; I am human. Yet, I would be slandered if I told anyone I am an atheist. It is a sad reality I live. I do not tell people of my lack of belief for fear of the hate or discrimination I may face. And why? I am not a monster, a terrorist, or even a criminal! I am the same person I have always been. I really wish people could accept that—accept me. It really bothers me that some friends or family would look at me differently if I told them I am an atheist. In fact, it makes me incredibly sad. Sometimes, like when I bow my head during grace out of respect for my family, I feel like I am living a lie.

For some reason, atheists are highly discriminated. There are many misconceptions about atheists, and most of them are not true at all. Disappointingly, we live in a world where fear is a driving factor in the actions and natures of people. Atheism, according to modern culture, is something that should be feared. People are taught to believe that atheism is wrong and cruel, but that is simply not true.

Religion is taught, unlike atheism. There is a reason all babies are born atheists, and there is also a reason atheists don't go to Sunday school. That's because religions are fake. Religion is taught to little kids, who believe almost anything they are told. That is the real cruelty. I was one of those kids, and it was painful. Luckily for me, truth has power over fantasy.

My dad and his parents—my other grandparents—are religious. Mostly, my grandparents are extremely religious. Unfortunately, my dad was raised as a religious person. Although, he is extremely smart and most definitely an avid lover of science. The only thing my dad has done from a religious view that I frown upon is having religious children's books read to me when I was a child. He taught me to believe in God by regurgitating all the information his parents told him. It is a sad cycle, and I am happy to break it. I'm very happy that my dad never forced me to go to church. I'm grateful for that, and I have a lot of respect for my parents.

I will, undoubtedly, talk more of the religious subject in the future. I do not wish to further delve at the current time for fear of exasperating the subject. And, please, dear reader, do not jump to conclusions because I have voiced myself as an atheist. Please respect me, and, in return, I will respect you. Thank you.

After dinner, we ate a lovely dessert of pumpkin pie and vanilla ice cream—a terrific combination. I felt like my stomach was going to explode. The food was absolutely wonderful. It was a great ending to a splendid evening.

Overall, I must say, Thanksgiving was a resounding success. Everything about it was wonderful. If only Charlie and Darla could quit their bickering. One miracle at a time, I guess.

NOVEMBER 30, 2015

People hardly notice me—a scrawny, quiet teenage boy. My frustration often gets the better of me, however; lately, my thoughts have been increasingly sporadic. My integrity hangs and dangles in the air, and it is about to drop. Consciousness is an identified enemy to me, and it terrifies me. Everything is a struggle. I hardly feel as if my existence is worth mentioning because, as is quite apparent, my presence should neither be welcomed nor should it be acknowledged. In short, I am depressed. I have just recently had my strongest suicidal urges, and yet my problems remain. My thoughts are terrifyingly detailed and descriptive—numerous possibilities to take my life. In fact, I doubt anyone would notice my absence. Not many people know my name, but maybe people would take notice if I was dead and my body was being mauled by vultures.

Would anyone notice? Would anyone care? If I jumped from a perilous cliff and my lifeless, mangled, distorted body rolled like a ragdoll into the middle of a busy road, would people swerve to avoid me? Perhaps a well-loved individual would exit his or her vehicle, displace my body into a ditch, and drive away as if I was never a living and breathing creature. I am unloved. The dark, tormented hole in my heart cannot easily be filled. I am just a lonely soul, demented and shunned by his peers.

My depression is an endless cycle. I contemplate committing suicide to end every problem I have ever had, have, or will have, but something always convinces me to continue living. For instance, if I die, that would cause problems for people involved in my life. Does that make me selfish? If so, my depression spirals to a barely comprehensible level of agonizing despair. What the fuck is wrong with me? This shithole is my life. I'm trapped in this shithole, but I'm crawling up out of this crevice. This horrid imagery is, sometimes, not all the time, how I see life. It is torture, and it is not easily escapable. Sadly, I am not simply a crazed and fiery-eyed lunatic, but I am sane. Sanity is the shackles that hold me to my cell. At times, it is an internal struggle to stay happy and on the path of life. The road of death is quite welcoming.

I often feel like the mighty Atlas; the great strain of the world sits like a crushing weight upon my aching shoulders. Or, as Isaac Newton kindly witnessed, every action has an equal and opposite reaction. I hold the pressure of the world, and it presses down on me as I feebly attempt to rise up like a rebellious force. But it is not easy. It is fucking difficult. This journal is all I have to look forward to, or at least it feels that way. Nobody will read this. I am not sure if that is good or bad. To be honest, if anyone read this journal I would feel extremely sad and embarrassed. Not only that, but what if the person did not like my journal? I am very self-conscious. In my head, compliments can turn into daggers that stab me repeatedly. Insults are much, much worse. My confidence—the small amount of dignity I retain—crumbles and shatters at any insult or criticism. I am a disgusting atrocity of a human being. Insults, from my own perspective, are death wishes from others. *Oh, you're good at school? Nerd.* I hope I am stabbed a hundred times and my body is impaled. *You're not good enough.* Douse my bleeding corpse in hydrochloric acid. *Kill yourself.* Maybe I will.

But laughter is the absolute worst. I cannot think of anything that hurts me more than the resounding laughter of my failures. Your humor is a tragedy to me. Your tears of laughter are my tears of sadness. And, just because I am smiling does not mean I am happy. Smiles are deceiving. Fuck it. Life is deceiving.

DECEMBER 12, 2015

More than a week has passed since my last journal entry. I tell myself that I was only busy, which is only partially true because I had extended periods of free time, although I really was busy at times. Why do we put off important parts of our lives? When a distant relative calls to wish a happy birthday, why are we so reluctant to talk back? Why do I not write in this journal every day? This journal is my life; therefore, I should take it more seriously. But, for some reason, I procrastinate my writing. Why do we procrastinate? The things we procrastinate are inevitable, and yet here I am, once again, procrastinating my journal.

To be honest, I have quite a bit to write about. But I am not going to write because everything I should write about happened a few days ago and hardly feels important now. In fact, I hardly feel like writing right now. A sudden and overwhelming sadness has taken over my body. I feel like a rock jutting from a cliff that is repeatedly beaten on by the ocean surf. Although I feel much better than from my last journal entry, I still feel awful. There is an emptiness that is eating away at my happiness.

DECEMBER 14, 2015

Sometimes I feel happy, but the happiness is short. Maybe happiness is like an ice cream cone on one of those hot summer days where it is too hot to be outside, but you go outside anyway because you will be upset with yourself if you waste such a beautiful day. And happiness is just like an ice cream cone. When you get a perfect ice cream cone it is absolutely wonderful, but it doesn't last long. The ice cream melts as quickly as you can eat it. No matter how you try to preserve your ice cream, it melts. Happiness is like that. No matter how hard we try to be happy, our happiness is only temporary. Then, after the happiness is gone, a sudden wave of sadness rushes through our bodies.

My first feeling of sadness is hard to describe. It is almost like a chill down my spine, but it feels different. The sensation—I think that is a more suitable word—washes over my entire body; it cripples me until I can only slump in despair. Slowly, I slump lower, lower, lower until my head is barely above my desk and the back of my shoulders are pressed tightly on my worn, black computer chair. When I feel as if my body cannot drop lower, I look up at my computer screen. The screen is always dark, and I can see my reflection in it; the screen is almost like a mirror, but it is not a mirror because the person staring back at my disgraceful body is a stranger. The stranger is dark and mysterious, and his eyes are blank and unloving. His face is covered by the blackness of the computer screen, and it obscures any emotions that may be hiding beneath his weak, pale skin. In his hand is a weapon of mass destruction—a weapon of his own destruction. He is holding a pencil, equivalent to my own, but his pencil only writes words of hate, jealousy, anger, and, strongest of all, sadness. There is no light in his world, and it noticeably affects his distorted image. One glance at this detrimental individual correlates a lifetime of ridicule. His eyes, although solid balls of darkness, are not impermeable, although the illusion remains. Behind his eyes, etched with an impeccable cruelty, are the hundreds and thousands of faults in his life, and it includes every word of every bully, and every mistake he has ever committed. Most frightening of all, his mind is an incredibly dedicated seismograph that intricately details the many faults in his life. He is hardly a real person, and, if he is considered real, a terrible embodiment for humans.

That is what sadness is for me. I become this stranger, and, yet, an unpleasant happiness floods my veins. The happiness is not genuine, but I accept it because I have no other options. It feels <u>safe</u>. But when I am a stranger, everything is surreal. Nothing matters when you cannot feel. That's what I've learned through my expeditions into the darkness.

The worst feeling is loneliness. I am alone. Nobody fucking loves me, and if I trick myself into thinking someone loves me I end up hurting myself. Maybe I am just a stupid rug because everyone always walks all over me. That is just who I am. I am a big fucking teddy bear, and I cannot fight back. Resistance is not an option. And, hey, maybe I am too young for love; I get that, okay? But I need love, and I need somebody to share my love with or I feel worthless. Completely fucking worthless.

That is what sadness is.

DECEMBER 17, 2015

Today was the first day of our final exams. Boring as fuck, as usual. My finals were easy, and, after chilling with my buddies for an hour or so, I decided to go home. No big deal, right? Fuck you.

My friend Jackson decided he needed a ride home, and so I came through in the clutch. Jackson is pretty cool. He is a little on the nerdy side, but I guess I am too. All my friends are nerds in one way or another. Anyway, Jackson has big, curly black hair. He is white as paper but his eyes are slanted like an Asian stereotype. Actually, he is part Native American; it doesn't really show. If he wore glasses he would probably look twice as smart as he already is. He is on the Trivia Team, and he is one of the best on the team. Second to me, of course. Obviously, that was a poorly tasted joke, but in all fairness, I am the captain of the Trivia Team. I always mess with Jackson, but, honestly, I am happy he is on the team. Plus, he has over a hundred pounds on me and he could beat a constipated piece of shit out of me if I say otherwise. He is not fat, but he is a fucking beast.

Anyway, Jackson gave me five dollars to drive him home. He only lives five minutes away, so it was a generous amount of money. His five dollars brought my daily wage to a grand total of ten motherfucking dollars. Ten dollars. Was all the shit that would soon follow worth ten dollars? Maybe. First, let me explain how I ended up with a few extra bucks.

After our boring ass P.E. final, which I got a perfect on, our class headed to the gym for a free day. My friends Ethan and Jackson were with me and we were playing football. Not even ten minutes into our fun, we were interrupted. The three of us were requested by Officer Lee; he needed a few helping hands. It really was not a huge ordeal, but we weren't doing anything important so we just followed him out of the gym.

Officer Lee is the only cop at our tiny school. He is big and black, but he is a gentle giant. His head is bald, and it gives him a high, mighty forehead. Muscles bulge from his monstrous arms, and his hands are as large as bear paws. But no bear would tangle with him. His presence seems unnecessary because our school rarely has fights. I guess it is simply a precaution. Either way, only a full-blown dumbass would have the guts to mess with him. Not only is he a physical specimen, but he is also extremely kind and generous. And his generosity fucked up my day, but I wouldn't know that until later.

But back to the story. Officer Lee pulled us out of class and we started walking. Now, Officer Lee is a fun guy, and this casual stroll was no exception. Throughout the entire walk, he was either pressed against the walls like a corporate spy, or he happily skipped on the echoing concrete. It was fucking great. Eventually, we made it to our school's auditorium.

"I need you guys to help get some stuff out of the car," Officer Lee said. He opened the front door of the auditorium and we walked outside into the freezing wind; you know, the kind of wind that stings your face and makes your ears bright red.

We went out to the car and each grabbed a box, turned around, walked back inside, set the boxes on a table, and that was all it was. The boxes were full of cookies and other shit for a holiday fundraiser. Easy job.

"Thanks guys, here's something for the trouble." Woah! He gave each of us five bucks—his own money—for our measly amount of work. I could hardly believe it, and it was very difficult for me to accept money for such a useful cause. After all, I was glad to help. But, no, I could not refuse his generosity. He is a wonderful person. But I will write about him another time if I have the chance because—believe it or not—I have an interesting story to tell about him.

That is where we got our money, and that is why Jackson easily passed it off to me for a ride home. So, after we finished our finals for the day, we grabbed our shit from our lockers and walked, once again, through the freezing cold to my car. For clarification, my car is a 2007 Chrysler. It is a fucking garbage minivan, but I don't mind.

I pulled out of the parking lot, and this is when shit turned south for the spring, considering it is already winter. I put on my left turn signal because I needed to turn down a side street. Well, as I put my signal on, I waited for the person driving toward me to turn right down the same street. I didn't want to cut him off.

Holy. Fuck. The dude driving was old as fuck and he was probably driving about five miles per hour. The speed limit is twenty-five. This guy took forever to turn. He took so long to turn that I was probably getting wrinkles watching him. His wife was sitting next to him, and she was old as fuck too. Why are old people either wise and lovable or dumb and ignorant? Seriously, this dude took a whole fucking minute to turn his car ninety fucking degrees to the right.

Finally, he finished his turn. Naturally, I followed suit and turned my own car down the road. Guess what? The old, wrinkly-assed, prune-sucking, dandruff-covered motherfucker in front of me was driving so slow I couldn't even move my van completely out of the intersection. In the process, the back end of my car pretty much cut off whoever was driving behind the old guy. I was lucky he or she didn't ram into the back of my car. Needless to say, I was furious.

"What the fuck!?"

"Yeah, I know," Jackson said.

"Do you fucking see this?" I asked him.

"Yeah. Old people, huh?" he said. Then he laughed because, for him, it must have been hilarious to watch me get pissed. If I wasn't pissed, I probably would have laughed too. But I didn't.

"Look at this! Seriously!" I yelled. The old ass had his turn signal on again and he was trying to turn into a drug store—as if he needed any more drugs. Except, to my dismay, there was not a car in sight. But fuck it. That old, shriveled dickhead sat there another thirty seconds before he turned off the road. Probably had to pick up medicine for fucking amnesia because he probably forgot how to drive. Or maybe he needed some Viagra. I don't blame him. His wife probably gets more entertainment from a feather duster these days. That lady is probably so old her vagina looks like it got hit by the Dust Bowl. Twice.

I drove Jackson home after that incident. Then I drove myself home because I was fucking exhausted. Did I almost get in a fender bender because I accepted ten damn dollars? Yes. Life is strange. Every decision you make has a unique outcome. Nothing else unusual happened today, but I don't care. I'm going to sleep.

DECEMBER 18, 2015

Today is Friday, the second and last day of final exams. It was interesting. A little scary, but interesting. Something to get the blood flowing, right? Sure. I got called down to the principal's office. *Fuck*.

I had just finished my last final of the day when my teacher gave me the bad news.

"Hey, Justin, you've gotta go to the office." For good measure he says, "I doubt you're in trouble." He was wrong. Unfortunately, I believed him. I guess that means I was wrong too.

I walked down to the office quickly so I didn't have time to be scared and nervous. By the way, I get nervous about almost everything. I have major anxiety. Getting called down to the office is a harrowing experience for anyone, but for me it is dreadful.

The secretary lady noticed me as I walked in. "Mr. Johnson's office," she said as she pointed to Mr. Johnson's tiny, pitiful office. Reluctantly, I walked into his office and sat down.

Mr. Johnson is the assistant principal. Overall, he's a cool guy, but he gets a bad reputation because he must uphold rules and expectations. It is a stressful job, but he handles his position well. I felt guilty for being in his office. Honestly, am I just another problem for him to deal with? Is that all I am? Why should I feel like nothing other than a problem? I may not look like one, and I may not act like one, but I'm definitely a problem. Maybe not a single problem, but maybe a bundle of problems strung together to form a giant ball—a snowball effect.

"Hey, Justin, thanks for coming in."

"Sure. What do you need, Mr. Johnson?" I asked. Really, I had no clue why I was in his office.

"Well, first I would like to congratulate you for helping Officer Lee. That was a very nice thing to do," he said.

"Oh, yeah, no problem," I said. Then he hit me with the real shit; you know, the reason I was being reprimanded.

"I also saw," and he pointed at the computer, which had security pictures from our school's cameras, "you and Jackson exit the premises through the loading dock doors."

Holy shit. I had no idea what he was talking about at first, and it took a few seconds to really click inside my head. Even then, I wasn't entirely sure why I was in trouble. But I knew I fucked up.

See, the school day wasn't over when my friend and I decided to leave. We didn't have any other exams to take though, and we decided to leave. That was my first mistake. Then, instead of going to the office, signing out of the school, and walking to my car, Jackson and I walked out a side door that was closest to our lockers. Apparently, someone saw us walk out the loading dock doors and he or she contacted Mr. Johnson. We made a major fucking mistake.

"Oh, sorry," I mumbled. Truthfully, I was mortified.

"That's a no-no. Students cannot simply walk out of the school. Safety reasons. Next time, sign out in the office."

In the end, Mr. Johnson was cool about the situation. However, I was still fucking scared. What if I had crashed my car during that little incident? That would have been a mess because I was out of school illegally, which can carry a fine up to $120, as Mr. Johnson kindly informed me, and I had a passenger in my vehicle who was also illegally out of school. Thankfully, I didn't crash. Damn. All that shit happened because of ten fucking dollars. Hopefully that is the last time it happens.

DECEMBER 22, 2015

Christmas break is boring. Seriously. It is freezing outside, and who would want to do anything outside in the middle of winter? Apparently, I did because today I ended up hanging out at my friend Michael's house. He wouldn't leave me alone so I knew I had to go to his house. And, hey, don't get me wrong, I had fun. We played football the entire time even though our hands felt like popsicles.

I guess this is an opportunity to introduce Michael in my story. Michael is one of my buds, and I've known him since second grade. Now, I know that means practically nothing, but I guess it struck a chord with me. He wanted to be my friend when I was a stupid second grader. I was a total nerd in second grade, too, which only adds to the mystery of why anyone wanted to be my friend. I was smart, my head was small and bald, and my mouth was always filled with something metal because my teeth were shit. Not only that, but I was also a runt. Fuck, I would have gotten my face beaten through my tiny ass if I lived in a rough neighborhood.

But Michael wanted to be my friend. That thought stuck with me for a long time because not many people—it hurts to say this—like me. I've had a lot of people pretend to like me, but they always ended up leaving. Everyone uses me. I feel like a fucking ragdoll; I'm always tossed around, stepped on, kicked, and beaten. I used to get bullied when I was younger, and there is one instance that I can easily recall. It always brings tears to my eyes, and this daunting memory will most likely haunt me for the rest of my life.

I was in kindergarten. School was over and I was walking to the bus, and as I stepped off the sweet, sweet sidewalk I was shoved from behind. Down I fell, hitting the pavement with an audible thud. In dismay and complete bewilderment, I slowly stood up and looked down to assess the damage. My knees were bleeding wildly, and hundreds of tiny pebbles stuck to the burning wound like a sticky adhesive. The pain, for a five-year-old, was utterly unbearable, but I looked over my shoulder into the dark, unforgiving eyes of a despicable disgrace of human existence. I knew exactly who he was because he was a grade ahead of me, but I doubt he even knew my name. He cackled at my demise. He laughed at my sorrow and pain! Oh, how that hurt! I hated him instantly, and I still hate him.

He walked past me and got on the bus, and, unfortunately, we rode the same bus, so I followed him. As we got on the bus, our bus driver said nothing about my injuries. Maybe she didn't see what happened, but it doesn't matter because I hate her too. And I hate all the stupid fucking kids that ignored my pain and anguish as I walked down the aisle and took my lonely seat against the window. I sat through the agonizing pain the entire bus ride, and I never cried. I'm not sure why I didn't cry, but I didn't.

When it was my stop, I slowly and carefully walked off the bus. Then I started crying. I was absolutely bawling as I took the long, painful walk down my driveway. I hobbled through the door and my mom saw me, a pitiful excuse for a human. That's when the tears really started flowing, and the entirety of my face felt like an explosive and powerful waterfall.

I can't remember anything after that moment, but I can assume my mom nursed me back to health. Still, that is one of my most haunting memories because it was the first time I realized people might not always like me. It is the memory that I can call upon to force tears into my weak and weary eyes, because sometimes people need to cry. That is all I can write today. The memory is extremely saddening and I cannot continue.

JANUARY 5, 2016

I have been extremely busy the past, what is it now, two weeks? Fuck. I don't even know. Honestly, I've had more than enough to write about, like, for instance, our family took a three-day vacation to the Wisconsin Dells, the "waterpark capital of the world." Or I could have written about visiting my aunt and uncle's new behemoth house. Or maybe I could have written about my delicious first time at Panera Bread. But, no, I chose not to write about anything because I feel so damn depressed all the time.

JANUARY 12, 2016

There are so many things I want to write about right now, but I don't have the time. The lack of writing is killing my motivation and my enthusiasm. Now, I blame my lack of participation on a limited amount of time, but is that even a credible excuse? Am I simply procrastinating? Probably. I hate myself sometimes, and this is one of those moments where I feel the desirable and unrelenting need to bash my disgusting face through an extremely sturdy surface, such as a wall or desk. Honestly, the past few days have been great for me, but right now I feel like I am Atlas, except I am most certainly not Atlas. If anything, my entire demeanor, not my body, would crumble at the weight of the world heaving down upon my puny shoulders. I am a despicable product of evolution.

Why do I write at my strongest feelings of despair? Why did I fail to write of anything that brought me happiness over the past few days? Fuck, I have no idea. But I did realize something today: the success of other people makes me feel terrible about myself. Maybe there is a scientific reason for this feeling or some stupid shit like that, but that doesn't matter to me. What matters is that I feel like shit just because I can't accept another person's success. It makes me question myself, my decisions, and my future. Am I good enough? What am I doing wrong? What future do I have? These emotions drive me insane. Seriously. I can hardly congratulate my friend on his new job because all I can think about is how I don't have a job. It probably doesn't help when some sly shit asks, "What do you want to do when you grow up?" and I have to fucking lie.

"I was thinking of being an accountant. It's pretty easy, and accountants make decent money."

That is a raining bucket of lies. The only thing I have ever wanted to do is write. I want to be a writer. But, if I said that to anybody that asks, like, for instance, my dad, I wouldn't get a pleasant response. It is the only job I have ever wanted.

JANUARY 26, 2016

The phrase is "time flies when you're having fun," but I don't think that is remotely true. Time is flying by and I am most certainly not having fun. At least, that's what I tell myself. I still smile and I still laugh, but behind the happiness is a resounding urge to maintain a previous happiness that I used to have. Honestly, and to put it simply, I am just not happy anymore.

Sure, I have reasons for losing my desire to continue life, but are those reasons better than the reasons I have to live? That is the question I am trying to answer.

FEBRUARY 3, 2016

I t's like I have so much to write about, but as soon as I open this journal my mind turns dark and foggy like a late summer night. That reminds me of something I wanted to write about.

There is nothing more depressing than walking to your car, the only car in the parking lot, guided by a few dim and insignificant bulbs of light that look weak and pale in comparison to the captivating darkness as it grips your entire body, climbs down your dry esophagus, and plants itself in your lungs until it's difficult to breathe. That's not mentioning it is cold as fuck and the wind whips harder with every step you take. Those footsteps echo off the concrete and make you feel like the loneliest person to ever walk the planet, but the feeling lasts only a few seconds before both darknesses swallow it entirely. Then, if you manage to walk the entire distance, you feel like you want to kill yourself inside the car because the silence is unpleasant and unbearable. Solutions are slim, but you only have to turn on the radio and drown out the silence with an onslaught of beautiful sounds. Unfortunately, upon hearing the beautiful talents of the musicians, you immediately sink into a deeper and darker depression because you remember you can't sing, but you try to sing along anyway. In your head, the scene becomes a cartoon and the windows crack and slowly fall to the ground because you are a terrible singer. Suddenly, you snap back to reality and realize you are still alone and nobody really loves you. The darkness is too thick; not even the sharpest knife could trim a sliver of the night, but it doesn't matter to you.

By the time you start your car there is nothing that could possibly make you happy. You start driving, but you are only focusing on your flaws. Occasionally, you drift into the other lane, but, for some reason, you slip back into your lane. The speedometer increases proportionally to the pounding pain in your heart, and maybe you glance down at it once in a while. You could be pushing seventy or seventy-five on a fifty-five road, but who gives a shit? Suicide seems inevitable as you drive, and you look for a telephone pole to smash. Nobody is around to notice or care, and, even if they were, they would not dare interfere or tamper with the darkness. After all, it is my darkness, and nobody loves me enough to end it.

FEBRUARY 17, 2016

I was standing in the lunch line today and I noticed something about the girl in front of me. She was incredibly fat, and I could only imagine the intense battles she must have in the morning as she struggles to put on her clothes, which, not surprisingly, were as ugly as she was: a plain brown shirt and baggy grey sweatpants. Her hair stuck out in odd places and it looked like she hadn't showered in a few days because I could almost see the grease and oils oozing from her pores. Her legs were giant balls of fat that shook like Jell-O every time she took a step forward.

As disgusting as she was, I couldn't help myself and so I started thinking about ugliness. How do you define a person as being ugly? Even though I thought that girl was not particularly appealing, someone else could have had the exact opposite story. Maybe someone out in this huge world thinks she is incredibly beautiful, and maybe I am ugly for even daring to think that this girl is not beautiful beyond compare. Am I ugly for thinking in this manner? For all I know, people probably look at me and notice my disgusting faults and think of how ugly I am. Except nobody will tell me how ugly I really am; they will just lie to me and tell me things I want—things I honestly need—to hear.

"You're funny!"

"You're cute!"

"You're nice!"

But how am I supposed to feel about these compliments? How do I know who is lying and who is telling the truth? Honestly, I don't know, and that is a scary thought. I wish I could figure out how to answer these questions.

Maybe everybody thinks I am ugly. Maybe, just maybe, there is not a single person on the face of the earth that thinks I am beautiful, and that makes me feel worthless. I mean, seriously, who the fuck would love someone like me? I have never really, genuinely expressed my thoughts on love or dating or marriage or anything like that, and I guess I have a decent excuse: why would anyone care for what I have to say, and who the fuck would care?

Not exactly the way I wanted this topic to lead, but, despite that, I feel compelled to write about other things. Not like anyone will ever read this anyways, besides myself, which makes me feel both happy and incredibly lonely.

I am, to put it simply, a nice guy. You know, the guy that does well in school, has good manners and a proper discipline, opens doors for people, never gets in fights or, for that matter, hardly gets in trouble at all. I'm also the nice guy that writes poems and other shit, and, unfortunately, I have written more than a fair share of love poems. Now, I guess I need a disclaimer here or something: I don't mind being a nice guy. It's just in my nature. But, and here is the big shocker if you want to call it that, I think I have a problem with trying to, and I am at a loss of words here, alter my nature. I guess that doesn't make sense, but I can try my best to explain my thoughts through these words.

FEBRUARY 22, 2016

I love to think. That doesn't mean I enjoy spending hours absorbed like a sponge in my studies. I just love thinking, and the ability to think, and sometimes I like to observe things. Humans are amazing creatures.

Today I thought about what kind of superpower I would want if I could have one. My mind buckled under the weight of every possibility, but I thought about it quite a bit and I narrowed my choices to two possibilities.

Although this may sound silly, I was in a sour mood one morning at school as I was walking to my algebra class. I had an appealing thought descend upon my head and I immediately felt every benefit from its existence. I wanted the power to walk on one leg while perfectly tripping every person who walked past me. I hated every person on Earth that particular morning, and tripping everyone was the only thought that truly satisfied my emotions. Never again would I have to look into the sneering faces of my idiotic peers and acquaintances. It sounds terrible, but at least I would limit myself by only using my power on people who deserve a blow to their despicable faces. Fuck all of them.

I guess that brings me to another option. I'd like the ability to freeze time and space. Something about freezing everything and capturing every second of every moment is fascinating to me, and if I could, I would. Photography is helpful, but it has limited abilities and can only capture so much before becoming useless. I want to be able to freeze everything, and then I could analyze every emotion and facial expression of every last person. I could tell who is lying and who is telling the truth. I could see who is making wrong decisions and who is making good decisions. Things like that interest me, and it's unfortunate I can't do that. I am an observer. I observe things, and I think about them until there is nothing left to think about, and then I have to think about the whole process again, but when I finish thinking again it just continues the cycle until, eventually, I exhaust whatever it is I am thinking about and I am forced to think about something else. Sometimes I think about odd things, and sometimes I think about normal things, but most normal things are not complex. Odd thoughts are complex and can transform into deeper and even more complex and intriguing thoughts.

For example, earlier today I started thinking about observing everything in the world at the same time. I figured being situated on the moon would be the best place to look over the entire Earth at the same time, but even this is not true because the other side of the Earth would be facing away from me. Anyway, I combined my ideal superpower of being able to freeze time and space with my new thought and it caused a torrential overflow of emotion that swept me off my feet and cascaded through my mind and body like a beautiful waterfall; except the waterfall rushes quickly in correspondence to how fast my thoughts were forming. But when I opened my eyes, the water fell to my feet and everything stopped.

MARCH 8, 2016

I haven't written in my journal in quite some time, and I guess that is unfortunate. You know, my friend commented today about my writing. He said I used too many commas and that my sentences were too long. He also made fun of me for using a semicolon; he's a dick.

But that's not what I wanted to write about. I want to write about myself. First, I'd like to admit I experienced a physical and mental meltdown two days ago. I felt stressed, and I guess it hadn't helped that I failed to write in here. See, I am feeling great right now, and I think that might be either my saving grace or my biggest fucking problem yet. Damn. I hope that last break in character was a one-and-done scenario.

Depression sounds extreme, but lately I have been wondering if I am depressed. The problem is, for me at least, it comes and goes. Maybe it is just hormones or stress or something stupid like that, but it feels so fucking real sometimes. I wonder if maybe I should go to therapy or a clinic, but, honestly, I don't think that would change anything. Really. Why the fuck should I listen to anything a therapist says or doesn't say? I don't know. I don't think a therapist is a good solution to any of my problems.

MARCH 11, 2016

The worst part about trying to write in this journal is the distractions. Funny, right as I wrote that sentence my phone buzzed. I guess someone wants to talk to me. That is exactly what will happen, and I will most likely let it happen. But that isn't even the worst distraction. No, the worst distraction is my own fucking family. I can't even write in peace or privacy. My head is hurting because I have to constantly worry about things. It is absolutely pathetic that my mind is paranoid about stupid shit like that. Fuck, I am not joking when I say my family has a sixth sense about me.

As soon as I start playing music quietly on my computer, my mom, dad, or sister walks downstairs and I have to shut it off. Or my brother barges out of his room like the oversized fucking horse that he is and stomps his two huge hooves against the carpet like an angry toddler in a tantrum. How the fuck do I deal with that? I have no choice but to turn off my music because it is more than likely music that grants me severe disapproval—or worse. Sometimes it makes me feel like a criminal with a secret. My family members are cops, and I have to stay under their radar. That is fucking ridiculous to me. Why should their presence play a role in how I wish to be perceived? Really, it shouldn't. But my parents would never tolerate any of my shit. They love me, but love can be a misleading emotion. If I told them how I really felt about things, they would still love me but that doesn't mean they will understand or even listen to what I have to say. So why should I even bother myself with the trouble of speaking? Truth is, most of the time I don't. I will just sink lower in my chair and pause my music and pretend to do something else or I will close any computer tabs that would make them suspicious. I am an observer. Who gives a fuck about me? Most of my old teachers can barely remember my name because I am so fucking irrelevant.

Unfortunately, my thoughts were steering me off topic. I just spent the past two hours being depressed and feeling sorry for myself. Now it is too late to continue writing in my journal. Plus, I forgot what I was going to say. I'm extremely tired.

MARCH 12, 2016

Although I have been slightly busy today (I had to periodically help my dad put down new flooring in the living room), I spent nearly all my free time thinking, relaxing, and listening to music. I adore music, but sometimes it still finds a way to depress me even more than before. Listening to perfect and successful people doesn't exactly make me feel better about myself. How am I supposed to feel happy when I am constantly in everyone else's shadow?

MARCH 20, 2016

I looked in the mirror this morning and there were three disgusting zits on my face. After I popped them, which was fucking torture, I stood in front of the mirror and stared at my face. Tears rimmed my eyes and a few rebellious trickles raced down my cheek, but I brushed them away. My brain started slow and meticulous, but it didn't take long for my thoughts to completely obliterate my mentality.

What the fuck is wrong with me? Is it just stress that is causing pimples to sprout from my face like some nasty and poisonous mushrooms popping out of the fresh soil? There were only three, but can I never catch a fucking break? I think the worst part is tricking myself into believing my complexion will improve as if by magic. Every day and every night I use Proactiv in the hope that all of the shitty things that pop up on my face every few days will just disappear. Proactiv isn't even the first acne medicine I've tried. This is the third fucking try to cure my problem. It doesn't work. No matter what bullshit my mom says about my face looking "a little better," I can always look in the mirror and see either new ooze-monsters forming or the remnants of their deceased relatives.

The worst part about any problem someone points out about me is that I can designate their face, their actions, and their words whenever I notice that problem. I'll elaborate on that. Whenever I look in the mirror and see a nasty, disgusting, gross-as-fuck zit, I think of my mom. More specifically, I think of a few choice words she said to me, or maybe I think of an entire situation. One situation that always comes to mind is the first time I ever got a pimple.

I don't remember how old I was, but I must have been six, seven, or maybe even eight. We were at my grandma's tiny fucking house, and it is usually a boring place where you have to stare at the hands on the clock to keep yourself from scratching your retinas off. That day must have been pretty fucking slow. I was watching a television show (probably Spongebob) and my mom came in the living room. She walked through my field of view and then towered over me in the same authoritative fashion that all adults tower over children. She must have noticed the pimple on my face. Little seven-year-old me probably shit his pants when he saw his mom slowly open her mouth.

"Ooh, you've got a pimple! Let me pop it!" My mom has an odd obsession of popping pimples and zits and any other strange blemishes produced by the human body. She probably used to be one of those kids that played with bubble wrap on a boring day.

I remember standing up with a roar of confidence, feeling like a real man. (Hell yeah! My first pimple!) But when I saw my mom's devious fingers stretching toward my face, almost in slow motion, I waited for a wonderful flood of relief to wash over me.

All I could feel was **pain**.

Her fingernails, long and untrimmed, dug deep into the pores of my face as if to excavate them of a precious treasure. I knew there was no treasure in my face. I was no fool. Stinging pain seared my face, and my mom removed her fingers as if nothing had happened.

"That wasn't so bad, was it?"

I don't remember exactly what happened after that, but I either drained my eyes of their precious liquids or I merely felt a salty embrace, the type that only fresh tears can provide, gently caressing my young and innocent eyes. I know if I did cry my mom probably told me to stop acting like a baby. Why was I even crying? Was I crying because the experience was painful, or was I crying because I knew it would mark the beginning of a long and painful road into adolescence? I don't know. I just can't remember. I only remember vivid images in my head. Fingernails slicing into my skin like a butcher's knife slices a fresh cut of meat. My mom looking at me and her eyes silently asking, "What is wrong about a tiny pimple?" She still looks at me like that sometimes. I fucking hate it.

Those thoughts and images often race through my head as I stare deeper into the mirror. My mom ordered Proactiv as a birthday present for me. All it does is remind me of how imperfect I am, and it brings back those fucking images of fingernails cutting into my skin and blood and pus oozing out of my pores. Then I look down at my own fingernails. What is wrong with me?

It's not just acne or my complexion. It's everything. A few choice words or certain situations are forever hardwired into the malfunctioning system I call my thoughts and emotions.

For acne, I think of my mom and her deathly fingernails dismantling my beautiful skin and reducing it to a cemetery of scars and craters. Maybe that is an exaggeration, but it certainly feels that way.

There are other things that affect me. I had a thought the other day when a girl in gym class scratched my hand with her fingernails. Is that a coincidence, or are my memories connected? Either way, my hand bled a little, but it was nothing to worry about. And you know what? I didn't worry about it, and I was proud of that. Pride doesn't last long, though, and it didn't take long for one of my friends to point out a problem. I kept talking about the cut and my friend finally got fed up with me.

"Dude, it's just a little cut. Get over it." Those words bounced around in my head like an echo in a deep and winding cave system that is so impossibly long there seems to be no imaginable ending. Infinite. But my head is not an endless labyrinth. I'm not fucking stupid. I looked down at my hand and I saw that cut for what it really was. It was just another imperfection. I say that because I can look down at my hand and I can imagine. What do I imagine? Well, I stare at my skin and I imagine all the tiny cuts I've ever had on that particular area of skin and bone. And that cut in gym class? That cut was on a part of my skin that had been previously unscathed by vicious contact. My skin was beautifully white and pure until some girl cut it. Sometimes I want to cry when I imagine things like that. Eventually, my entire hand will be covered in nothing but a hideously red and oozing parade of neglect that will forever bleed frantically. It hurts my head just thinking about it.

You know, I looked at my friend when he told me that, but I didn't say anything. I wanted to collapse on the floor and cry until my body was physically incapable of producing enough tears to keep pace with my constant flow of suffering and misery.

"It's just a little cut."

"It's just a little pimple."

The memories flood back into my head either instantaneously or over a certain length of time. And it's not just my hand or my face; it is everything. I can look in the mirror and imagine every pimple I've ever had. Together they would probably cover my face in disgusting fashion. Who cares if my acne is hardly noticeable? I notice it every fucking day. I look at myself and I can see deeper. I can look beneath the flesh and straight into the soft, cracked shell I call my mind. I can't tell if the shell is cracked or if it has been broken apart before. Maybe now it is held together by some cheap Elmer's glue or maybe Crayola's shitty substitute brand of glue. Honestly, it wouldn't surprise me.

My insecurities, if that is an appropriate title for my problems, are more than physical. The other day I accidentally created a memory that will undoubtedly haunt me for the rest of my life, or at least as long as I let it float up from my other memories and to the forefront of my mind. It hasn't bothered me much yet, but if I give it time I know it will resurface and provide another insecurity. It's a new one, and one I've never really thought of before. Until now.

I guess my voice is kind of deep. I never really paid much attention to how my voice sounds, although my mom used to tease me a lot when I was going through puberty because my voice cracked sometimes during the transition. But that never haunted me. No. Something one of my friends told me has continued to haunt me, however.

"Your voice is deep. You sound like a forty-year-old man. Or a child molester."

Thanks. Thank you for giving me another reason to doubt myself. Thank you for insulting a part of me that I loved and cherished. Thank you for providing me with another insecurity to add to a long and increasing list that I have thoroughly kept in check since I was four years old. I don't even want to write about my first insecurity right now. It'll happen eventually, but as of now I don't have the time.

That is all I can write about for now. My mind is stressed and exhausted. I didn't even write about some other insecurities I have that I wanted to talk about. There are so many things wrong with me.

MARCH 26, 2016

O kay. Here are some things I like about myself, or at least on a good day. Hopefully I can always find things to like about myself. So, before I talk about all of my insecurities and shit like that, I figured I should write about things I like about myself.

I like my eyes. I don't like having bags under my eyes, but they aren't that noticeable unless I am stressed or tired. My eyes are a dark blue color that I absolutely love. I like to think my eyes are like the ocean—dark, deep, and mysterious, with a light touch of calm and gentleness. Like a soft and soothing ocean breeze, my eyes glide across everything, touch everything, feel everything, and, finally, analyze everything. My eyes are exactly like an ocean. Most people only see the glinting surface and may take a quick swim, but most of the people who swim will retreat to the safety of the soft, hot sand on the shore. Maybe the water was too cold. Maybe the water was too deep. Maybe the water was rough and choppy. Well, some people might get past those parts of the water and they'll decide to swim farther out. Or maybe they want to go for a dive, and so they bravely plunge into the depths of the water. But everyone will eventually leave, like they always do. The people who swim the farthest out will see the sun receding into the horizon and will turn around to swim back to shore. The people who plunge deep into the murky depths of the unexplored and dangerous waters will be scared off by an oddly glowing fish with razor teeth and seven eyes. Or maybe they will need to surface for air because their oxygen supply is dwindling and they know their stay is limited. The sun will set and everyone will leave the beach, as they always have. Sure, maybe people will return the next day, but they will do the same things as the people from the previous days. I hope someone comes along and decides they love my ocean. I hope someone decides they'd love to stay with me. That person would not be scared of the deepest and darkest trenches in my ocean. That person will lovingly bask in my waters and will enjoy it, savoring every moment. And if the waters get rough and the waves get stronger, that person will bear the roughest waves until the sea is calm and all returns to normal. Then, the surface will glisten and twinkle; it's almost as if there is an invisible happiness and calmness resting upon the water. The waves will relax.

My eyes are oceans. I really want to love my eyes, but sometimes that can be difficult. For instance, I remember one day in eighth grade when I was eating lunch. I sat next to a group of stoners because we had assigned seats. Well, one day the lighting in the room must have been completely fucked up and one of the stoners noticed it. Kind of.

"Dude, your eyes," he says. "You look stoned." Then they all laughed because my pupils must have looked ridiculous. I'm not sure why, but that memory bothered me for a long time. It doesn't really bother me anymore because I realized how stupid it was.

Another reason I find it difficult to like my eyes is because of other people. Like, there is a senior in my accounting class who is fairly popular. Every day someone makes a comment about how pretty his eyes are. In fact, he got voted as "Prettiest Eyes" in the yearbook or something like that. Perhaps that was only a joke, but you get the idea. Ordinarily that wouldn't bother me at all, but it does bother me because it makes me notice how nobody makes comments like that to me. I don't think anyone has ever complimented my eyes. I have never heard that my eyes are pretty. Maybe my eyes aren't pretty. Why do I even like them? Nobody looks at my eyes and sees an ocean. They just think my eyes are normal. Completely fucking normal.

I like my hair. At least, I think I like my hair. It hasn't always been easy, but I think I like my hair right now. I used to despise my hair, so I guess this is a positive change.

When I was little, my mom would practically shave my head bald and that was how my nearly nonexistent hair would look. I'm surprised more people didn't make fun of me. Some people did make fun of me for looking like a bald man in second grade. Whatever. I'm just glad most people forgot about that phase of my life. Well, everyone except me, of course.

As I got older I got fed up with my bullshit hair and so I decided to grow it out a little. There was a small problem though: I had no fucking clue how to style my hair and so I always looked like a dork. I guess I still do, just not as much.

A few months ago, I changed my hairstyle a little and I absolutely loved it. I was so proud of my new hair and I couldn't wait to hear all the comments people would make about how they liked my new hair. They made comments, and that was basically all they did.

"Justin, did you change your hair?"

"Yeah."

That's all they asked about. They probably thought I looked like the dumbest person in the entire universe. *Wow, he sucks at styling his hair. What an idiot.* Fuck those people. I like my hair how it is and nobody should force me into changing it.

One reason I love my hair is because it curls when it gets long. One girl told me she liked the curls, and that made me like my hair even more. It really was a motivating and powerful moment for me when she told me she loved my curls. I felt like I finally had something to like about myself and take pride in. So that is exactly what I did, and it has made me feel so much better about myself. Maybe I still mess with my hair and try to keep it as perfect as I can make it, but it is less often. Maybe I still worry too much about how my hair looks, but I'm trying my best to minimize how much I worry. Baby steps. One foot in front of the other. Take a deep breath. Count to ten in your head. Do all that other shit that is supposed to help relax people, but never seems to work with me.

As for my physical traits, there isn't much left that I like. Most of my body I either hate or I feel it is neutral and average. My eyebrows, nose, ears, feet, and things like that feel normal. I don't have a reason to not like them, but I don't necessarily have a reason to love them. Now, those are just physical parts of my body. There are many mental components that I love and despise about myself.

But back to physicality. For the most part, I despise how I look in every single way. I think I hate my skin more than any other part of my body. My skin is like a fossil record in the manner it preserves the toughest conditions only to provide an accurate representation and image of every physical injury I hold on to through some feeble effort. Not to mention my acne problems.

And that's all I feel like talking about for today.

MARCH 29, 2016

I thought I was finally happy for the first time in a long time. No. I was wrong again. I am always fucking wrong. Everything I do is always wrong. Even if I do the exact same thing as everyone else, somebody will tell me how wrong I am. Nothing I do is ever right. I feel so fucking helpless. Eventually, there will be nobody left to help me and I will lie in the middle of the street and plead for someone to flatten my body with a preferably large and heavy vehicle. I doubt anyone would even do that to ease my pain. It would be too much of an inconvenience for them.

MARCH 30, 2016

Thinking about last night gave me an incredible sense of relief today. I felt calm and relaxed the entire day. I felt like I was floating on the fluffiest cloud in the sky. Right now, though, my legs feel numb and weak. But it is a pleasurable feeling.

I worked out today for the first time in months. If I remember correctly, the last time I exercised was toward the end of December. This is a huge step in the right direction. I stopped working out because I felt a lack of motivation, but there was a deeper reason that compelled me to stop exercising. Unbeknownst to me at the time, I had a serious reason for discontinuing my exercise regimen. I was setting my body up for suicide. I was subconsciously executing a plot to aid me in ending my life. That is fucking terrifying. I believe my head told my body to stop engaging in excessive physical activity. Who cares what condition my body is in if I am dead? That's probably the main reason I stopped exercising.

I wonder what other measures I took to set up for my suicide. How close was I to committing myself to death? Was there a time where it was inevitable? Did I ever fully latch on to a plan, or was it only an idea?

Now that I think about it, my room and other personal areas were always messy around that time. Why clean up after myself if I was going to die soon? But, you know what, I cleaned my entire desk off not too long ago. Cleaned most of my room.

I hope that means I am improving.

APRIL 1, 2016

My hands are freezing right now. They're starting to turn slightly blue, which worries me a little. My hands are always cold. I think I have a circulation problem or something because my hands are always cold, even when the rest of my body feels warm. Or maybe I am too skinny and scrawny. Fuck. I really hope it's not a circulation problem, though, because I don't want to have an aneurysm or a major blood clot or a stroke or some nasty disease. With my luck, I'll probably have a heart attack due to high cholesterol. Both sides of my family have had heart problems and a bunch of different types of cancer. I fucking despise my genetics, as I've previously mentioned. Hence, fuck Gregor Mendel.

Maybe I'm just skinny and that makes me cold. I look like a skeleton, and I doubt that's a coincidence. I may be a skeleton on the outside, but that's nothing compared to how dead I feel on the inside. If I were to be dissected, the inner portions of my thoughts would be covered in cobwebs, and tiny tumbleweeds would gracefully roll around like in any stereotypical Old West movie. Or maybe I am an arctic tundra and my thoughts and emotions are sealed deep beneath a thick and expansive permafrost. That would probably explain why I'm always cold.

Spring break is almost over. Where the fuck does time go? How can all this time elude me so cleverly? Today is Friday, April 1st, which means one-fourth of the year is over. That's not a prank, either; it's a disappointing fact. Fuck April Fool's Day, and I say that because it is the dumbest day of the year. If you have ever used the internet before, you know that the last thing anyone needs is a day of increased stupidity and foolishness. It is fucking ridiculous.

Three months of this year are gone forever. That terrifies me because it makes me realize how quickly time flies without anyone even noticing. I am sixteen and time is hurrying me along. I got my driver's license a couple of months ago. This summer I need to find a job. Then I need to go to college and get a degree that means absolutely nothing to me. Then I need a real job to support myself. Then, before I know it, I'll be retiring and my entire life will be a bleak and meaningless existence. Then I'm going to die and a bunch of people I don't like will show up at my funeral. All those shitty people will say stupid shit about me and shed a tear or two, but that's all the affection they'll show. They don't care if I am dead or alive. I bet some asshole kid at my funeral will keep asking his or her parents when it will be time to leave. I can read that kid's mind right now.

"Who died? Who? I didn't know him. I don't care. I just want to get home."

Want to know how I can visualize that asshole kid? I was that kid when I was little. It wasn't exactly the same scenario, but the general principle is the same. Let's delve into my memories, shall we?

We drove up to Wisconsin to visit our aunt, uncle, and two older cousins. I must have been little because I can't remember very much about the memory—only brief snippets of important moments. Anyway, we had to go to the hospital in Milwaukee or Madison or somewhere else that I don't know about. I was little and I didn't understand what was happening. I also didn't care, so I guess ignorance really is bliss.

I remember sitting on the floor in the waiting area and working on puzzles. Someone must have bought me a Gatorade or a Powerade from a vending machine because I remember I drank a lot. Every five minutes I kept asking my mom to take me to the bathroom. I was probably a distraction to everyone in the waiting room, but it must have been slightly entertaining. I had no idea what was happening or why we were in a hospital or why everyone looked so grim and sullen. Little me felt fine. What was wrong?

One of my cousins had a massive tumor on one of his lungs. He was a teenager. But I had no idea what was happening. I was sure everything would be fine. Why was everyone crying? What was wrong? The doctors and nurses will fix everything. Luckily, that was true for my cousin. His artery was nicked with a knife, causing the operation to turn into a life or death procedure. But I didn't know that at the time.

Although that memory is vague and diminishing, it is still traumatic and it resonates strongly for me. I may not remember much from that day, but I will always remember how sad and worried everyone looked. I wasn't worried at all. Except now the roles are reversed. I am always sad and worried and depressed. Sometimes I become incapable of feeling emotions. My body shuts down and every defense mechanism is suspended in action. Anyone can attack and destroy me. I have been beaten near to death mentally, although my physical body remains unharmed. Eventually stress and worry will destroy my physical entity in addition to my mental state of being. But, remember now, the roles are reversed. Nobody cares about me. Everyone becomes a version of little Justin in that hospital waiting room. Nobody really cares. They don't take notice of my pain and suffering. They just see my fakest smiles and my strained laughs and create the assumption that everything is fine. They can't see the tears in my eyes. They can't see my eyes receding to the sunken depths of their pitiful sockets. They can't see the tumor inside me that is slowly digesting my existence. It is black and grotesque like a disgusting creature that is so unfathomably hideous there is no possible way it could exist.

People who don't care will deny any knowledge of my problems. They choose to disbelieve in any evidence I provide of the huge dark tumor making a gruesome feast of my worthless body. Why? Why do they dispose of me in this manner? But a jolt of adrenaline answers my questions swiftly. It's because they don't care. *You are nothing. Your existence is a shame. Nobody loves you.*

But I try to resist this inner struggle. *Ha, look how far you are in this journal and still nobody seems to care. When will you learn, little boy?* I keep denying it. *Someone cares? Who? Look around, you have nobody.* I look around and I see people. Then I look closer and I see that they are not really people after all. They are nothing more than skin, bones, and a few random strings of thought. And then it dawns on me that everybody else is secretly that little asshole at my funeral. None of them really give a shit about me. They don't care if I live or die, breathe or suffocate, swim or drown, fly or fall, walk or limp, smile or frown, laugh or cry, or any of that. They don't even care if I shit or piss myself when I die. My body could be buried beneath multiple layers of piss and shit inside my casket, but it doesn't matter. Nobody cares.

Nobody.

APRIL 6, 2016

A friend tried to kill herself the other night by drinking a cup of bleach. I was so scared. I talked to her for hours trying to calm her down. I was very lucky to have talked to her or otherwise she might have committed suicide. Thankfully, she ended up falling asleep and she never acted on her desire to make the bleach a new companion. I care about her a lot and it really hurt me to see her like that. That's not mentioning she cuts herself almost every day. Poor girl. I hate to see her in so much pain, but her entire life has been full of pain. As her friend, I will try my best to relieve some of her pain. Hopefully I will bring her a little bit of happiness. If I am unable to help her, hopefully someone else does. She could use some important people in her life.

Fuck. It is just so difficult to help my friends right now. I can barely take care of myself. But I still help them because I care about them. It's just difficult. I love my friends and I would do anything within my power to help them. I just wish I could get some help myself.

I say I want help, but do I really mean it? Or am I just saying that because everyone else wants me to get help? I've got some serious problems, so I better get them fixed. I don't know. I don't want to become a different person. I don't want to lose some of the aspects that make me feel like myself. But I want to be able to function correctly. I don't like how I have moments where my life falls apart and I can't perform any basic human functions. I don't know.

APRIL 11, 2016

I didn't sleep last night, and if I did it was hardly worth mentioning. I felt fucking awful when I woke up, and by woke up I mean checking the clock for two hours until the alarm sounded and I woke up without raising suspicion. That's what happened. I guess it's only fitting that I had a shitty start to a shitty day. People say it depends on your outlook and how you view things that makes things good or bad, but I bet those people don't feel very good after not sleeping for an entire night. Fuck those people, honestly. They make it seem like life is so damn easy and that everything is cheesy and happy and shit. That's not fucking true.

My day started out rather normal as I went through my morning routine. Shower. Put clothes on. Put on stupid fucking acne cream that hardly fucking works. Try to style my obnoxious hair. Eat breakfast. Wait for my stupid brother to get out of the bathroom so I can brush my teeth. Brush my teeth. Grab all the shit I need for school. Walk to my car. Start my car. Wait for stupid brother. Drive to school. Maneuver through a parade of cars and drop my stupid brother off at his stupid school. Drive the short distance over to my school. Park my car. Walk the loneliest sidewalk in existence. Go inside the school. Walk to my locker.

That's when my morning routine ends and my school routine begins. Today was particularly interesting because I defied both routines. I didn't sleep last night, so I never really woke up, which set off a chain reaction that ruined my morning routine. Then I ruined my school routine. Fuck.

After I went to my locker today I remembered I hadn't done my algebra homework over the weekend. I took my homework out of my folder and instantly realized why I hadn't even attempted it: I had no fucking clue how to do it. My friends were messing around and talking so I figured one of them could help me, considering they weren't busy. I should have said, "Hey, you have nothing better to do right now, can you spare thirty fucking seconds and tell me how to do this worksheet?" That's not what happened. I walked up to my friend and asked him how to graph secant, cosecant, and cotangent. From his immediate response, I could tell I was wasting my time.

"You didn't do any of it?"

No. I didn't do any of it. Why the fuck would I be asking you for help if I finished it? Why the fuck would I even bother talking to you about it? Why the fuck should I even talk to you at all? Those thoughts bounced around in my head like an endless ping-pong battle. Fuck. But, hey, I broke the routine. I broke every piece of criteria I'd ever set. Most days when my friends say some stupid shit like that I just wait for them to finally help me. It makes me feel so fucking stupid and helpless. They just keep talking and ignoring me as I sit there, clock still tick-tick-ticking away, but they don't even give a shit. What great fucking friends I have.

I broke the routine because I just walked away. It was ten minutes until final bell, but I just started walking to class. I could hear my friends asking me where I was going. I could hear them whispering behind me as I walked farther away from their pitiful and meaningless words. I could feel their eyes searing the back of my head like a scolding hot iron. I just kept walking. I wasn't about to succumb to them or anyone else. I felt so sick of dealing with their shit. Don't I have enough problems already? Can't they fucking see how troubled I am? Do they not see the bags under my eyes from how stressed I am? No. Apparently, they cannot see anything. I won't let them see who I really am, or how I really act.

They also don't know how I have to help my other friends because they are fucking suicidal. That is stressful, too. Everything is stressful to me. I guess it is not always evident that I am stressed. The only real physical signs of stress are probably the bags under my eyes. And maybe acne is a sign of stress. Fuck. I don't know.

By the time I got to French class, I had completely given up on any chance of completing my homework. I just stopped doing it. That's another routine broken. I always do my homework every day. Except today. Today, I didn't do my homework. I broke three routines in less than two hours.

The girl who sits across from me in French class was a little concerned about me. Her name is Ashley. I noted her concern for me, but I don't think she is a prime candidate as someone I would open up to. She is just a French class friend. Either way, I did notice that she was concerned about me. She has a strange sense of knowing when something is wrong with me. Maybe I just don't hide my problems around her because I don't care if she knows something is wrong with me. She asked me today if something was wrong, and I told her no. Denial.

I didn't say another word that entire class period. I kept thinking about one thought over and over. It was very intriguing and my mind decided to pounce on it, wrestle it to the ground, and snatch it up. My thought: the mechanism in my jaw is broken and now I cannot speak. My mouth would not move, try as I might. The harder I tried to talk, the harder it was to speak.

The rest of my school day was a little more difficult to handle. I had to put on my fake smile and my fake laugh and my fake persona so nobody could see how badly I was about to fall apart. Maybe I didn't even know it at the time, either. It doesn't really matter.

Chemistry was oddly my best class today. Funny, but I just thought of something about that. That's another routine broken. Chemistry is my least favorite class. Except today. Today it was my favorite class. I loved chemistry today, and it must have showed. I kept having spontaneous thoughts that were very random and inappropriate, but otherwise entertaining for myself and everyone around me.

"Don't you hate it when you get the shit beat out of you by a panda bear in a foreign restaurant's bathroom?

"I always wanted to be a time traveling, shape shifting, drug dealing teletubby."

It was one of the best moments I had today.

After school ended, I decided to drive to the dollar store and look and see if they had any composition notebooks. I needed to buy a new journal. I *needed* to. If the dollar store didn't have any, I would have immediately drove to another store. If I had to drive an hour away, I would have. That's how badly I needed a new journal. Luckily for me, I bought two composition books at the dollar store. They were both wide-ruled and that was slightly disappointing, but I didn't care too much because I finally bought a new journal. It was the first time today that I felt genuinely happy.

Having another journal means I can finally write about my rainbow whenever I want and however much I please. Rainbows are very reassuring. Usually rainbows come after a storm, and, hey, maybe the storm caused some damage. Maybe there was some wind damage and a few trees and powerlines collapsed. Maybe there was some flood damage from all the water. But looking up in the sky and seeing a rainbow can be very reassuring. Rainbows might not seem like much when everything feels like shit, but they can be so, so reassuring. My rainbow means a lot to me, but that's probably because my journal is more than just a rainbow. If anything, my journal is the rainbow and the giant pot of gold at the end of it. That's my rainbow.

Driving home from the store felt like a relief. Finally, I was going home, where I feel so safe. I feel like myself. It is a nice and welcoming feeling, and so I eagerly embraced it in the hope of redeeming my day.

I played a couple of games for an hour or two to relax. I started to feel better and more powerful with every passing minute. When dinner was done, I took my food downstairs and sat at my desk, the secluded exclusion zone. That's probably when shit started to really go downhill, tumbling past Jack and Jill. My therapeutic dose of happiness was being chipped away, and my mental state crumbled. The beginning of my day caught up with me and exposed my flaws once more.

"Justin!" It was the signal call. My heart leaped, then dropped like a bomb, but then leaped again. I ran upstairs to see what my dad needed. He told me to follow him outside, and I did. Things were about to get messy.

He hooked up a black wagon to the back of our lawn mower. Then, he placed a shovel in the back of the wagon. He started explaining why we were outside. It was about seven o'clock in the evening, by the way.

"You're going to have to clear the burn pile. Shovel the ashes into the wagon and then drive the lawn mower up to the dumpster."

That was all fine, I guess. We rented a dumpster for a week to clean up from our kitchen and living room renovations. My dad thought we should make the most use of the dumpster by using this opportunity to clear up the burn pile, which is what our massive fire pit is called. You know, it's a place to burn cardboard and branches and boxes and twigs and leaves and anything else you feel like burning. Over the years, the pile of ashes and dirt and debris started to pile up. Now it was time to get rid of it. I was excited, honestly. That is, until I asked the second dumbest question ever to my dad.

"Should I grab another shovel?" It seemed like such an innocent question. But as soon as the words left my mouth I felt a wave of regret wash over me. My dad replied effortlessly.

"You only need one."

Ouch! That hurt me. I could feel the sharpened points of daggers poking at my skin and prodding me. I knew exactly what those words meant. I was going to be working alone. It's not like I'm not used to being alone, but I really had a small and insignificant hope that my dad would join me. It would have been nice to just shovel ashes and talk. No. Instead, the only thing I received was a rush of memories and flashbacks from my past. Specifically, one question flooded my head with an influx of torment.

I was in eighth grade. It was the middle of December and, much to my delight, there was hardly a flake of snow in sight. I was in school at the time, but I remember being excited because I was going to a Chicago Bulls and Milwaukee Bucks game. My dad was going to pick me up early from school so we could drive to Milwaukee. Why were we going to Milwaukee and not Chicago? Well, we got tickets from our uncle and he, along with my aunt and cousins, live in Wisconsin. That's not to mention that Milwaukee tickets are incredibly cheap when compared to Chicago tickets. They are probably a few hundred dollars cheaper, which was amazing because my uncle gave us four tickets. One for my mom, dad, brother, and myself.

Unfortunately, things don't always work out like they are supposed to. My mom was sick and my brother had bronchitis. Our family can never catch a fucking break, you know? It's always one unlucky occurrence after another. That's life, like it or not. I don't like it.

Anyway, it was just going to be my dad and me. Damn, I was so excited! Finally, a chance to spend some quality time with my dad. I had been waiting for this moment my entire life. There would be no more waiting. I was determined to have a great time with my dad, whether the Bulls won or lost.

We drove through Milwaukee, a truly beautiful city, as a few light flakes of snow drifted quietly in the frosty breeze. After a bit of driving, we found the BMO Harris Bradley Center, home of the Milwaukee Bucks. My dad parked the car and we started walking toward the entrance.

I'll never forget those next few moments. I can't forget. I am diseased, and my disease is traumatizing me. I must remember. Quietly, oh so quietly, the memory sneaks in and nonchalantly eradicates me. The memory becomes my past, present, and future. I cannot escape its vicinity for fear of becoming entangled in an endlessly spiraling web of superb and superior darkness. The darkness has arrived.

There was a man shouting outside of the venue. He spotted us and started talking to my dad as we quickly approached. I was an observer of this conversation, as I always must be. I stood still and scrutinized my father and this stranger conversing so freely. Something felt wrong. I felt confused, like a tiny child. I felt helpless and insignificant. But, still, still I listened. I focused my eyes and ears on the exchange of words between those two people. What choice did I have? I must observe so I may use memories to torture myself. The voice inside my head told me to observe. *Do not move a muscle.* When I freeze, I can feel the voice smirk and whisper to me. *Good boy. Freeze. The words, the words! Digest them! Listen!* I obeyed the voice. I stood and listened to the new memory forming in front of my eyes. I saw it. I heard it. I felt it.

The stranger weaved an innocent story about his wife and kids, and I listened intently. I studied his facial expressions, eyes, and body language. I stared at his lips and watched them move gracefully and effortlessly. It looked so easy. Then, I looked at my dad and studied him. I watched him nod his head and I watched him study and listen to the stranger. I felt like time had frozen and I was staring at a set of pictures, and, no matter how much I did or didn't try, I knew I would go unnoticed. But I noticed.

The stranger kept talking about how he had no tickets and how he was separated from his wife and kids. My dad told the stranger that we had two extra tickets. The stranger's eyes lit up, and at first glance I thought he was happy. Surely, he was happy, right? What else could it be? I kept looking at the stranger, staring beyond his eyes. What was I missing? I decided it was nothing of importance, and I instead focused my thoughts on what had just happened.

My dad gave away two tickets that were supposed to be for my mom and brother. The stranger handed my dad ten dollars, which was an unfair exchange. We had great seats, located a few rows behind the center of the court. Those tickets were probably worth a hundred dollars, but my dad didn't seem to care because he was just going to throw them out. Better to make a few dollars than to make nothing, right? No. Right after that unfair exchange, I started thinking about how that stranger would be sitting next to us during the game. I don't know why, but I decided to confirm this thought with my dad. At this point, my memory turned into a horrifying nightmare.

"So that guy will be sitting next to us, right? Dad?"

As soon as the words left my mouth, I mentally retreated into the darkest and loneliest corner. I felt numb. How could I be so fucking ignorant? The truth behind my question choked me viciously. I was suffocating beneath the weight of my thoughts. I tried to speak, but the words couldn't vocalize. The harder I fought and struggled, the tighter I felt my throat close. Soon enough I wouldn't be able to breathe because my windpipe would be crushed. I wanted to cry out in desperation. *Help! Help me! Can't you see what is happening to me?* Nobody answered. All I could hear were throbbing echoes of my stupidity and ignorance. *That was a ticket scalper. How much more obvious could it be? What the fuck is wrong with you?* The voices attacked me. They beat me until I could no longer feel, and then their assaults intensified. *Can you feel it now?*

Are you still numb? What does your dad think of that stupid question you just asked? Silently, I pleaded for help. *Why do you even speak? Stop asking questions. What is wrong with you?* I don't know.

My dad didn't respond. I like to think that he didn't even hear me, but maybe I am in denial. *He heard you. He just couldn't answer such an ignorant question.* Stop! Those fucking voices are always attacking me. I'm just lucky my dad never answered my question or the voices would have attacked me twice as much. *First you asked a stupid question. Then you embarrassed yourself. HA! How pathetic, little boy.* Please stop hurting me. I feel so helpless and defenseless. Why are you attacking me? This is hurting me deeply. Please stop. Please leave me alone. Why do you have to constantly attack me? What did I ever do to you? I feel vulnerable all the time. It's because of these vicious attacks that I am incapable of handling any criticism. Insults are torture because they have the potential to become a new memory. Everything is so difficult and stressful. But I need to get back to what happened afterwards.

The rest of the night was perfect. My dad and I had great conversations before, during, and after the game. We both complained about how terrible the teams were playing. Then, almost like magic, both teams seemed to come to life in the fourth quarter. Swish! Mike Dunleavy threw up a three-point shot with a few seconds left. The Bulls took the lead! Game over! Bulls win! The stadium went ballistic, and the cheers of Bulls fans drowned the words of anybody in the building.

My dad was happy. I was happy. It was a wonderful night. How come I can't think about that? Why does my mind force me to recollect the memory of my ignorant question? That memory haunts me every day. I question everything, and I love that about myself. But when this memory surfaces, I can't question anything. I become vulnerable and incapable of asking questions. It terrifies me.

It all rushes back to the present. My dad walked away and went inside the house. He left me alone. I could feel my mind buzzing and whispering. Trigger! My heart was racing and my body was shaking, but I somehow found the strength to hop on the lawn mower and drive it to the burn pile. I hopped off and grabbed my lonely shovel and started scooping ashes and dirt and shit and debris into the wagon. My shovel scoops became increasingly angry and upset. I could sense my mental state deteriorating slowly, and I knew I was going to collapse. But I kept shoveling that pile into my wagon. As my pile of ashes grew, my thoughts grew with it. My thoughts grew in anger until I started stabbing my shovel into the pile over and over. But I tried to calm myself. *It'll only be a few minutes. Just do your job and head back inside.* Calm down.

After my wagon was full, I drove the lawn mower to the dumpster. I hopped off again and started shoveling the ashes into the dumpster. Then I repeated this process four or five more times until the sun was starting to disappear behind the horizon. But that didn't bother me as much as my overwhelming thirst. Suddenly, I felt dehydrated and weak, and that's when it happened again. I had another flashback that captured the undivided attention of my mind.

Eighth grade. Baseball practice. The late summer heat blazed through the air across the entire baseball diamond. Sweat dripped from everyone's hair, face, neck, and arms. Practice was brutal, and we never stopped running. There were no breaks.

One moment I felt strong and confident, although slightly tired, and in the next moment I felt like I was about to die. My throat was dry and no sound could escape from its torturous, hollow chambers. I began to feel lightheaded, and my balance teetered. Water. I needed water. Right now! I sprinted toward the dugout and fished around in my bag for my antidote. I felt like I was seconds away from passing out and smacking my soft and gentle head against the unbudging concrete floor.

Finally, I found my water and chugged it until there was none left. My vision returned. Then, I felt steady and strong again. Well, I felt strong until I looked out of the dugout and met eyes with my coach. I could feel his eyes piercing me, but his disappointment is what dealt the deadliest blow. *You are weak. You needed water before the water break. I am disappointed. Weak.* My eyes retreated into their sockets, but I stepped out of the dugout and back onto the gritty dirt of the infield.

And then the memory ends and the moment rushes back to me with a sharp and renewed pain. I could feel the echo pounding me every second. *Weak. Tick. Weak. Tick. Weak. Tick. Weak.* I felt so weak and dehydrated. I needed water.

I put my shovel down and walked up the steps and into the house. I reached for my beautifully wet salvation, tipped it back, and allowed the pure, clear liquid to fill my throat. I felt better, stronger, and more confident. I was ready to get back to work, but my dad stepped into the kitchen.

"Good job, buddy, thanks for helping." His voice startled me, and I looked over at him.

"I'm not done," I told him. I walked out of the door before he could respond.

I quickly got back to work and started shoveling, shoveling, shoveling. I felt so weak and tired. My wrists felt like they were about to snap off at any moment. My back felt like someone was stabbing daggers between my spinal column, trying to make me flinch. I was in pain, but there was nobody else to witness my pain. Pitying myself, I kept working. I never stopped.

I looked into that pile of ashes and I saw years and years of memories. I saw dreams, hopes, and memories, but they were all ashes. Everything turned to ashes one way or another, and it was my job to move the ashes. I had to bury the ashes and the memories. For years, I had piled memories into that fucking spot on our lawn. Sometimes the memories were tiny branches with razor thorns that sliced my arms and legs. Or perhaps it was leaves from years of raking and raking. Or maybe cardboard from boxes of appliances or parts my dad ordered for one of his projects. Fuck, I don't know. Everything was set on fire. Everything was reduced to black ashes. Except me. I used to just stand in absolute silence and listen to the crackling noise that fire makes as it slowly eats the memories. I stared into the flames as they flickered brilliant oranges and flashed crimson reds. I watched the memories burn.

It was finally dark outside, complete blackness. The moon had already taken its pitiful throne as the celestial king of the sky. I struggled to see what I was doing because everything was black and grim. But after ten trips or so in total, I was shoveling ashes into the dumpster and my dad walked outside. Shit, that's not good.

"Make this your last load, okay?" That's what he said. Ordinarily,

I would have obeyed him and put the shovel down and walked away. Today was not ordinary.

Something happened to me in that moment. Looking back on it now, I still can't tell exactly what happened to me. It's quite probable that I will never understand it. But something happened. I'm not sure if it was stress or adrenaline or weariness, or even something else, but I do know one thing for certain. Momentarily, I had another flashback.

It was a beautiful day at the park. I was probably nine or ten years old, so I guess I was old enough to behave myself. My mom, brother, and I were at the park with my mom's friend and her kids, including one of my best friends. We indulged ourselves with the park's atmosphere. We had a wonderful time eating and playing in the park together. Well, we were having a wonderful time until the memory happened and everything changed.

It started off as a simple walk along the park's trail. At a certain point, I remembered something I had always wanted to do. I wanted to walk the entire circle of the trail in its entirety—one giant loop. So, what did I decide to do? I asked my mom about it. She promptly responded to my question.

"Sure! Of course you can!" Sarcasm. That meant she was saying no to my request. I was being denied. I was always either being denied or being ignored, and I was sick of it. I would be denied no longer. I would not be ignored.

I stopped walking in their group formation. Instead, I turned around and started walking in the opposite direction. Thankfully, nobody noticed me right away. I often wonder, when thinking of this traumatic memory, how long it took for anyone to notice my absence. It must have been at least a few minutes. *Minutes.* There were entire minutes that ticked by without anyone noticing that I was nowhere to be found. Where did I go? Well, let me explain.

I walked straight along that trail without a glance over my shoulder. How long did I walk? I don't know, honestly, but it must have been at least half an hour. I don't remember much about the walk and, thinking back on it now, I probably didn't remember anything at the time, either. I was mentally and physically focused on one thing: the walk. It fascinated me. Every pebble under my foot and every crack in the pavement felt like a story, and I decided to follow that story. I read that story with every step I took, and, when I felt like the story was ending, I wrote my own story. I etched a delicate and elaborate pattern in each individual groove of that trail. Each twist and turn yielded another chapter in my story. I was determined to complete my story. No exceptions. No excuses. Well, unless you count getting caught as an exception or excuse.

A park ranger drove up beside me in her little Jeep. She asked me if I was Justin. I told her I was indeed Justin, the mysterious child. She said she came to pick me up and drive me back to my mom. She also said my mom was very worried about me. Therefore, I decided my little expedition was over, and I climbed through the passenger's side door and buckled up.

The ride back to my mom was surreal. I felt like it wasn't truly happening. I remember the park lady talking to me and asking questions. She told me I had walked a couple of miles. *Miles.* But, for some reason, I didn't feel exhausted. I don't know what I was supposed to feel.

My mom and the others were waiting at a picnic table for my safe return. I stepped out of the car and walked toward them. My mom started crying, and she came over to me and hugged me and told me how worried she was about me. I hugged her back and told her I was sorry for walking off. She just kept hugging me, and I hugged her back. Usually that's where my memory ends, but sometimes it ends earlier than that. Today, my flashback ended as soon as I started walking.

White light from above our garage flashed through the black night and stung my eyes. Reality flooded back into my lungs with a deep breath of the cold, April night. I felt that strange feeling again. My muscles tensed and then relaxed, then tensed again. My fingers gripped tighter around the shovel; I could already feel blisters forming across my sensitive fingers and my delicate hands. I felt that strange feeling and I embraced it.

What was the feeling? Was it adrenaline or was it hormones? I don't think so. It was a necessity. It was a compulsion. It was a force of sheer will and determination. I was not going to put my shovel away until every last speck of ash was gone. The fires had left too many unspeakably horrifying remnants. Memories. I had to dispose of the evidence. I *had* to. I was compelled to shovel until I collapsed in exhaustion or the pile disappeared, whatever came first. There would be nobody to tell me when to stop shoveling. Nobody would grab another shovel and move a single scoop of ashes. Those were my ashes. I died in those fires. Nobody is worthy of disposing my remains. Only I can dispose of my remains. If someone tried to touch the ashes, my shovel, or myself, I would have bashed their inferior skull with either my shovel or my fists. Nothing would have stopped me, and I didn't believe anything but myself could end this compulsion. If my dad tried to take the shovel out of my hands, I would have fought him, too. I felt disgusted. *This is it,* I thought, *this is the moment where I relinquish my flaws.* In that moment, nobody could have related to me or understood how I was feeling. The only thing that mattered to me in that moment was clearing that fucking pile of ashes. I didn't care about anything else. Nothing. I would have stayed up all night if I had to. It didn't matter what time it was because the only thing that mattered was destroying my ashes. If I had to pick up the ashes by hand and carry them across the yard and throw them into the dumpster, I would have. The feeling was powerful, but it cannot be replicated or explained. Give me the greatest minds in history and the combined writing capabilities of Shakespeare, Hemingway, Dickens, and all those other famous authors, those poor inglorious bastards. That won't change anything. The feeling cannot be reproduced or described. I could write an entire journal dedicated to the feeling, but nothing would change. Nobody would be able to grasp its dominance. Nobody would be able to comprehend its utter brilliance. It was a powerful feeling. But why was it so powerful? Why? Where did the feeling originate? I know one thing: that feeling was a result. That feeling was the result of my life and every fucking moment leading up to it. That feeling was every pain, scratch, word, thought, attack, abuse, laugh, smile, frown, gift, loss, emotion, and memory I've ever experienced. That feeling is the result of my life. That feeling is an external extension of my innermost trauma. I was prepared to swing my shovel like a baseball bat at someone's head. My mind was controlling my body parts. My trauma was controlling my mind. It was all connected, and that fucking feeling was the brunt of everything. Most of all, that feeling motivated me and forced me to be confident. If I felt like that all the time, I wouldn't have any problems in my life. But why did I feel like that? I felt the same as in my park memory. Nobody takes me seriously, and that is a mistake. I felt sick of not being taken seriously. I felt like a fucking pawn. Fuck everybody in this world. What do I have to do for someone to take me seriously? I told my mom I was going to walk that trail and she thought I was fucking joking. When I walked away, not realizing the trail is a straight line and not a loop as I had originally thought, that's when people realized I was being serious. What if I said I was going to kill myself? Would anyone take me serious? Or would they try to be witty cunts and make a joke out of it? Do I have to kill myself to receive sympathy and remorse? What the fuck? Is that what it takes for anyone to notice me? I've gone unnoticed for so long that finally being noticed terrifies me ceaselessly. Would anyone notice me if I killed myself? Would they finally take me seriously? I don't know. The only thing I know is that feeling.

There were a few times where I almost collapsed from exhaustion while shoveling. I have scoliosis and my back was twinging, making it difficult to stand. Every part of my body felt sore. My wrists were in pain from the constant motion I used to shovel. Everything was aching. I had to stop shoveling for a few moments because I was worried I was going to hurt myself. I would stick my shovel in the grass, hold it, and crouch down into the surrounding darkness. Then, I would look up and stare at the moon until my agony subsided. That was the signal. It was time to get back to work.

At one point, I was shoveling ashes into my wagon when I saw a bright and irritating light stabbing through the darkness in my general direction. It was a flashlight. One of our neighbors was outside, and I could see his figure walking toward me. I was pissed at him. I told myself that if he came near me or asked me to stop running the lawn mower, I would bash his fucking brain with my shovel. I didn't care. I was not about to let some asshole try and push me around. I was fucking sick and tired of being pushed and prodded. Nobody was about to tell me what to do or how to do it.

But the man turned around and, in the pale illumination from his flashlight, I saw he was only taking his dog outside. That was a relief. Why am I so fucking paranoid? I'm basically a wasted entity.

I always feel so vulnerable. I felt like that stranger was going to do something or say something to me, and I was scared because I knew I'd be traumatized. Also, I felt like smashing his head with a shovel. That would be a regrettable decision, and I'm glad I didn't act upon that impulse. I'm not violent. It was the feeling that was violent. That feeling would have made me do anything to ensure my pile of ashes was handled properly.

My mom yelled at me to get inside because it was past nine o'clock. She said it was my last warning. That was a fucking threat. I completely ignored her. I was thinking about flipping her off, but I decided against it. I debated it heavily. I've never sworn around my parents out of respect, but I would have flipped my mom off without hesitation in that moment. The feeling is too powerful. Hopefully it never tells me to kill myself. I would do it.

Not long after that, my dad came outside and told me again that it was my last load. He said he was serious, but I could hear the exhaustion in his voice. Normally, that should have intimidated me until I succumbed and reduced my pride to blackened ashes. But I didn't listen. I had to tell myself when to stop. That's exactly what I did, too.

After I finished shoveling my "last load," I went back to the pile. I picked up two metal pieces, carried them to the dumpster, and heaved them over the side. I told myself that was my last load. When I looked back at the burn pile, I saw nothing. The ash pile was nothing more than a flat, black blemish in our yard. My task was complete. The feeling left me, and a wave of satisfaction washed over me. I finally felt satisfied. Not only that, but I did everything by myself. I didn't let anyone manipulate me. I didn't conform to someone else's desires. I cleared the ashes.

My state of satisfaction didn't last long. I felt like shit. My muscles were practically begging for me to sit down and relax. I listened to their whining. I went inside the house, and I could feel eyes following me. Every action from my body was being scrutinized, and questions were forming. They were all looking at me, and I knew exactly what that meant. When people look at me, they're thinking, judging, and questioning me and any decisions I make. Decisions is a powerful word. Maybe if I had control of every single decision I would be a perfect person. But I don't always control my decisions. Sometimes I must alter my decisions based on various reasons. Maybe one day I want to do something, but I have to make a different decision. Usually my mind starts racing and gives me a thousand different fucking reasons for why I should or shouldn't make a decision. Then, as soon as I decide, I have ten different people trying to tell me how wrong I am.

What the fuck is wrong with me? That's my mantra. I keep repeating it to myself until that's the only thing I'm capable of hearing. Why would I do that? Maybe it felt like the right decision at the time. Why is everyone looking at me like that? Why is everyone asking me questions? Everybody looks at me like I'm doing everything wrong. I can't stand all of those eyes digging into the back of my skull and clawing out my own eyes until the only vision I have is darkness. Constantly, I worry that the darkness is going to be permanent.

Sleep tight.

APRIL 17, 2016

My family is fucking stupid and poor and they make bad decisions. My stupid great-great-great grandfather made the dumbest decision and now it is costing our entire family as the unlucky trail continues. My dad's uncle killed himself because of it. I can see that affected my dad, too. What did my grandfather do? My dad told me a little story about him.

He owned 120 acres of land. He, for some stupid reason, gave away the rights to the minerals on the land. That meant anything underground was not his property. He no longer owned anything beneath the surface because he relinquished those mineral rights. He only owned the surface.

As time went by, it was discovered that there were massive oil and natural gas reserves beneath the property. This was years later, long after the mineral rights were given away. By this point in time, the property had been divided into six sections with twenty acres per section. My dad's side of the family are mostly farmers; that land was a valuable asset. Each family member or group of family members owned one section. My grandparents owned, and currently own, one section of that land. That section has oil and natural gas reserves.

A company told my grandparents that they were going to mine the oil and natural gas out of the ground. My grandparents must have been happy because they went along with the company's orders. They must have assumed they would receive profits from the mining. But nope, that company built a giant rig on their property and didn't pay them a single penny. My dad's uncle ended up killing himself over the battling that ensued. Maybe he couldn't handle the stress of the ordeal. I think he realized it was over and that no money would be received.

My grandparents were too poor to sue the multi-million dollar company. So, for the past however many years, they have been paying taxes on that property. But they don't get any money from the millions of dollars that company has made off the oil and natural gas. That is how the cookie crumbles in our family. We are poor and we make stupid choices, and then it becomes a cycle.

My dad told me how upsetting this memory is for him. He says he has spent countless nights thinking about it, and I believe him. It surprises me, though. Nothing has ever made my dad that upset. You know, I've got a couple of thoughts about that, too.

I have watched my dad work every day of his life. Every single day. Sometimes, I feel like I missed out on a lot of my own childhood because of that. My dad was always gone or working or sleeping or trying to recover from work. My dad never even had a childhood. He had to work every day of his life. It's not fucking fair. It was only one bad decision. Our family could have had some money, and maybe then my dad would have been able to have a normal childhood. Maybe then we wouldn't have to do shit the hard way. Life is so fucking unfair. I hate it. It's terrible.

What is going to happen to me? Am I just going to grow up and have some unlucky thing happen to me? Will I have to work and work for nothing? Life is so unfair.

One bad decision. That's all it took. I didn't even know about it until my dad told me. I don't know why I'm so upset. I feel like years and years of struggle have reduced our family to nothing, and now I am the burden. I must carry this burden with me always. My family has a history of struggling and working and struggling more, but they rarely display emotion. That's just how our lives work. Now, I will carry their burden and my burden and everyone's burden. All of their struggles are somehow mine.

We aren't poor anymore. It feels strange and I hate it. My dad told me today that the lowest amount of money he ever had in his bank account was seventeen dollars. We used to live paycheck to paycheck. We were seventeen dollars from nothing. My dad grew up poor, but my mom didn't grow up as poor as my dad. She never had much money, either. But my dad had it the worst.

One time, my dad told me about how embarrassing it was to go to the grocery store. He said his parents would pick out all their groceries and then proceed to checkout. There was always a problem. His parents couldn't write a check because they didn't have enough money. They had to go and put some of their groceries back because they couldn't afford them. Their bank balance would have dropped below zero. My dad said that was always embarrassing.

Why does that memory affect me? That memory makes me feel sad and embarrassed and it didn't even happen to me. I might have a strong connection with my dad, but I shouldn't be able to feel in that manner. I'm not sure. What the fuck is wrong with me?

A friend told me I may have Post-Traumatic Stress Disorder, or PTSD for short. She said every symptom sounds like me. I asked her what the symptoms were and she told me: "Recurrent, unwanted distressing memories of the traumatic event. Reliving the traumatic event as if it were happening again (more commonly known as flashbacks). Upsetting dreams about the traumatic event. Severe emotional distress or physical reactions to something that reminds you of the event." There are also symptoms of negative changes in mood and thinking, as well as changes in emotional reactions. She also told me that it can happen to anyone, including me.

So today I found out I most likely have PTSD. A doctor's diagnosis is needed to officially verify I have PTSD, but I'm not sure I will tell my doctor. Either way, I am going to refer to my problem as PTSD. I have PTSD. It makes sense. I will talk about it more at another time. For now, this story goes on to the next important date.

APRIL 21, 2016

I'm living my life on this chaotic timeline. Prince died today, and it oddly triggered my PTSD. I flashed back to a memory where I was riding in a car with my mom and her friend.

Michael Jackson had recently died, and one of his songs, probably as a remembrance, started playing in the car. I had never heard the song or its singer. I was ten years old. Being an inquisitive child, I asked about him.

"Who is Michael Jackson?" The words vibrated from my lips and shattered like glass. I wished to put those pieces back together, but it was hopeless. The damage was finished.

"You don't know who Michael Jackson is!?" They yelled at me. I shook my head, feeling silly and stupid. My mind wandered from my paralyzed body. Why didn't I know who Michael Jackson was? How come his terrific voice never reached my tiny ears? I don't know. It bothered me that I was one of the few people who had never heard of Michael Jackson. How did everyone else know Michael Jackson? I felt extraterrestrial. I quickly realized that I was an outcast, a rogue. There were the people who knew Michael Jackson in one group, and there were people who didn't know Michael Jackson in another group. And then there was me. I was stuck between knowing and not knowing, knowledge and ignorance.

Similarly to Michael Jackson, I had no clue who Prince was. I had heard his name before, but it never concerned me until my chemistry teacher started talking about him. She is a huge fan of him, apparently. She mentioned him over and over and I fought the temptation to ask about Prince. I knew how embarrassing that would be. My teacher would humiliate me in front of my peers.

"What? You don't know who Prince is? How is that even possible?" That's most likely what she would say to me. It would have hurt more if I asked a question. Questions are the beginning of disappointment.

In addition to that fiasco, my stupid fucking friend triggered me this morning. I was sitting down against my locker with a few other people, and we were minding our own business. My friend was standing in front of me. He kept kicking me in the fucking leg. I told him to stop multiple times, but he kept kicking me. Lately he has been more physically aggressive than ever before, and I feel football has made a large impact on his behavior. He triggers me all of the fucking time. His kicking triggered a memory to surface in my deluded mind.

It was Halloween. I went trick-or-treating around town with a friend named Joey. After we were done, I followed Joey to his friend's house. We sat on the lawn and started eating our candy. Remember that we were young, and candy still excited us and gave us unparalleled joy.

Well, my friend and the other guy were both much larger than me. They both played football together, too. They decided it was an appropriate time to go on the trampoline and wrestle. They were both much more aggressive and physical, unlike me. I was (and still am) a skinny twig. I knew that if I went and wrestled with them I would get snapped in half. They took it way too seriously. So I just sat there on the lawn, eating my candy and keeping to myself. I watched them wrestle. Alone. I felt so left out, but I was choosing to be left out. They had asked me if I wanted to wrestle, and I said no. I told them no.

Today, my friend kept kicking me and that was the trigger memory that I flashed back to. I don't fully understand how my PTSD works. I don't expect people to understand, even if they wish they could understand. I just want people to listen. Listen to my story. Listen to my struggle. Listen to me. Attempt to understand, but do not stress if you cannot. Sometimes I have a difficult time understanding these things, too. Heck, for all I know I might not even have PTSD. I'm still trying to figure everything out. I've been trying to do this for years, but I never had a name for my problem until now. PTSD. The more I know about it, the better chance I have to limit it or prevent it entirely.

I read that PTSD can be short term, meaning it disappears after enough time has passed. I don't think mine is temporary. I don't know. This has been happening for too long. These memories have been tormenting me far beyond a short timeline.

Another thing I found interesting is that some, if not most, people's PTSD stems from one specific event, but I can't seem to single out one event that would have solely caused my PTSD. If I had to choose, I think the memory that started it all was four-year-old me being terrified and traumatized by our basement filling with smoke. My dad and uncle were in a panic that day, screaming and yelling for me. All I could see was gray, dirty smoke. Everything felt distant. It was one of the most traumatizing moments of my life. I haven't written about that memory yet. It's too powerful. It must be recorded perfectly or it will bother me forever.

My biggest problem is that I am still creating memories. I live in fear every fucking day. I don't want to be traumatized again and again and again. I have to relive every single memory over and over and over. I remember a frequent nightmare I had when I was little, and how much it scared me.

My dad was on an impossibly tall ladder against the side of our house. He was trying to climb onto the roof, which, for a child, seemed like a skyscraper. I was watching him, observing him, detailing him as he climbed up the ladder. Then I could hear myself yelling at the air in my feeble attempt to move those floating particles. Everything happened in slow motion. The ladder buckled and fell backwards, and my dad's flailing body hit the concrete with a bone-crunching echo. I screamed for my mom to come outside. I ran toward my dad, but there was nothing I could do. His lifeless body was crumpled and distorted, forever vanishing from the realm of life.

And then I would wake up crying because I had just watched my dad die. Waking in a cold sweat and terror, I would stay up late and relive my dad's death until my head became exhausted from thinking. I remember being terrified to go back to sleep for fear of having the same nightmare. Instead of sleeping, I would stay awake and contemplate my nightmare. Maybe it was my fault. Was I supposed to be holding the ladder? Why did the ladder buckle? Why was I a witness to this atrocity? I hope it was not my fault. How could I, a child at the time, take responsibility for my dad's death? How can anyone carry that burden for the remainder of their pathetic and miserable existence? Nobody would place the blame on me, would they? How could they blame such a seemingly innocent child? It was only an accident. Only an accident…

It wasn't even a real memory; it was a nightmare. But it felt real to me, and I kept it. I cried over this nightmare more times than I can count on my fingers. I felt like I had actually witnessed my dad die. There were many nights where I had that same nightmare when I was little. I would wake up, cry, think about the nightmare, and then go back to sleep. Repeat. A cycle. A routine. Repeat.

I have to relive memories like that every day. It makes life difficult. Everyone around me has no clue what is happening. For them, bad memories happen and then they are over. For me, I am always at risk. As far as anyone else is concerned, I could be mourning the death of my father throughout the day. Nobody knows that vulnerability. Inside, I am fucking dying. They just can't see it. So when I'm not talking to my friend and he asks me why I'm not talking, what am I supposed to say? What if I had just watched my dad die in that nightmare?

"I was crying and watching my dad fall to his death. What do you want?"

He would assume I am joking, or insane. But I am neither. Everyone else is living without this constant fear that I possess. This is my burden. When they try to act like I am just a normal person, I know that it won't work. They bother me when I shouldn't be bothered. They question me when I shouldn't be questioned. They insult me when I shouldn't be insulted. They don't know any better, but it still makes me fucking sick. Can they not at least see that I am struggling and that whatever they are doing in that moment is wrong? I could be losing a mental battle at any given moment, and when someone tries to make me lose a physical battle it's going to hurt me even more. I tell my friend to stop kicking me, yet he doesn't listen. What if I was that scared four-year-old Justin who was standing in the corner of the room, terrified by how quickly the room filled with smoke? I can't see anything. I am terrified. I am alone. I am going to die. I am going to die standing against this wall without a word, and nobody will ever know what happened to me.

No. My friend doesn't understand. Nobody understands. How can I even explain it? It's not something that can be easily explained. Physical disabilities are easy to explain. Those are easily visible and incredibly more understood. Oh, this person can't walk? I guess I won't ask them to play tag. Understood, right? But nobody knows that about me. They don't know about my PTSD. They can't see the hidden anguish and fear that I live with every moment of my life. Sometimes I have a difficult time seeing it, too. But it is always there.

I don't even understand myself sometimes. Hopefully this journal will help me grasp a better understanding of myself. I can look back at all my entries and finally analyze myself. I don't know. I can only hope to do that.

How come I wasn't triggered the other day when I visited a college and asked a professor my simple question? There were people watching. I felt their eyes on me. I asked a question. I should have been triggered. I almost expected to be triggered. I should have lost my functionality as a basic, compatible human. But I didn't. The professor answered my question and immediately placed his attention on the next question. What happened? How come that didn't trigger me? I don't understand.

APRIL 22, 2016

I woke up early and drove to my school on a Teacher Institute day. Why? I was going on a field trip to the county jail and courthouse. That was definitely an experience, but for some reason I feel like it would be useless to write about. It was boring and extremely disappointing. Every inmate seemed like a normal person, and there was only one inmate I felt I could relate to.

That one inmate was sitting on a tiny bench in the middle of the room. He was white, middle-aged, and balding. His back was turned to me, but he didn't appear particularly menacing or dangerous. In fact, quite the contrary, he was crying. I couldn't see his face, but I could see his body rising and falling in rhythm with his sobs. I thought his breathing was ragged and irregular, but it was his repeated sobs. He went on crying for nearly twenty minutes. Then he got up, albeit slowly, and proceeded to walk to his cell. The only sound was his cell door shutting behind him. He cried in front of me for twenty minutes, but his silence is what made me feel such a strong connection to him. The power of his silence nearly reduced me to tears, as well. I wonder if he went into his cell to cry alone without our tour group staring at him as if he were a lonely animal in a zoo. In a certain sense, he was a lone animal trapped behind bars. It was very surreal to watch that man cry, even though I couldn't hear him. I know he disobeyed the law and he was being punished for his crimes, but to see his punishment made me emotional. I couldn't help it. I felt sympathetic for the sobbing man.

After visiting the jail and courthouse, my government teacher drove our group of students (six of us in total) to a restaurant. I didn't know what to order and the thought of ordering was killing me. I ended up buying a chicken sandwich because that was the only item I felt familiar with. Everybody else ordered more elaborate, fulfilling meals. I couldn't help but feel like an outcast from the rest of my group. Trying to ignore it, I quickly ate my sandwich and shared some onion rings with a girl in my group. It didn't help anything.

The ride back to the school was a nightmare from which there was no escape. Why was it a nightmare? Well, everybody started talking about superheroes and movies and shows that I knew nothing about. Knowing I had nothing useful to contribute to their conversation, I stayed quiet. As my silence encompassed many minutes of observation and intent listening, it was only a matter of time before someone noticed I was still a breathing member of the car. I had to speak before they noticed, but there was no time to speak.

"Oh, Justin, I forgot you were in the car," my teacher said. "What do you think?" Suddenly, there were a dozen piercing eyes attached to me, following every movement I made. My heart dropped into my stomach. I swallowed my fear, pondering what to say next.

"Yeah, I think teleportation would be an awesome superpower." I probably said some other useless garbage, too. I was more worried about having everyone's attention for those few seconds. I had intervened with their conversation and I had stolen their attention.

The only other interesting note to be made from this day is that I started to feel sick. My throat was hurting, and I may have a fever.

APRIL 23, 2016

My stress levels are going off the charts. It was my sister's birthday party, although her real birthday was weeks ago. We invited friends and family over to celebrate. Normally I would put on a mask of happiness and pretend to be enjoying myself for the occasion, but I felt terrible and sick. I decided to use this to my advantage to avoid making social interactions with people. If they got too close to me, I reminded them that I was sick and not feeling well. I spent the majority of the day on the computer, playing games.

There is one moment that sticks out in my head from today. I was standing near the wall in our kitchen, and people must have noticed me. Maybe it was because I looked so pale and sick.

"You're so skinny! You're like an x-ray. Look, I can see straight through you! It's seventy degrees in here!"

I turned around. I was standing in front of the thermostat. I laughed along with everyone else, but on the inside, I felt even worse than I did before.

APRIL 24, 2016

I noticed music and song lyrics are an important part of my daily life. Some days, I get certain sections of songs stuck in my head and that seems like the only thing I can concentrate on. My mind becomes a single-track operation. Music affects my emotions and manipulates my thoughts and actions. If it doesn't manipulate, it plays a role of heavy influence. Interesting, very interesting.

Also, one particular memory hit me hard today. It is a short memory, but I feel it is worth mentioning.

I was playing a video game once, a long time ago, and I was looking up cheat codes on the computer. I had already completed the game and I wanted to mess around as much as possible. But my dad saw what I was doing and he asked me why I was cheating. I told him. Then, he had a witty response.

"What's the point of playing the game if you're just going to cheat?" He walked away after making this comment. The memory ended.

Today, I realized what that memory means to me, and I felt terrible due to this newfound realization. I realized I cheat at life. I've been cheating at life for as long as I can remember. I hate it, but I have to do it. Then, I remember my dad asking his question. It hit me like a punch from Ali's flying fists of fury. I struggled a lot today with that thought.

I often think about suicide to end the game of Life, and not the board game that I've never played. Life. I need to stop my cheating. Today was tough, but I managed to stop thinking about suicide. Thankfully, that thought didn't last too long. PTSD is an aggressive force.

Sometimes I wonder how much longer I'll be able to cheat at life. By cheating at life, I mean all kinds of shit. Mostly making excuses and avoiding things. For example, if I know my dad or mom needs help with something really quick, I will go in the bathroom and pretend to take a shit or something so they don't ask me for help. Usually, my plan backfires and I end up helping them after I get out of the bathroom. Fuck. That's still cheating. I don't do it because I'm lazy, either. I do it because I'm terrified of everything and I don't need any additional traumatic memories.

I also came up with an interesting thought about PTSD in an attempt to visualize it. I thought about sitting in class and how most of the chairs have little holes in the back. Having PTSD is like having someone sit behind you with a needle. That person will poke you with the needle through those tiny holes, and it hurts so fucking bad. All you can focus on is not getting poked again. Except you can't always tell when that person is going to poke you; it's a bit more complicated than that. You may anticipate being poked by the needle, but that's when it doesn't happen. When everything seems perfect and normal, the needle stabs you in the back.

Perhaps you try blocking the hole. Maybe you use a book or another object to block that tiny hole. But then you feel uncomfortable and your back hurts because you are constantly leaning against a book. Nothing helps. Even if you find a way to block the hole, a malicious person's needle will find a new approach to attack you. Instead of poking through a tiny hole in the chair, that person will send his needle of misery into your exposed neck. Nothing can stop it. That's one way to visualize PTSD, my disease.

APRIL 26, 2016

I was scheduled to take an ACT Compass Test at the local community college. If I passed the test, I would be able to take an advanced, college-level math class at my high school. I was feeling nervous the entire morning. My anxiety was pressuring me. Pressure, stress, and fatigue were all factors that consisted in my morning bowl of cereal. Commence my suffering.

All students who would take the test, including myself and my friends, hopped on the bus without a care in the world. I heard people talking about how easy the test would be, and their words softened my mood. Passing time on the bus, I listened to music and became lost in the lyrics.

Only eight students could test at a time, so the majority of us went into the cafeteria to await our impending failure. I spent a few mindless hours in the cafeteria until the mind-numbing boredom curdled into dread. It was my turn to take the test.

Before entering the testing room, I gave photo identification to a disgruntled man. He grumbled about something and handed my driver's license back to me. What an asshole.

I pushed the door open and walked to my designated computer number. If I remember correctly, my computer was number forty-five. I sat down and quickly completed the instructional page of the test. The test had begun. Resume suffering.

My mind receded and left me with a blank slate covered in emptiness. I couldn't remember anything. I completely forgot how to do basic algebra problems. Why couldn't I remember? I was terrified. My hands shook and my body temperature plummeted. Cold, shaking, and afraid, I finished my test. I vaguely hoped that I had somehow passed. I exited the testing session and walked back to the grumpy old man.

"Justin?" he asked. I nodded. "Eh, yeah, here you go, one second."

Observing his movements, I watched him circle two words on a piece of paper. College Algebra. He handed me the paper and he told me to leave. I glanced at the paper as I walked away, and I almost started dry heaving. Trigonometry, the class I was attempting to enter next year, was left uncircled. Realization jabbed me in the stomach and kicked at my kidneys. I didn't pass. I failed. That stupid sheet told me I failed.

The walk back to the cafeteria was like a death march. There were no oppressors to murder me if I stopped walking, but it certainly felt that way. I was so close to collapsing on the floor, yearning to be trampled and crushed beneath an unforgiving and relentless stampede. Who makes up the body of the stampede? Everybody else that passed. They would trample me and stomp me into the floor until I am reduced to ashes. Everything is reduced to ashes.

I failed. Everyone else passed. I couldn't get over that moment when the man nonchalantly circled College Algebra. I felt numb, if numbness is a feeling; it is mostly a lack or absence of feeling. This test was the beginning of my future. It was my life. And I failed. When I failed, nobody steadied me and told me it was okay. No. My friends looked at me like I was stupid and helpless. I couldn't even look into their eyes because I knew they would have noticed my problems. They would know. "What is wrong? Why do you look like you're about to cry? It's just a stupid test." They say those words, but their actions make their words feel detachable. They pretend they are concerned for me, but secretly they are only happy to pass the test. They couldn't care less about what happens to me. All they did was whisper to each other about how high their test scores were while I was sitting there trying to think about how my life would pan out. That test was supposed to be the first step in the correction of my life, but I failed the test and hurt myself in the process.

I thought about how much of a relief it would be to kill myself and end my problems. End the flashbacks. Erase the memories. How am I supposed to lead a normal life when this burden chokes me until I asphyxiate? I can't think, move, or speak. That's not even mentioning that I'm sick and my nose is runny and then stuffy, runny again, then back to stuffy. It is an alternating cycle of discomfort. My head hurts sometimes, too. I always feel too cold, too warm, or a disgusting combination of the two. I feel weak all the time, as if my other symptoms were the tip of the iceberg. I'm what lies beneath the iceberg, somewhere lost in the overshadowing darkness. Most of this is a result of stress. I was stressed so much that it physically made me sick. How depressing is that? Meanwhile, everyone else is living within completely normal lives; the same lives I cannot live and I'll never be able to live. But they keep acting like I am normal and I will live a normal life. I'm not normal. I will never be completely normal. I carry the burden.

The rest of my day was a mixture of numbness and defeat. I could hardly speak, but I spoke to provide a fake aura of indifference. My life, following an incredibly stressful month, was falling apart. Death seemed to be a close companion during my rough moments, but I shunned death. It is not time for me to die.

Later on, I found out I actually passed the test. I was in disbelief. It was very anticlimactic, but I accepted it. I passed.

APRIL 27, 2016

Nothing bad happened today, but I did notice something rather important. Recently, my grades have been slipping, or at least it feels like that. I try not to check my grades because it is too stressful, but I noticed my scores were lower than usual. Anyway, I've been slacking a little because some things hold a higher priority than grades. Can you blame me? I thought that my mental health was more important than a few letters or numbers on a piece of paper. I'm sick of priorities.

My English teacher wrote a short message on my paper. She said I needed to include more information in my notes about *The Book Thief*, by Markus Zusak. I thought about that a lot. It was bothering the fuck out of me. She was right. My work has been sloppy and pathetic lately. I'm struggling, even though the book is considerably easier to decipher than any previous works of literature we've read this year, such as *The Iliad* and *Dracula*. I found my struggle to be strange until I realized what was happening to me. I couldn't focus on the book because I was too busy focusing on myself and my life. My English thinking translated into my thoughts, and now I'm deciphering myself. I'm analyzing myself like I'm a book or a character in a book. I'm looking for metaphors and similes and themes and all kinds of fancy literature shit like that. I'm searching and digging for connections. It's very strange, but I think that's what happened. Either that or I'm just thinking too much.

MAY 1, 2016

Why do I make people laugh? I don't know. I guess I want people to like me. Nobody likes me. If I didn't make people laugh I'd just be the smart, quiet, nerdy kid nobody talks to. If I make people laugh once in a while they won't completely ignore me. That's the only reason my friends probably talk to me. From time to time, they know I'll do or say something funny. Otherwise, they leave me out of everything, and I hate it so much.

Looking around the room for a partner in chemistry class, I noticed there were seventeen people. That's an odd number. Who is the odd man or woman out? Guess. Enough guessing. It's me, as always. I do a mental count of people in the room every fucking time. When there is an odd number, I have to ask to join my two friends, who always partner together.

"Yeah, can I be with you guys? There's an odd number…"

This weekend, on the surface, looks like it turned out great. But if you dig a little deeper it's not that hard to see how fucking terrible it was. While it was certainly an improvement from the last few weekends, it still bothered me. Honestly, I only had two goals for this weekend. I only met one of my goals. That drives me crazy because I'm trying so hard to help myself and I'm failing. Or half failing, considering I did meet one goal.

My first goal, which I accomplished, was to play video games for quite a few hours. It's usually a great way to relax and relieve stress. It's a wonderful distraction, too. I played a lot of games this weekend and I'm proud of it. What's my problem? I've got a hundred thousand fucking critics always taking my life and splitting it apart just to analyze it and then spit it out as if it tastes like shit.

"Oh, wow, you played video games all day. You must be a lazy piece of shit!"

"You're so spoiled." My parents tell me that far too often. They're trying to make me feel worse when I'm trying to feel better. I'm like a nail and they're the hammer. I'm trying to stay up but they keep pushing me down into my coffin. Pretty soon I'll run out of nails. What will happen then? The coffin will be sealed and nobody will be able to face me.

My parents try to erase any progress until I relapse and have to recover again. Another fucking cycle. If it's not my parents, it's somebody or something else. It's always a constant battle. I always push up to survive or else the nails will close my coffin and I'll be shut and sealed.

My dad says I'm spoiled. He goes off and tells me how shit his childhood was, how shit his life was, how much money he never had, and I sit and digest it until I feel the same. I walk around and fucking hate everyone and everything. I feel disgusted all the time. I look at some of the old shit I have and I realize how grateful I am, but, when I turn around and see my friends, my gratefulness disappears and my hatred returns.

My friends have all the updated games and all the new improved systems and shit, and I'm busy playing with the same games my dad played when he was a teenager. They look at me enjoying my games and assume I'm insane, even though I'm trying to stay sane. Everything seems insane to me.

They complain about how outdated I am and how much it aggravates them. I look at their fancy shit and I feel disappointed. They send me on guilt trips regularly. But I look at my dad and notice all of the shit he never had as a kid. I glance at my friends again before I look at myself and all the shit I do or don't have. There are two sides to my story. I have my parents telling me how spoiled rotten I am and how I should be more thankful, and I have my friends that all have bigger houses, more luxurious cars, and anything they want. All this shit seems so insane.

I get so hateful and I start to pull this shit apart from both angles. I attack one side of the equation and form my thoughts like a mob lynching a black man. I'm seething in rage and biting down a wave of anger as it rushes my head and swarms all its chambers.

I look at all these people buying pairs of shoes they never even wear. I get so angry and I want to say shit to them, but I back down like a dog that barks and never bites. It doesn't bite until you push it too far and its bark quickly transforms into a nasty bite. Some spoiled kid with a collection of Jordans is going to step on the poor dog's tail. Maybe slap the dog across the face for barking too loud. We'll have a serious problem in formation. The dog formulates a plan for its retaliation attack against the perpetrator.

When the dog attacks that spoiled kid, there will be issues for the kid because he knows he'll get chewed to pieces if he stays. He takes his shoe collections and his money and carries on his business elsewhere, but the damage is done. The dog may have won the battle, but is it fair to say it won the war? That spoiled kid caused that little dog too many problems. Years of rubbing new and expensive things into its face have passed, and now the poor puppy needs some serious loving before it can be normal again. There is still hope for that dog, but it will be a difficult recovery.

I'm that fucking dog. I look at all these kids with their shoes and they look at me in mine—the only pair of shoes I have. I've never owned two pairs of shoes at the same time, but these kids are out swapping theirs with a new pair for every day of the week. They have the nerve to laugh at me when they see my kicks. Damn, it's just a pair of shoes, right? I never saw a problem with it because all I ever needed was a pair of comfortable shoes to wear, but I guess that's wrong. They keep looking at my torn and tattered shoes and they ask me how much they cost. When I throw a price in their face, they spit it back at me with a laugh and a sneer. They smirk and they sneer and they won't drop the fucking subject. I tell them to stop, but it doesn't matter. They talk about how many hundreds of dollars they've blown on new shoes. They brag as if it is some sort of achievement. As if that isn't enough, they look at me like I'm the one who's missing out. Deep inside, I feel slightly attacked by their actions. I can sense their malicious intent, but my defense mechanism is slow to kick in.

Before my defense turns to offense, I know that I've got a little secret to offset them both. Before I realize what is happening, something in my brain takes an instant to turn my instance into an image. I take that image and consciously and subconsciously use it to beat myself repeatedly. I'm a victim of this abuse and I decide to seek the help of strangers, but when I put my hand out for help nobody reaches for me. They're all too busy gazing at the new pair of Vans that came out. See, I've already got too many problems. It seems like each new pair of shoes brings another image into my head. All my friends talk about the new pair of shoes they're going to buy, and I can see their desire and greed burning passionately, but nobody can see how it silently slaughters me. I take their little snippets and segments and I smush them and smash them and pocket them in a little nook or cranny inside my mind until the time is right to replace them.

They continue talking about their shoes. They talk about my shoes, too. Secretly, I feel myself searching and seeking a way to pry myself out of the conversation, trying to seek some sort of isolation. They never directly say those two words I fear, but I can feel it resonating from the tips of their tongues. That's the only evidence I need. Cheap. Poor.

As if that's not bad enough, I come home with my worn and beaten shoes and I take them off. I need to clear my mind from all the shit I have disputed in my head from earlier in the day. I casually relax until something prompts my dad to lecture me on how spoiled and ungrateful I am. He says I need to be more appreciative. He tries to put it nicely, but I know what he's implying. I take his words and I feel how sharp, pointy, and dangerous they are. The sharper the words, the deeper I drive them into my skin.

People tell me to toughen my skin, but let's not be brash about it. My skin is soft and gentle like the creature it contains. When you try to turn me into a monster, I slowly become one. Pent-up rage is released and unleashed like the fury of a thousand and one armies marching to an attack or battle. Now that my skin's been punctured, it's time to reverse the process of abuse.

There are two sides to every story and it's about time I've told mine.

I've got two sides to my own story. If I could tell each of them apart and learn to separate them, there would be hope for a brighter future. The only future I have seems foggy, but I can't see clearly in the fog. Nobody has the necessary fog lights to lighten my vision. I need to lift this fog in order to restore my future to the bright and happy place it used to be when I was young. When I was young and dumb, I never had to worry about the kind of shoes I wore or what people thought of me.

I used to wear my light-up sneakers and think I was on top of the world. Everything was great, but dig a little deeper and you'll find the sinkhole. The shoes I thought were cool and comfortable were probably the cheap Walmart version of every other kid's pair of shoes. My parents probably lied to me about how much my shoes cost or how much money we had left. See, I never worried about it back then because I was too young to grasp the concept or begin to understand it. Except now I'm old enough to visualize the lies, and it makes me realize how close I came to placing my parents in a desperate place. Money was on low fund, but nobody ever told me that. I'd go around the store looking for the newest shit to buy, but I know my mom was secretly dying on the inside. She knew things were too expensive, but she couldn't figure out how to explain it to me. She would always lie her ass off or she'd find a way to distract me with something cheaper.

I sit and contemplate these thoughts and memories from both angles, trying to analyze each individual side of the story. Now I get these strange vibes when I buy some new shit because my parents have more money than they've ever had before. I can go out and buy a new shirt without worrying too much about the cost. It doesn't work. I still find myself checking the price tags until I find the cheapest clothing item. If I find a price that's higher than I am comfortable with, I just move on to the next rack of clothes. I end up finding most of my shit in the Clearance section, at least until my mom comes by and tells me to put them back. She always wants me to find a better selection. I go back to the rack containing the expensive clothes and grab a few of those. It pains me deeply, and I am ashamed to admit it, but every time I buy something I mentally slap a dollar sign on it. I think of all the pain and stress my dad had to go through to get me this shirt, or these pants, or those shoes. It hurts me.

All this shit seems to cost too much and it drives me insane. My mom isn't too bothered by it because it isn't her money, and my dad is too stressed to worry about it. But I look around at all the shit I've bought or haven't bought and I start to worry. As soon as I try to unwind and relax a little, my dad visits me and tells me how spoiled I am.

I look at my friends with their shoes and clothes and watch them buy video games before they hit the stores. It all feels distant and strange to me. They go to the mall on weekends to spend extra money they don't need. While they're busy doing that, I'm dying as I try to battle these depressing images. All this shit seems unfair and wrong. I get so jealous toward people I shouldn't, and I get sympathetic toward people I otherwise wouldn't. I've got people mad at me, and I've got people who feel sad for me. I can't tell who is in the right and who is in the wrong.

I've got a nasty case of debilitating memories conking and knocking on my conscience until I'm knocked unconscious. Each side of this argument tries to persuade me, but I won't move, budge, or talk. I keep all of these battles locked up inside so when the time arises and arrives they can be used as a tool to detain me. Anyway, I am getting off topic.

My second goal for this weekend was to write in this journal. I keep getting distracted and thrown off course by all the other people in my family, chores, and other shit. I spent all weekend trying to write in my journal, but the only thing I ended up doing was hiding my journal from everyone. I hide my journal like I hide my battle wounds, and it ensures people look at me as a normal person having a typical day. But, on the inside, I'm really fighting a war. Each day is a new battle. Even when I'm smiling and laughing, there is a war being fought inside my head. Nobody notices these battles, and sometimes I don't notice them until it's too late. I am as wounded as a combat veteran, but there is no sympathy for my wars. Where is my Purple Heart? Where is my Medal of Honor? Where are the parades and holidays dedicated to my survival? There is nothing. All I have are memories and wounds—invisible, deadly, and incurable wounds. Sometimes I'll sit and think everything is fine and dandy because I've won a few battles. Maybe the tide of war is shifting. Except as soon as I think positive thoughts everything seems to darken; a sneak attack by the enemies just broke through my line of defense.

My offense has shifted into a struggle and a defense against all the extraterrestrial invaders that attack and invade me. I try to be evasive and act like nothing's happening, but somewhere deep inside me I can feel my brain shift. I'm transforming into a war zone, and I'm catapulted into the middle of it. That's where I get attacked from all angles.

Even when I'm smiling and happy, you don't see the struggle that lies underneath. Sometimes I have to fake my happiness or otherwise I would collapse from the pressure. I have to sacrifice a smidge of my sanity to keep myself moving in the direction I'm pushing my life to flow.

I've got a million responses to each attack, and for each response I've got about a billion more excuses. People say I make up a lot of excuses, or that I complain a lot. I guess that's true, but I'm just trying to save myself. Excuses are my last resort to an attack. They're like my reinforcement soldiers who come to defend me and take back a battle for at least one solid victory.

Trying new things is disastrous for me because it just opens the gates wide and open for any new army to come marching in. The army may hold a truce flag and appear friendly, but as soon as they get inside I can feel their pulses racing and I know they want to hurt me.

Say what you want about me and the way I think, but it's too difficult to make you understand. Let it be known that I can only write about the things I know how to write about. Some of these things can't be explained. These feelings and images and memories just keep on degrading me with no true explanation.

I could really keep writing and using my abuse as a tool to relinquish my fury, but I know the surface of my body needs to be replenished. I need to sleep and prepare for tomorrow's battle. I am just a warrior, but nobody gives me the credit I am due. I feel jealous of everyone around me, including my friends. They don't even comprehend the scope of my issues. They just see the surface and figure it's some trivial bullshit that is bothering me. Maybe if they read these words they would see how complex I am and why I can't explain things to them. They wonder why I don't talk much because they don't realize all the things I am thinking. If I were to talk, they would be stunned. They would think I'm crazy.

MAY 3, 2016

I have nothing important to write about, although I wrote an interesting paragraph that I'd like to record.

We are just tiny floating specks of an equally tiny speck that we call our planet. Our civilization is merely an illusion that we associate with because it is something our minds are capable of understanding. We cannot grasp the concepts of the universe due to our limited cognitive capabilities. Our tiny floating speck of a planet is inside a galaxy with millions and billions of other tiny floating specks, and then our galaxy is, on a similar scale, an even smaller speck. The universe is incomprehensibly vast and endless, and our lives are meaningless and insignificant. We are dust particles that are consumed by each breath of the universe. For all we know, our universe is just a floating speck of an even larger universe that consumes all the tiny specks in our universe. Nothing matters.

MAY 4, 2016

I don't have much to say because nothing has happened yet. I'm just a pilot spinning out of control. My jet just got shot down and I'm frantically trying to save myself before I smash into the earth below. I look around and all I see is my descent. I tell myself to look up, but when I look up all I see is the sky getting larger as I approach the ground. As I accelerate like a heated fireball, I gaze around and observe my scenery. There's water below me, but at my trajectory I'll pass right over it. A collage of trees stamp the land almost everywhere, except for a few pastures and ponds. Flowers sprout from the grass, looking so beautiful you could copy and paste them right into a movie poster.

My plane begins to spin faster as my engines completely die and I lose all control. I'm helpless. No matter how hard I jerk the wheel I know I'll never be able to regain control. I'm hopeless. Looking around the cockpit, I notice that I'm out of parachutes. Ejection is not an option. My heart beats faster and faster, trying to explode from my chest. Realization grips me and my mind turns to a blank slate covered by a still image of my impending destruction. Knowing I can't escape my fate, I brace myself for impact. The water is so close I can almost taste its salty spray. Tree needles are poking at my skin. Grass rubs against my ankles and I almost reach to itch it, but I'm not there yet. I'm still in the cockpit, awaiting my doom.

I brace myself. My eyes go dark and I can't tell when I'll hit the ground. It's a mystery, but I count the time away softly in my head. *Tick.* Three more seconds. *Tick.* Two. *Tick.* One and a half. *Tick.* One heartbeat. *Tick.* Boom.

I'd describe my crash, but each time is different. Some days I land in the water and I manage to survive the initial crash. Another day I'll get trapped beneath the fuselage and slowly lose consciousness and drown to death. Other days I wipe out half a forest before a tree branch gets lodged inside my windpipe. Every crash is unique.

It's been a hectic month.

MAY 7, 2016

I make mistakes. Allow that information to digest your cerebral instincts. It's probably worth mentioning that I am human. Do you have any idea what I could be implying when I say that? Let me repeat myself. I make mistakes. That means I am never entirely authentic or accurate when I write. I am merely a confused and weary archeologist. Instead of digging up fossilized remnants of our prehistoric ancestors, I dig up thoughts, feelings, emotions, and memories. I use my discoveries to tell a story. Similarly to any of my archeologist counterparts, I attempt to put puzzle pieces back together. They dig up bones and try to create a replica of an extinct animal. They dissect and decipher every piece in the vain hope they discover, through their careful analysis, a unique history behind that particular animal. Hold on a second. Shit. Those are paleontologists, actually. It's too late to go back and erase my words. See? This only proves my point. I make mistakes. That means no matter how detailed my descriptions and explanations are, I'll never be able to replicate exact thoughts, feelings, or memories. I simply translate these images to the best of my abilities. I am a translator and I'm having a difficult time deciphering these thoughts. I'm missing my Rosetta Stone, but I carry on without it. The path is difficult and unsteady, yet my mind tells me to position my feet between the splitting stones. Except I miss a stone and my limp body flails through the air and plummets to the ground below. That's another mistake.

I often wonder about how many mistakes I've made in my writing. How many moments did I forget to write about? How many thoughts went undocumented in this journal? Every word I write is an epitome. I strive for every detail to be recorded and presented in this journal. I want to look back at my words and be able to feel them. Placing a memory in the palm of your hand, you should feel it. Does it sit in the palm of your hand or does it glide effortlessly to the tips of your fingers? Does it feel warm and bubbly or does it peel and shed? Does it attempt to flee or is it difficult to leave your hand? Does it feel wet and sticky or does it slide around? What are you witnessing? Do you truly appreciate these memories and the imagery I have provided? I'm not a painter. I do not possess the ability to create art. The only option I have is my words. Words are worth a million Mona Lisas and so much more. Mona Lisa is pampered with her secured glass and monitored temperatures. She is always protected and guarded. Her temperature is controlled to assure her beautiful face stays young forever. Imagine a man sticking a thermometer in Mona Lisa's mouth to check her temperature. Then, imagine him talking to her as if she had a fever.

"I'm sorry, ma'am," he says, "but it appears you have a fever. Not to worry! I have it under control." He adjusts the temperature to keep Mona Lisa healthy. Her face and its colors are forever preserved.

She is deemed a priceless artifact, completely irreplaceable. Money cannot buy her. Why are words not priceless? Are words not the most priceless information available? The first amendment protects and upholds the freedom of speech, but does that offer the same value as a Mona Lisa? Are words priceless? Words are valuable. Words are my form of art. Sometimes, these words are all I have. They kept me alive; I was resuscitated. At the same time they resuscitated me, they equally tried to suffocate me. Words are incredibly powerful and influential.

When I forget to write certain things, I feel terrible. Sometimes I will be in the shower and I'll have an interesting thought, but I will usually forget it by the time I get out of the shower. Of course, I make mistakes. I probably made mistakes writing this entry, too.

I am a mistake.

MAY 8, 2016

My sister threw up and started crying today. I started to help her, but my mom woke up and took control of the situation, thankfully. I looked at my sister and it brought an abundance of memories to the surface of my head. They weren't insanely crippling flashbacks, but it was enough to stir my emotions.

I flashed back to every time I was sick when I was little. My immune system must have been complete shit because I was always puking or shooting it out the other end. If I were born before vaccinations, I'd probably be one of those kids that got mumps, measles, and chickenpox. Unlucky, but I'm grateful for modern medicine.

I remember throwing up and waiting for my mom to come into my room. She would bring a trash can and she would place a towel on my pillow. If I threw up multiple times, she would make me drink Ginger Ale or 7-Up to calm my stomach. This was always in the middle of the night. My mom always helped me when I was sick. If I had to choose, that would be her greatest trait as a mother, in my opinion. When I think of how wonderful my mom is, I usually think of situations where I was sick because I knew she would always be there for me.

That memory morphed into a different one. I remember asking my parents what I was like as a baby and their answer stuck with me. Apparently, I was a terrible baby. I constantly woke up in the middle of the night, crying for no reason. I was hungry, but I never wanted to eat.

As it turns out, my parents argued about me a lot. Were they arguing about me, or were they arguing because of me? I don't know. I have no clue what they argued about. But it was almost always about me.

My mom was upset because I stopped taking naps at two years old. I wasn't officially potty trained until I was four or five. I had a lot problems, and I caused twice as many. Emotional. Financial. Mental. Everything. My parents rarely got into fights, but most of their fights were because of me. I've only been able to recount a select few of their fights. I was too young to remember most of them, but I can almost hear their voices in my head. Yelling. Arguing. Fighting.

I remember one time my parents got into a fight. They had argued over small things before, but this fight was extremely verbal. I can't even remember what they were fighting about. Yelling. Angry faces. Spiteful words. I remember how it ended. My dad punched a hole in their bedroom wall. That was the end of the fight, or at least that's where my memory ends, so I'll assume the fight ended, too.

I imagine the aftermath of that fight. My dad had to fix the hole in the wall. I wonder how he felt as he fixed a problem caused by his own hand. What was he thinking? Did it upset him? Was he bothered by it? What were they fighting about? I don't know. Do I want to know? Yes, but I don't think an answer would benefit anyone. Was the fight about me? I hope not. I hope it wasn't me. I was too little, so young. I hope it was about money. Not me.

My mom had a miscarriage before she had me. I never thought about it much until recently, when I realized the scope of my issues. Would I have less problems if I had an older sibling? A role model or someone to guide me? Or would that sibling cause more problems for me, like my younger siblings already do? I don't know. I like to think that I would be better. But a darker and more secluded part of me wishes that I was the miscarriage.

There was another fight between my parents when I was twelve or thirteen. We were planning to drive to visit my dad's parents in New York, as we do every year. My parents got into an argument over it. My mom was frustrated because we never visit her dad, who lives in Georgia. We had never visited him before. We visit my dad's parents every year. My dad countered her argument by reminding her that she still lives close to her mom, brother, and sister. My dad has no relatives in this state. They argued back and forth, but I kept quiet. I am an observer.

Those are the thoughts I had when I saw my sister puking. She reminds me of myself sometimes, and it worries me. I couldn't bear to see her deal with the pain I have. When we play together outside and I want to go inside, she grabs my arm and blocks the door.

"Nooo Justin," she says, "I need two people to play. Please, Justin."

I look into her eyes and I can't help but feel my eyes brimming with tears. It makes me remember how many times I played by myself as a kid. I used to play football by punting the ball to myself and running across the yard. When I went inside, alone, I would cry in my room because I had nobody to play with. My brother never wanted to play with me.

My childhood upsets me. Everything about it traumatized me. It's not like I can tell people about it. They would tell me I'm a liar. My words are supposedly fictitious. My memories are artificial. I am making it up. They will tell me I am selfish for thinking like I do. They will tell me how great my life is and how wrong I am. My mom tells me how easy my life is. Ha! I wish it was that easy.

Fuck. I made it through the week without any complete mental collapses, but barely. Chemistry class was so damn close. I struggled through it. You could tell me how strong I am for battling through my issues, but every strength has a weakness. Strengths are bipolar in that sense. My weakness is thinking I am safe and everything is fine. That's when I am attacked and my strength becomes a weakness.

Our chemistry lab involved pipetting hydrochloric acid into a flask and filling a buret with an unknown base. An indicator was to be placed into the acid. It was very confusing to me. I looked at everyone else doing their labs and I read the directions over and over, but my mind was numb. I wanted to punch myself in the face. Why can't I remember what I'm supposed to do? How do I do it? Fuck. I hadn't even started the lab yet and I was terrified.

I was sitting at my desk waiting for an open station to start my lab. Nine people were working on their labs while the rest of the class, eight of us, waited. I was terrified. The lab looked complicated and I wasn't sure how to do it.

The period was coming to a close and I figured I wouldn't have to start my lab. I let my defenses fall. My weakness, my Achilles' heel, my pain. I'd have to wait to start my lab. Except one person finished their lab with fifteen minutes left. My nightmare progressed.

The teacher told us there was an available lab station. Nobody moved a muscle. She decided to choose someone to go to the station. There were eight people. She picked me. She instantly stared me down, and I felt challenged and threatened. I wanted to sink lower and lower in my chair until I crumpled to the floor and melted through the cracks. She told me to go to the open station. I was terrified. I tried to make an excuse. I told her I had no problem allowing someone else to take my place. I didn't have to go that day. She shrugged her shoulders as if she could care less. It didn't matter to her, but to me it meant everything.

At this point, she started to get finicky. Again, she told me to go to the lab station. I was still terrified, and I didn't budge. I was freaking out. How much time had passed? My heart was pounding, as it usually does when I feel anxious.

I jolted back to the present moment when she raised her voice at me. She was close to yelling at me, and it reminded me of my dad. *Trigger.* She told me I didn't have a choice. I **had** to go. She said I had to. That bothered me beyond reason, but what was I supposed to do?

I could feel people turning their heads to look at me, and I could feel my teacher's eyes burning an eternal gaze into my skull. Despondent and defeated, I subdued and obeyed her command. I walked over to begin my lab. My hands were shaking, but I managed to perform a successful test trial. It was a struggle, but I did it. It was a highly emotional start to my lab.

An interesting thought has been in my head this entire week, so I figured I might as well share it while I have the opportunity. "I'm out of my comfort zone so often I have no comfort."

With that thought, I am tired. To be continued. My life.

MAY 9, 2016

When I was younger and I got bullied a lot, I would always stall so I could stay up as late as possible. My mom would get livid with me because she knew exactly what I was doing. I didn't give a fuck. I knew that the earlier I went to bed, the faster I'd be asleep. The faster I went to sleep, the quicker I'd wake up. What happens when I wake up? School. I hated school. I knew that every time I walked through those damn doors I would be attacked by someone.

I liked to sit up late at night because I knew the longer I stayed awake meant more time before school. It definitely didn't do anything to help my procrastination problems. I was delaying the inevitable, as I always do. But it made me feel a little better.

I realized how often I still do things similar to that. I stay up late because I want more time to relax and recharge my defenses. I need a break from being vulnerable all the time, you know? In the morning, I stay in bed as long as possible because I know I'm vulnerable as soon as I step out of my room. My mom wakes me up every morning because otherwise I wouldn't wake up. I would just stay in bed all day and stare at the ceiling, closing my eyes and relaxing. It would be an end to all my petty worrying.

It's late and I'm still awake. Some nights I stop caring about life. I care too much about shit, but am I to blame? Am I the problem? Or is everyone else the cause of my problems? Am I the abnormal one? Or is everyone else jealous that I'm the only normal one? Are they aiming to hurt me? Or are they perched in precarious positions pretending to befriend me? And again, I apologize for any alliteration, it's just that when my mind is pacing and I get to facing all these premonitions I start to stress a little too much.

I know that if I go to bed I'll be bound and gagged by each alternative method of torture. Of course, the main method of torture is just another lesson of unfortunate nurture where my learning curve is spurred off course. Words are sticking to my head and I can't seem to shake them off. What?

People keep talking about my future because it's approaching quickly. They don't seem to notice the obviously oblivious signs that the scope of my problems is larger than previously thought. I don't think they realize how troubled I am or how much work it'd take to fix me. Let's face it: my head is an attic cluttered with mental spider webs. It hasn't been cleaned in recent memory. The attic is filled with broken items, which consist of a boat and a giant clock. Who would dare venture inside my attic and attempt to dismantle these broken gears and puzzles and piece them back together? I used to work right until somebody took a hammer to my clock and smashed it. Or maybe they grabbed a pencil and stabbed a mannequin man in the hand. That mannequin is me. I've been stabbed in the hand.

I feel like staying up late and rising with the sun each morning. At my funeral, I hope the mourning is reserved for those few who felt concerned. At this rate, I'm plotting my death and strategically formatting the outline. I want a grand show for my first, last, and only showing. I bought a ticket to my death, yelling at people with silent words.

"Sir, please take your seat so I may save this breath!" My words seem desperate, but I say them casually in an attempt to see if anyone feels concerned for my casualty. Nobody gropes for my dangling hopes, and so I smile and laugh to continue the show.

"Ladies and gentlemen, boys and girls, a spectacular show has been prepared for your entertainment! Please, take your seats and remain quiet. Remember to enjoy the show. Without further adieu, I present my death!"

Before the show begins, let it be known that nobody was kind enough to usher at my funeral, so I felt the need to do it myself. I ushered folks to my own death. One time, I tripped in the aisle, and I could tell someone was dying to laugh. Get it, dying to laugh? He nearly pinned his sneer against my back. I can't even catch a break at my own fucking funeral. I smile ceaselessly and the torment seizes me behind each grin. Captured and captivated, I struggle against the dark hand covering my mouth and nostrils. I am slowly suffocating, but people point, stare, and laugh as if it's the prologue to my show.

Somehow, the show continues despite all of the aforementioned issues. On stage, my story begins. The curtains to my life flaunt open and wide for the whole world to see. Behind the scenes, they probably had trouble capturing some of these images. My entire attire feels stretched and hopeless, as if some wretched person had brutally used it before. My arms dangle at my sides as each despicable aspect of my life is described. Finally, these people can see what it's like to be me, and I feel so relieved to have these few in my close company.

The audience watches carefully as each scene is scripted, each set is placed, each camera rolls, and each memory is shoved in their faces. Each scene becomes more detailed and complex than the last. My first day of kindergarten, I'm standing against the wall bawling my eyes out as my mother tries to soothe me. Flash forward to another memory down the line. I'm being stared at by an entire class of lunatics. Or am I the true lunatic? Each memory appears in a sequence, and each sequence appears in a series. It's so organized, it almost feels like it needs to be slightly disorganized to destroy any strike of consistency.

I've gotten so used to acting out each scene that I can practically finish the lines in my dreams. This is my life, and this is my show. Every person in attendance, whether they like it or not, bought a ticket to my death. Maybe they were obligated to attend, but I pretend that I didn't notice. I have the world at my fingertips. Each and every person can experience the reasons and feelings behind each of the individual divisions of my mind. Throughout my show, I enjoy an aside for my patient audience.

"Hey there! Having a good time? How's the show? Are you tired yet?

We've only got one hundred thousand more scenes to go!" People sneer in disgust until I jump off the stage and commentate their fate.

"You were never much of a friend to me, so I guess it's no surprise you'll die as alone as can be."

For each retaliated snarl I spit, the rest of the audience gobbles it up. Now, I return to my show before one of those loose-lipped reptiles decides to poke its teeth and hiss. There is no intermission for fear of losing attention, but I often pause the show to demonstrate my train of thought. My train of thought is an Amtrak, which means it moves quickly until it derails.

"What is the coincidence of meeting the prerequisite incident since a certain instance distanced its innocence?" I say these words and they gawk at me like an animal caged backwards in a zoo, where animals are the gawkers and the people are the caged entertainment.

It takes some time to explain to them that my mind is an interesting piece of an intricate puzzle, and the puzzle is missing so many pieces that it's no longer possible to decipher or solve. They concede to defeat as they realize my problems are unsolvable and each complex arrangement of thoughts and memories is more indecipherable than the last. My brain is morphing and going through metamorphosis while my mind races to maintain tabs on each and every aspect of life through its peripheral vision.

Nobody seems to understand how much time has elapsed as I stand on stage and relate my struggles. I announce each section equally. Memories deserve to be equal because I fought for all of them. I will not stand idly and allow my tragedies to lay to waste and disintegrate to dust.

I stand on stage being devoured and swallowed whole like an antelope in the mouth of a hungry Eskimo. I say these words and everybody stares back as if my lips and mouth are under attack. I flip them the bird and resume my position of spitting out my conscience until this malicious bitch down in the front row thinks she delivers a more delicious pitch. She forks me her story, but I chuck a spoon into her face and jam my fingernails into her dismantled frame. I place my burden on her head until it crushes her skull and peels off two pounds of skin. Once again, I begin to push my story.

About halfway through my story, I begin to feel horny so I scratch at my pickle and tickle my balls. The audience giggles because they think it's funny, but there is nothing funny about me or the way I perform my irresponsible acts. I perpetrate my memories and utilize them as torture devices. My mind splits like wood from an oak tree, every hair on my neck raises, and an ocean washes over me. That's how I feel every time I retrieve a memory. I can't tell you how much I'd give to relieve this tension, but I pass off my apprehensiveness as nervousness and forfeit, or relinquish, my basic rights to the watered-down version of a monster. Why am I rhyming? There are no rhymes to describe these feelings. I only hope that you feel for me and listen intently.

The show is close to closing, for I have chosen a death over the glitz and glam of real life. I'm not sure how I die, but I know the story ends because I can feel myself being suspended in everlasting relaxation inside a coffin. Isn't it amazing how many words come to mind at times like this? I close the show with a few choice words directed at my audience.

"My audience, thank you for contributing. Your participation has neither gone unnoticed nor will it go unrewarded. This show wouldn't have been possible without each and every one of you." Here, I pause and gaze into the eyes of each onlooker, bystander, and properly seated individual. I fixate on their flaws and take extreme precautions to avoid their temperamental states of being.

"In return for your services, I now present the moment you've all been waiting for." Everyone slides up a few inches in their seats, arching their backs and craning their necks for a better view. They had listened to my story. Now, it is time for the ending. A grand finale.

"And now," I calmly say, "I present to you: the mistreatment of life and the pursuit of death."

I die, the curtains close, and I can feel roses brushing against the base of my coffin. The crowd clears with one last glance in my general direction before they leave and return to their normal lives.

The show is over.

MAY 15, 2016

I see why my dad tries not to worry about it. It is so fucking depressing, and it makes me angry. I can't even imagine how angry it makes him. Well, I guess I can imagine. My dad claims he was an angry teenager, but I think he is an angry person. I don't blame him. He realized how unfair and cruel his childhood was. It's not like that situation improved for him as an adult. No, I can't blame him for that. I've been to his parents' house more than a few times over the course of my lifetime. I've seen that disgusting piece of shit that he had to grow up in. The house, if you can even call it that, is over one hundred years old. When our family visits our grandparents, we have to stay at a hotel because my grandparents' house isn't safe or suitable for living. That's sad.

When I was little, we used to stay in their house. I remember every detail of that house. I remember one time my grandma opened the closet to give me a toy and the entire ceiling of the closet was rotted and moldy. I remember how the doorknobs on our bedroom doors didn't always work because they were falling off the doors. I remember how cold it was because they couldn't afford a furnace. I remember their wood stove sitting in the middle of their living room, the only heated room in the house. I remember taking showers in the bathroom, marveling at how rusty the tub was. I remember how the faucet for the sink was broken. I remember how the toilet seat swiveled on its hinge. I remember how the floor was so dirty it would make your socks black. I remember having to wear shoes because I was running out of socks to throw away. I remember how cluttered and unorganized their house was. I remember how one corner of the house was sagging into the ground. I remember everything.

They have so much junk in their house that one side of the house is sagging into the ground. Allow that thought to sink into your head. Last time we visited, my dad and I went into the basement. He took out his pocketknife and studied one of the support beams for the house. He stuck his knife into the beam, and, hardly a surprise, the knife went into the beam as easily as if it were made of paper. Honestly, the wooden beam was weaker than paper. My dad walked around the basement and stuck his knife through every beam. Every single one was rotted from the inside out. My dad couldn't believe it. His parents were fucking clueless.

My dad suppresses most of his traumatizing memories. He rarely talks about his childhood, and when he does it is only a brief snippet. I wonder how many childhood memories he hasn't shared. He keeps every memory locked inside, somewhere, but he never outwardly allows these memories to bother him. He shared something with our family once when we were driving.

Not too long ago, my grandparents were sleeping in the middle of the night. They woke up and sniffed at the air. Smoke. They exited their bedroom and started searching for the fire, but they couldn't find it. They couldn't find the fucking fire inside their own home. Eventually, my grandpa realized where the fire was. It was *inside* one of the support beams. He couldn't see the fire because it was inside the wood. In order to extinguish the fire, he had to cut through the beam.

What started the fire? It was their wood stove, which must have heated up the beam until it caught fire. If my grandparents hadn't woken up, the fire would have collapsed their house and they would have died. Actually, my dad was rather pissed that they put the fire out. He thought they should have let the house burn to the ground in order to collect reimbursements for the damage. Maybe they could have found a better place to live. No. They didn't do that.

That's why our last visit to New York, where my grandparents live, was so important. My dad spent eight hundred dollars of his own money to help his parents. He spent the entirety of our three-day reprieve installing a furnace for their house. He worked and worked constantly, never stopping. Honestly, it was even a struggle to pull him away to have a family meal. That really pissed my mom off.

As for me, I had nothing to do for three days so I made puzzles with my mom and grandma. I hated it. I never want to see another fucking puzzle again. Puzzles remind me of that trip and it pisses me off.

My grandma had the nerve to ask my dad to go on the roof and investigate a supposed noise she heard. That was the final straw for my mom and I. We were both livid with my grandma, but my dad completely contrasted our anger. He was concerned with helping his parents. They needed his help, otherwise they would die. I'm surprised they're still alive, in all honesty. My love for them has diminished significantly after that last trip. The love for my family is weakening.

Anyway, I think I've exhausted that topic. I want to talk about my dad for a minute or two, and how he moved away from his parents. His pursuit to get away from his parents, and his dream of being an automotive mechanic, brought him to where we live now. Now, he told me this story once, long ago. He had one hundred dollars and a yellow Mazda truck when he drove away from his parents' house, unsure of his future. He didn't have anything other than that. He was eighteen or nineteen, if I recall correctly.

Speeding things along here, he went on a blind date with my mom, who was still in high school. She was a senior, and he had graduated. They started dating and they moved into an apartment after my mom graduated—she barely passed. My dad was working as a mechanic. My mom was working retail at the mall.

Later on, my dad told me those first few years were the hardest. He said most of his lunches consisted of bread and a block of cheese. He would cut a piece of cheese from the block, place it on the bread, and stick his cheese sandwich into the microwave for a few seconds to melt the cheese. That was a meal to him. They couldn't afford anything else.

Over time, they made money, but it wasn't much. Their apartment was trash. Cockroaches roamed freely, and they must have gotten fed up with it because they started looking for a house to live in. After searching for quite some time, they found the house we currently live in. It's an old house; it was likely built in the 50s or 60s. It was a complete dump when they bought it. My parents didn't have any better options; however, they slapped one hundred thousand dollars down on the house, and the rest was mortgage. Debt city, baby! It's depressing. The house was disgusting, old, and a mistake. Everything in the house was dull and brown: the carpet, the walls, the windows, the closets, the doors, the kitchen. It was cramped and tiny. But that was never a problem until they had me.

When I was born, I brought a warm, heaping bundle of problems. I was covered in dollar signs. I often wonder how many arguments my parents had because of me. Anyway, I grew up and caused new problems. I was always, always causing issues.

I remember my fourth birthday. I was at the hospital because my brother was born—two days before my fourth birthday. We were going to take him home as a lovely new addition to our family. This action doubled as a birthday present for me.

I was sitting in the hospital room, looking like the bored child that I probably was. My mom handed over my new baby brother, and I held him for the first time. It felt incredible to have a little brother, no matter how small or squirmy. I think he was sleeping because I don't remember seeing his eyes. But I remember he was wrapped and swaddled in a beautiful yellow blanket. I had the same blanket at home, but mine was blue. Having a little brother made me realize that I was now a big brother. That was an incredible feeling, and I embraced it. I loved that feeling of knowing I was the protector of my little brother. I was so excited to have a baby brother. I could hardly wait to play with him, and I imagined all the amazing moments I would share with my brother.

At some point, I handed him back to my mom. My parents knew it was my birthday, and they didn't forget. They told me my new brother was my present. A new brother? In my four-year-old mind, that was the greatest present ever received. How could any present possibly be better than a new brother? I didn't realize that my brother was a present because my parents couldn't afford to buy me anything. I didn't understand. How could I have comprehended the thought of money? I didn't know anything about money or finances or rich or poor or struggle or wealth or standards of living or anything. I was officially a big brother, and that's all I cared about. That thought seemed to satisfy me.

For the first few years, I loved my brother. I loved my parents. I loved going to my dad's shop and I loved watching him magically repair cars. I loved sitting in the office and watching all the people walk into his shop. I loved sitting in the chairs and observing. I loved sweeping the floor, although I made sure to avoid any areas where my dad or his employees were working.

But, as I got older, I realized and understood more than I could before. Was my brother a gift, or did my parents think I wouldn't notice if I went without a birthday? I started to ask myself questions because I knew nobody had the answers. Or, I knew their answers would be lies. I didn't want people to lie to me. Later, this fact became an obsession. I refused to be lied to, or denied the privilege of having my question answered. This most likely aided my isolation.

Why did my brother tattle on me for things I didn't do? Why did he tattle on me for things I did do? Why couldn't he keep a secret? Why wouldn't he play with me? Why wouldn't he listen to me when I talked to him? Why did he hurt me so much? Why did he claim I hurt him? Why was I being punished for his lies?

I thought having a brother meant I had a friend, someone to play with me. Someone I could trust. Someone I could talk with. The only thing my brother did was tell me to leave him alone. He never wanted to play. He would yell at me, attack me, or both. I remember one time, a long time ago, I made him upset before one of my baseball games. The result was easily predictable, but it still had a large effect on me.

We were getting ready to leave for my game. I was dressed in my tiny uniform, infinitely excited about playing baseball. Standing near the door, ready to leave, my brother and I must have gotten into an argument about something. Before I knew it, my little brother was in a fit of rage. He placed his fingers (and thumb, but I will call it a fucking finger because it is on his hand) at the top of my shoulder. He dug his fingernails into my skin, and all I could feel was a deep pain vibrating from my shoulder. Slowly, he slid his fingers down the length of my arm. His impenetrable grip spliced open my arm. The sound was like the screech of multiple nails on a plethora of chalkboards. His touch burned my arm, and I started screaming. When he pulled his hand away, I investigated the damage. Five bloody streaks ran from the top of my shoulder down to my elbow. It was my left arm. I remember that because the right side of my body was pointing toward the front door. My entire left arm was bleeding profusely. My mom scolded my brother, spanked him, and proceeded to yell at him as she walked me into the bathroom. She helped me wash my arm and clean my wounds. We didn't have time to properly cover the scratches, but my mom managed to slap on a couple of Band-Aids to block most of the wreckage. My arm looked rather pathetic by the time this process was complete, considering it was covered in scratches and bandages.

My brother was four years old when he scratched me. I was eight years old, and it was only four years earlier that I'd held him in my arms at the hospital. I thought he was the most beautiful and amazing sibling I could have ever had. But when he scratched me, I realized he was deceitful and menacing. I didn't want him as a brother anymore. He hurt me with a malicious intent and a deceitful heart. He hurt me. Brothers aren't supposed to do that, are they? I don't know.

I hate that fat piece of shit. He is a deceitful, violent, lying excuse for a brother. That scratching memory is one of many traumatic memories I have because of him. He is, as dramatic as this may sound, one of the banes of my existence. Anyway, there are many more memories of my brother.

One time, we were outside on a beautiful, sunny day. I must have been seven or eight years old, which meant my brother was three or four years old. My mom had bought us a plastic hockey set to play with on the driveway. There were two plastic sticks and a plastic puck. My brother was having trouble hitting the puck because he couldn't control his stick, and my mom told me to help him. I went over to my struggling brother and started to help him.

The puck was on the ground and the stick was in his hands. I stood behind him and held his arms in an attempt to visualize the motion of hitting the puck. All I wanted to do was **help** my brother. But he wouldn't listen to me, and he kept thrashing in my arms. I couldn't control him or his stick. I let go, and he wildly swung his stick at the puck.

I can't even remember if he hit the puck. Knowing my brother, he probably missed because he is extremely uncoordinated. But I do remember his vicious backswing as the stick whipped through the air—straight into my forehead. He slashed a chunk out of my forehead with his stick. Immediately, and instinctively, I put a hand to the point of impact, directly in the center of my head. When I pulled my palm away, it was covered in blood. The blood was gushing, pouring out of my head like water running out of a faucet.

My mom probably swore as she raced me inside the house to clean up my wound. It's strange, thinking back on it. I didn't cry. I must have been in total shock at the sight of all that blood. It was my blood, spilling profusely from my broken head. But I remember sitting on the toilet in the bathroom as my mom tried to stop the bleeding. I would be traumatized forever.

If it's not enough to bear the burden of that memory, I guess I needed a scar, too. I still have that scar, right in the middle of my forehead. Most people wouldn't notice it unless I mentioned it. But I notice, and that's significant enough for me.

I remember how my mom debated taking me to the hospital because she thought I needed stitches. I probably did need stitches, but my mom decided against it. Maybe she didn't want to pay for it. I don't know, but my injury managed to heal on its own. All that's left is a scar, a memory, and a traumatized child.

I only wanted to help my brother, but he ended up taking a chunk out of my face. You can argue that it was just an accident, and maybe it was, but I don't believe his resentment of me was an accident. I don't know. He has caused me too many problems. I hate him so much. Of all the siblings in the world, I got stuck with that piece of shit. At least I have my sister. I love her, even though she annoys me sometimes. I gladly accept her as my sister.

My asshole brother tries to ruin her, too. I can see it already, and I do everything in my power to protect her. When I look at my little sister, I see a part of myself. Maybe that's why I love her so much. That's not an egocentric statement, either. That's an "I-wish-I-had-somebody-who-loved-me-when-I-was-little-so-I-could-avoid-being-traumatized" statement. My brother still physically and emotionally abuses my sister. I always hug her and remind her that I love her to try and save her from the clutches of my estranged sibling, my brother. I don't want her to have the same memories I have. Nobody should have those memories. But I do.

Nobody should have a memory of their younger brother putting clean dishes away in a fit of hysterics. I tried talking to him, but this psychopath took a knife out of the dishwasher and pointed it at me. The tip of the knife, although at a safe distance, was aimed at my throat. My mom screamed at him to put it away. The damage was done. I saw the unfazed gaze in his cold, unloving eyes. He would not have hesitated to hurt me. Nobody should have that memory.

Nobody should have to go to sleep in a worrisome mood because they are worried that their psychotic brother is going to attempt to kill them while they're sleeping. I had many nights where I waited to fall asleep because of that same reason. If I knew he was angry with me on a particular day, I would stay up later than usual to ensure he didn't sneak and slither into my room and try to kill me. Paranoia.

I don't want my sister to live like that. I want her to feel safe. Nobody should have to live like that. My dad knows. He might not understand a raging lunatic for a sibling, but he understands how unfair life is. He knows nobody should have to live like they do, yet people do. That's why he works all the time. He wants to give us, his children, a better life—a life he never had as a child. In doing so, he unintentionally aided in my own destruction. He was never home.

I remember so many days where my brother and I would get into fights and I would sit in my room and cry because I was anticipating the moment my dad walked through the door. I knew he would be upset with me and he would spank me. I didn't want to cause any problems for my dad, either.

One reason I loved my mom was because she often wouldn't tell my dad about any of the fights unless it was extremely severe. She wouldn't tell my dad, and it saved a handful of problems for everyone, including me. I loved her for doing that. I was a momma's boy, anyway. I'm not ashamed to admit it. I loved my mom more than anyone.

I didn't love my dad for the longest time, unfortunately. In my little eyes, my dad brought nothing but problems. He spanked me when I misbehaved. He ignored my side of every story or argument. He never played with me. He was never home. I hated how he had to work every second of the day. I ignorantly blamed him for his schedule, but it wasn't his fault. Whose fault is it? I don't know. I could place the blame on anyone and it'd make sense to me. Of course, I was always told to not point fingers because that is considered rude. I only need to point two fingers, one on each hand. I will gladly point my middle fingers at everyone equally, including myself. I blame everyone for my problems. I blame myself, too, even though I shouldn't. Society claims rape victims and war veterans and other victims shouldn't blame themselves. Does that logic not apply for me? Why am I not allowed to blame others for my problems?

"My brother forced me to be a social outcast. He tormented me with unsolicited violence and anger. My dad isolated me from a young age, which caused me severe psychological damage. My mom stayed at home because she couldn't get a job if she tried, not because she wanted to spend time with me. My school was filled with kids who constantly found flaws with me, and they bullied me because of these flaws. My friends were quick to abandon me and now I have trouble trusting people. Most of all, I secluded myself from mostly everything because I was too scared. I forced myself to become a lonesome warrior."

Am I not allowed to say those things? What am I supposed to do, blame all of this on myself? Is it my fault my brother threatened me with a knife? Is it my fault my parents had no money and therefore couldn't afford to spend time with me (because the most valuable asset money can buy is time, and my parents couldn't spare me any time)? Is it my fault?

I can't shake these memories or these thoughts. I look at my brother and I am able to laugh and talk with him, but I know it is an illusion. I have seen his true colors, ugly reds and murderous intentions. I know that, if given a chance in a fit of rage, he would not hesitate to murder me. If nobody can admit that, I guess I will be the first. He, in his blatant ignorance, would deny my words. I doubt he even remembers these memories. He doesn't fucking care.

I hate it when people act as if my life is normal and I'm supposed to get a job, be happy, focus on school, and go to college. Maybe if I had time to talk to them about my life, my memories, and my thoughts they wouldn't badger me constantly. Maybe I wouldn't have gotten bullied as much as I did. Maybe, maybe, maybe. I hate it when people tell me not to say, "Maybe if…" or "What if…" because they think it provokes bad thoughts. Those statements don't provoke bad thoughts. My bad memories provoke bad thoughts. Maybe if people were halfway decent in this world I could be halfway decent, too.

I remember having terrible days where I would go to bed without a word. I would lay down in bed, stuff my pillow over my face, and muffle the sound of my crying. I would cry, and then I would wipe away any loose tears still sprawled out upon my face. Then, I would pray. I would pray to God because that is what I was taught to do. What did I pray about? It probably went a little something like this:

"Please, God. Please help me. Please make the bad people stop hurting me. Please. I could use somebody right now because I have nobody. I'm tired of being bullied. Please help me. I am incapable of defending myself. Please help me, God. In Jesus' name I pray, amen."

And I would go to sleep and hope my prayers came true. I thought God would surely help me in my darkest times. No. He didn't help me. He didn't even answer me. He didn't leave a message or a symbol of His presence. I sent Him my message and He promptly ignored me. I hated God.

Nobody helped me. I hated my dad for teaching me how to pray. I hated how he prayed with me before bed when I was little. I hated the children's books he read to me about Jesus and God and how much they supposedly loved me. Their love wasn't even platonic. It was nonexistent. I hated everything and everyone. I realized the only person willing to help me was myself. Nobody else cared. Eventually, I stopped praying altogether. Years later, I stopped believing in God or Jesus or any other deity. I tried my best to fix my own problems. It didn't completely or permanently work, but it worked more than any prayer. Prayers are as false as the words that create them.

When I think of my grandparents praying and worshipping, I feel sick to my stomach. I despise them for their actions. I hate how their lives are garbage, but they are far too blinded by illusions that God is good and loving to realize how shitty their lives really are. Not only that, but they also shoved years of religious hogwash down my dad's throat. Next in line, my dad taught me about God and Jesus when I was little. I guess I'm the first one to realize that the concept of religion is fake.

What is my goal in life? On a simple scale, I want to be happy with myself. On a broader scale, I want to make a difference. This world is filled with disgusting people performing equally and increasingly disgusting actions. Maybe if everyone on the planet read my words they would act slightly different. Maybe they would stop spewing toxic religious and political propaganda. Maybe they would stop bullying. Maybe they would stop the pain and misfortune of those who suffer. Maybe my words can end starvation and inequality. Maybe my words can end murders and rapes. Maybe my words can stop little brothers from pointing knives at their older brothers. Maybe, maybe, maybe.

Writing is not an option for me. I *have* to write. I have to record these memories and these thoughts. When I don't write, for a variety of various reasons, my mind is inflicted with pain. It hurts me. I can feel the scratches on my left arm. I can feel my forehead throbbing as it squirts and oozes blood. I can almost feel a knife slicing my jugular, teasing my audience. Almost. Writing helps a little. A little is better than nothing, and nothing is better than something.

My English teacher expects me to write an essay. In my darker moments, I often think about that. It is a recurring thought I've had for the past few months. I wanted to turn in my journal entries instead of an essay. Then, I would kill myself before she realized the horror of my desires. I had this thought planned in my head, planted and fertilized like a gardener's seed. I nurtured that seed, tended to its needs, and kept it growing and alive. It is depressing that I used to think about this so often. In my defense, I knew it would be a glorious exit from existence. Do not worry, innocent reader: I have no current intentions of acting on this thought. I will attempt to write my essay, but the literary quality of the essay will undermine my potential capabilities. Basically, my writing is going to be complete garbage. Why? Take a look at this entry. I only have so many words to utilize, and I need to recharge my batteries, as the expression goes. I'm so, so tired.

I slept until eleven in the morning for the second day in a row. I am disappointed in myself, yet I continue to sleep into the early afternoon. I have to relax and allow myself to return to equilibrium before I collapse again beneath the weight of my stress. I am a result of the world and every memory I've ever had. I'm an interesting product. Maybe if someone had taken pity on me I would not have been a result. Maybe if someone had taken pity on me when I was being bullied. Maybe if someone had stepped up and told my bullies to scram. No. Nobody showed remorse for me. Nobody, nobody, nobody. Only I had remorse for myself. I pitied myself because I felt so fucking pathetic. I still do. I pity myself because nobody else pitied me. They only assume I am lazy and worthless.

Assumptions can be deadly.

MAY 21, 2016

I woke up at noon again and began my morning routine. After I showered, I decided to shave because I had noticeable stubble. It was a seemingly innocent decision with disastrous consequences.

Normally, I take my sweet, sugary time in the bathroom, especially when I shave. Today was different. My family complained about how much time I spend in the bathroom. They pressured me, and I, like an unsuspecting salmon, took the bait. I rushed my shower and the fishing line caught between my teeth like dental floss. I quickly started to shave, and that's when I realized my mistake.

Shaving above my upper lip, the deceitful fisherman's hook ripped my mouth to bloody shreds. I cut myself with my razor. I watched the blood trickle out from my new wound and I felt my heart bounce. *Calm down,* I told myself. *It's only a little blood. A small cut.* Wrong. I started to wash my wound with water before dabbing at it with tissues to soak up the blood. At first, I was pissed because I cut myself, but I swiftly realized I had a problem. The cut wouldn't stop bleeding. I kept rinsing it with water, but my efforts were futile. I applied a forceful pressure to the cut, but nothing changed.

Now, here's some quick facts about me. I am nauseous around blood, or thinking about blood for extended periods of time. I have been told I have a weak stomach, which I inherited from my mom, but I think there may be an additional reason for my nausea. Many of my traumatic memories involve blood, which may be a reason for my inability to handle the sight or thought of blood. There are more memories about blood that I haven't wrote about yet. But, coming back to the present, a new memory was in formation.

My head swirled and I felt lightheaded. I felt like I was about to throw up, pass out, or both. My vision started to fade, and I knew I had to do something. I was on the verge of fainting. Wearing only underwear, I crouched on the floor in a feeble attempt to rush the blood back to my head. It didn't work. I decided to lie on the floor for a few minutes. The blood slowly returned to my head, and I cautiously stood up. As soon as I glanced in the mirror and saw the blood, my head began to feel dizzy again. Once more, I dropped to the floor and again repeated this cycle.

I must have looked ridiculous. I was lucky nobody could see me lying on the floor, disoriented and nauseated, with half of my face clean shaven and the other half of my face covered in stubble. I was a literal two-face. My identity divided down the middle of my face. One half of my face was clean and smooth, like the image of my life. That face is the false persona I possess in order to repel inquisitive intruders. The second half of my face is murky and bubbly, covered and veiled from the air that borders it. This face is who I am. I hide myself in the shade to avoid the danger of the sun. In the middle of my face there is a dividing line that separates falsehood from reality. It's a bleeding, rugged line that separates my life.

After twenty minutes of avoiding my cut, I decided to cover it up so I could finish shaving. Unfortunately, I had to use a huge fucking Band-Aid to cover the cut because I couldn't find any small bandages. It looked like I had a mustache, but I didn't give a fuck because I was desperate. My mustache scheme worked, and I finished shaving without any other altercations.

I felt so fucking stupid. I walked out of the bathroom and my mom saw me. She started laughing at my bandaged face, then jokingly asked if I almost passed out. I nodded my head. I felt so pathetic. One tiny cut and I was on the floor for half an hour trying not to pass out.

Embarrassed. Humiliated. Defeated. A terrific beginning to my summer vacation.

MAY 28, 2016

My journal means everything to me, you know? I think it saved my life, honestly. When I came close to giving in to my suicidal thoughts, I would think of my journal. I would tell myself, "Look, you dumb fuck, you haven't finished your journal." How could I leave this planet without sharing my story? I kept living, and the story continues.

I have been extremely productive lately, and I love flipping through the pages in my journal. I hope this doesn't sound egocentric, but I'm proud of myself for writing. I feel like I have finally accomplished something of worth. I love having a passion that I can actively pursue.

Lately I've had a lot of confidence, probably because I'm alone with my words. I have been infatuated with the thought of being an author. I want people to read my journal, or an edited version of my journal, or a book based upon my journal with an engaging storyline that follows the original. The storyline would be my life, and the characters would be myself and any people involved in my life. I don't want to be any ordinary author, though. I want to be the best fucking author in history. I want to capture the attention of the world until everyone reads my words. Maybe I crave attention because I have been alone my entire life.

I want the entire world to read my writing when I'm ready to release it. I realize it is a stretch to assume people would enjoy my words, but that is the type of confidence I felt today. And why is it such a moonshot idea? Why can't my writing be recognized and embraced? Why wouldn't my words give cancer patients the strength needed to continue their battle? Why wouldn't struggling people digest my words and relate to them? Why wouldn't my words inspire humans to soar for the skies and achieve any unfulfilled dreams?

Kids at my school talk about having followers on pointless social media websites. If I was social, I bet I would be pretty fucking popular. But that's not what I want. I want my writing to receive attention, but I want the attention to be useful. I don't want my writing to go to waste; my writing is my life, and I don't want my life to be wasted. Do you understand? If I could have the attention of the world, I'd direct it at my writing. These words are life-changing and lifesaving.

I want my writing to be featured everywhere: libraries, schools, bookstores, and the internet. I want my books to be given away on television shows when a contestant wins a prize. I want Ellen, Conan, and both Jimmy Kimmel and Jimmy Fallon to invite me on their shows so I can talk about myself and my words. People notice I don't talk much, but that doesn't mean I have nothing to say. I want to be the person people admire and idolize. I want graffiti artists to adopt me and my words as part of their art. I want my words to be used in inspirational and motivational quotes. I want my words to be quoted from every corner of the globe. I want my story to be translated into every major world language. I want to have money so I can support myself, but I want to be able to hand money to people who need it. I want to pass out one hundred dollar bills to people in homeless shelters. I want to leave thousand dollar tips for struggling waiters, waitresses, and chefs.

Thoughts like that are what helped keep me alive. Dream big, be big. I don't crave attention at the moment, but that's only because I want to save it for later, when it really matters. My friend recently told me that I have a distinct writing style, and that made me feel incredible. I have a writing style? That's what writers strive for. Nobody wants to be compared to someone else, someone who may have a similar style, or even an entirely different style. People strive for their own style, an identifiable personality. I want people to appreciate my style. I want people to crave my writing like a heroin addict craves a needle. I want people to feel an addiction to my words. I want people to read every sentence twice because they're afraid of skipping any precious words. I want people to read my story over and over because they feel they have a reason for doing so.

That's the type of confidence I've been oozing all day. If I had that type of confidence daily, every eye would shift in my direction.

MAY 30, 2016

I need to push this weight off my chest. The bar is crushing me and puncturing my lungs, but what am I supposed to do about it? My spotter ditched me again and I dropped the fucking bar. No problem, right? It's only a routine. By now, I'm used to being ignored as I struggle and suffocate. I can't handle pressure, and I am certainly unable to handle this physical and mental exertion. Calm down, you stupid fucking imbecile. Exhale. The bar rolls off my chest, and I'm free to breathe once more.

What happened today? First, we need to examine the past. What past are we examining? I'm glad you're interested. We will be quickly examining yesterday's events to achieve an appropriate attitude for today's catastrophe.

What happened yesterday? Thank you for actively participating in this conversation, but please don't ask questions until the end! As I was saying, yesterday was the instigator of a preventable series of nightmares and triggers. Yes, this is pathetic. Most traumatic incidents are highly preventable, and it would serve me an enormous favor if they never happened. But they did happen, and now I must pay the price because the world is focused on punishing me. I feel like a victim of the world's oppression. Am I a real victim? Is my trauma fabricated? I don't know.

My dad came home from work yesterday in a terrific mood. Incredibly rare, yet oddly disappointing. Why was I disappointed?

Obviously, he had a special treat for my brother and I. What? Treats are not disappointing? I beg to differ, and please refrain from arguing with me. If I were an engine, which I'm not, arguments would be my fuel. Be reminded that too much fuel causes engines to overflow and explode. Boom. This treat was not an ordinary gift. No, never ordinary. This glorious gift from my father was nothing other than a job. It was more tenacious work and stress, the only gift my dad knows how to consistently give. It was the only gift his father ever gave him. It is a family heirloom, passed and exchanged between countless generations. Now this intangible treasure is bestowed upon my scrawny shoulders, draped around my neck, and drenched down my spine. I have been anointed with this slippery gift. There is no way to deny this ancient artifact, a timeless relic of dedication and sacrifice. Denial results in punishment as fearful as Death himself, an uninterrupted stream of viciously tormenting screams and an unparalleled beating of my ass. Deny and be beaten, or accept and suffer. My options are limited as I accept this gift, a decision I have made effortlessly my entire life.

I followed my dad and brother into the garage, and my dad explained our gift. He didn't explain it correctly, though; I can attest to that. He left out a crucial piece of information. He forgot to mention that the reason for our gift was because he hasn't had a day off in over a month. He works twelve hours a day, and we only see him for two. During those two hours, he is usually busy eating, relaxing, or talking on the phone. Twelve hours a day, seven days a week. What's a nine-to-five job? Try six-to-six, and toss in an extra hour or two for commute. He even worked on Memorial Day. Fuck it. He works on Labor Day, too. It is inhumane and insufferable. He forgot to mention that to us, but I know it. It's the gift that keeps on giving, as the saying goes.

Nothing is easy for our family. Everything is difficult, time consuming, and expensive. Nobody seems to grasp the concept of this overwhelming difficulty on a daily basis. How can a person even begin to understand what it is like to live in this family? That's considering that the word living is an acceptable term. Dying at an exponential rate seems to be a more suitable term. Exponential decay, not growth. A simple scenario for any other family is a nightmare for ours.

My parents' credit cards get stolen. There are errors in their taxes.

The numbers in my dad's paycheck are horrendously wrong. Pizza deliveries are delivered to a house with a similar address. Delivery trucks deliver wrong items, broken items, or they simply forget our items. My bus route was suddenly changed and my mom had to start driving me to school. Everything at our house breaks or falls apart constantly. By the time we repair one thing, two more things break. It's an endless battle, and we are on the losing side.

Insects find ways into our house no matter how many times we spray the perimeter of the house with insecticides. We used to catch mice often, and then at night we could hear more mice scurrying in the attic. Every time my dad hired a professional to fix something, the professional did a terrible job. In one case, my dad found out the carpenter he hired was a crook. The carpenter was arrested, which meant my dad was forced to do work on the house himself. The roof used to leak before my dad fixed it. The water from our well always smells like sulfur and rotten eggs, not to mention it used to be dirty. The water pressure is low unless we change the water filters every few days. We live a hundred yards from the river, but we have no riverfront access. The river floods our yard and we have to clean up the contaminated debris. There used to be mold under the carpet and we couldn't figure out why. The basement used to flood every time it rained. Some of these problems have been fixed, but you understand. Everything is a problem. Everything is difficult.

Anyway, my dad told us that we had to set up the pool by ourselves because he can't have a day off. It's not like his "days off" are full of luxury or relaxation. He works so much that by the time he has a day off there is a new set of problems and chores awaiting him. Hooray! As for the pool, I will explain why this is such a difficult task.

We've never had money, but that hasn't stopped us from trying to have fun. I said try; that doesn't mean it isn't a stab in the ass. We could never afford an above or in-ground pool, a real pool. You know, the kinds of pools that you don't have to set up and take down every year? Real pools are too expensive, but five or six years ago my dad bought us a pool. Usually, we set it up every year together in our backyard. It is always a pain, but we manage to help our dad set it up. Not this year. No, no, no. This year my dad put me in charge of setting up our watery sanctuary. He expects me to handle this immense responsibility. He might as well have labeled a boulder with the word "STRESS" and dropped it on my deformed head.

He reminded us how to put the pool together and how to take care of the ground beneath it. We have to make sure the ground is leveled out and clear of any sticks, rocks, roots, or any other shit because they could poke a hole in the pool. Plus, nobody wants to step on pointy roots or sticks while they're trying to enjoy a wet and slippery haven. Clearing the ground and leveling the pool is not an easy task. Our yard is on an incline and, although the dirt area is somewhat level from prior pool-digging excavations, it requires a mutilation before we can begin to place the pool down.

That was yesterday. He told us to start today and, from the way he worded it, he expected us to be finished by the time he got home today. More expectations. I fucking hate the standards that hang over my head like a menacing noose. People expect everything from me, but they offer nothing but agony in return. A gift, it's only a gift.

I woke up later than I wanted to. Eleven in the morning, to be exact. Shit. I went to take a shower, like I do every morning, but today was not normal. When I exited the bathroom, my brother came inside. His face was red and I softly imagined white puffs of steam gently sliding out his ears. He was dripping in sweat. Judging from his facial expression, and his hateful gaze, he was visibly pissed. Ignoring him, I started to make a quick brunch. That's when he started berating me for his own belligerent impatience.

"Thanks for the help! Where were you? Why do you take so long to shower? I've been outside for half an hour! Why haven't you done any work? Why are you so lazy? Why, why, why…"

I ignored him because his words are empty shells that rattle around somewhere in the abandoned and void space I keep for a brother. He was upset with me for not participating with him even though I didn't have an opportunity to start. His stupidity baffles me.

By the time I made it outside, I noticed two things. The first thing I noticed was that my brother hardly did any work. Fucking hypocrite. The second thing I noticed was that the amount of work he clumsily accomplished did not healthily correlate with how much he was sweating. It was hot outside, but, damn, he is fucking fat. I tried to help him lose weight a few times and he wouldn't listen to me. It's not my problem, but it is my problem because I have to deal with his fat and lazy ass. Expectations.

Anyway, my brother had pulled the tarp off the dirt area and into the grass to dry, as my dad instructed us to do. Next step, we needed to use a hoe (the tool, not the harbinger of diseases) and our hands to pull any roots, rocks, and sticks out of the ground. See, our property is lined with trees. Our pool area needs to be cleaned and groomed because it is too close to the trees. It's too close to the trees because there is no other place to put our pool. Problems, problems, and more problems.

I started using the hoe (still talking about the tool) to snap roots. It was difficult work, and eventually I put the hoe down and started pulling roots, rocks, and sticks out of the ground by hand. My brother, who had contributed next to nothing, picked up the hoe and lazily pushed and pulled it around.

"You know, it'd be a lot easier if you use the hoe," he said to me. "Why aren't you using the hoe? Why are you using your hands? What are you doing?" He repeatedly asked these questions. How am I supposed to use the hoe if he is using it? Did he not see me using the hoe for half a fucking hour? He is oblivious to anything that does not concern himself. I hate him. He is a selfish prick. He is aggressive, impatient, antisocial, unobservant, oblivious, untrustworthy, violent, threatening, unhealthy, and most likely undiagnosed for bipolar disorder. He could easily be bipolar based upon his personality traits. I don't know if genetics are at play, but one of our cousins is bipolar. If I remember correctly, I think our cousin takes medication. As for my brother, sometimes he has good days. Today was not a good day.

I told him to keep pulling out roots. No. He grabbed a rake and started leveling the ground even though we hadn't pulled out all of the roots and rocks. We had been working more than an hour and we were both sweaty, dirty, and exhausted, but we had to work. We had a deadline. My brother chose not to listen to me. That's the only thing I ask of him. I want him to fucking listen once in a while. He can't listen, and he probably never will. I told him to keep pulling roots, and what does he do? He took the rake and started leveling the dirt. I took the hoe and used it to beat at a patch of roots in the area he raked, practically erasing his supposed progress. Now the area was no longer level. Our work experience was the equivalent of drawing a picture and every time you draw something another person erases your picture. Not only that, but he acts like I'm the one causing problems. If he had listened to me, which he never does, there wouldn't be any problems. Right? Am I not delusional in thinking that? I don't know.

After some time, my brother got fed up and left me alone. He went inside to return to his secluded lair. Good riddance. Although I was alone again, this time I derived a certain pleasure from it. The pleasure didn't last long because I felt stressed and overworked. My work had to be perfect or else I knew my dad would be disappointed. Hours of pulling roots and weeds left me with dirty fingernails and bloody fingers. My back was flaring up and twinging in pain. I pressed my fingers against my scoliosis-diseased spine. Sweat dripped down my skinny arms and legs. Grime smeared the acne-plagued pores on my face. My shoes, an old pair that I use for work, were caked with dust and dirt. Bugs attacked me, spiders creeped and crawled across my body, and ants bit my vulnerable skin. Then, standing there in the blazing sun, I looked out onto the river and I heard a faint and distant noise drifting to my ears. I heard it before I saw it, but I recognized it immediately.

Boats rode by with fishermen and laughter, and then those boats were pursued by a collage of jet skis. I heard their laughter and excitement sailing in the wake of their desirable and unflinching happiness. As it entered my damaged eardrums, I felt a twinge travel down my spine. The twinge hit the bottom of my spine, and I shuddered at the sensation. I relaxed slightly, allowing my bones and muscles to droop and collapse.

I was upset, but I wasn't sure if I wanted to cry in sadness or scream in anger. I envied those people on the river. Why couldn't that be us? Doesn't my family deserve to be happy like other families? Doesn't my dad deserve to relax for once in his life? What about me? Have I not earned the right to be happy after enduring years of anguish? It made me sad, and I almost dropped to my knees and started crying.

I wanted it so bad, and I felt like maybe if I wanted it enough I could have it. But it doesn't work like that. That realization escalated my emotions into frustration and anger. My fists clenched and my face scrunched. Although they couldn't see me, I flipped off all those river people. I fucking despised them for being able to do things I can't. Why can they afford to buy big boats and jet skis? Why can't we do that, huh? Is there something wrong with that? We don't even have fucking access to the river. I felt envious and jealous. I wanted to push those people off their expensive and luxurious boats and hobbies. I didn't care if that was right or wrong. That is simply how I felt. I'm not going to gloss over any details or sugarcoat any emotions. I fucking hated those people for enjoying their day while I felt miserable. They were enjoying their lives while I slowly perished.

But I got back to work—a gift from the river. Out of the murky depths crawled my heinous gift, beckoning to me, waning me in its direction. Work. So, I did. I worked and worked, like my dad always has, and his dad always has, and so on and so on. That's fucking miserable. A gift, a gift.

I finished pulling the roots, and with the completion of my work meant the return of my biological brother, an estranged sibling. He came back outside and we got back to work. We positioned the dark blue tarp over the dirt area (which I had crudely leveled out because the sun was going down and we were running out of time) and dragged the wrinkled pool on top of it. We stretched out the pool and started putting the pipes through the plastic sleeves in the lining of the pool. This action was filled with arguing and bickering between my brother and myself. Quite cutely, my little sister also joined us. A gift.

Fast forward to later in the evening, our shitty attempt at putting up the pool was complete. We were supposed to clean it out, too, but we didn't have time. I was worried my dad would be pissed and disappointed. We had been working all day, so I figured my dad would be satisfied with our efforts. My brother and sister went inside because we were finished. Strangely enough, my mom replaced them.

She went to water the garden, but the hose was tangled up. My brother had reeled it in before, and he fucked it up. It took the combined effort of my mom and I to untangle it. Twenty agonizing minutes. The hose started leaking, but I managed to fix it. My mom swore throughout the ordeal, saying she is sick of this fucking shit never fucking working and everything fucking falls apart and everything is so fucking difficult. A gift, a gift.

I went inside after that, hoping my day was over even though I knew it wasn't. I dreaded the moment my dad would walk through the door. I always dread it. I never know what kind of mood he'll be in when he gets home. I'm fucking lucky and grateful he isn't a drunk, deadbeat, abusive asshole because he would probably beat me any time his temper sparks and ignites. That's what work does to you, though; it beats and batters you, abuses you, and drains your body. A gift, a gift.

My dad came home and he seemed to be satisfied with our work output. He asked me how it went. You know, setting up the pool? I glanced at him and looked away, gazing outside. I was looking at my watery grave. I told him the truth.

"A nightmare."

JUNE 4, 2016

What is a heritage? I am unaware of my heritage, but I'm more than aware of who I am. Who gives a fuck what race I am or where I come from? The only thing that matters is who I am and what I achieve. I will achieve the most I can possibly achieve.

What the fuck is a heritage? The only known piece of the matter I care is that I am the residing heir of my lineage, and of that I am more than sure. I am the king of my lineage, and all those who precede me are nothing more than my loyal subjects. Perhaps they are even less, nothing more than horses in my stable. In my lineage, I feel regal and royal when I bounce in life like it's a battle royale. My story is able to contain any intrusive fables. I deter any arising threats that attempt to label me as someone who is best left alone. I am the king, and of this I am certain. My royal blood runs straight in my veins; that's why it's called a bloodline.

I am a loose cannon attached to a noose. I'm holding aloft any impatient patron who waited too long to acknowledge my royalty. I receive royalties from my kingdom for each life that I've touched and blessed, an unending fortune of love. Anyone who dares to mess with the king deserves a message, and that message is delivered by mail and an impounding storm of hail. From the skies and the waters, I pound each and every deceiver with a cleaver of misfortune as my fortune grows and increases like a leech at an excited beach.

I approach any who boast more than their fair share, and I crush any who dare slander my grandeur or pounce on my chalice throne. This is my home, and I do not tolerate those who debate my prevalence in the industry of the most loved and benevolent. I am the undisputed ruler of each individual who bestows upon me an unlimited supply of power. I am the accomplished, and those below me are left to fend for themselves. All who sit below me on this throne, and most who sit close to me, adore me. I rant and rave, and they chant my name louder and higher every time I finish writing a page.

I sit on my throne, so peaceful, and I wonder if there are any below me who would dare to squander with greatness. They wander aimlessly, aiming to stab an attack at yours truly, the truly moving power. I conceive a test for those who wish to best me. The rest of my loyal and adoring fans cheer my name; they jeer at any unlikely victor that jabs at the reigning champ. I am a champion, and my rules are as follows:

One, I am the sand beneath your feet and the breeze gliding where your fingers meet the air. Two, I am the holy light shining in your complex apartment, arranging your arraignment. Three, I am the power that flows like a clock striking the top of every hour. Four, I am the heritage from which your marriage is inherited. Five, I am the man with the eccentric smile who stole the moon and set a monsoon on a land of bumbling baboons. Six, I pretend to mend your wounds so I have an excuse when I dab them with an additional dose of salt. Seven, I am the king, and you will obey my orders.

I am the conquest on any of your successful quests. I am the gratification of any eternal suffering suffered under any internal injuries. I am the moon, screaming at your son to retract his dreaming trance. I am the sun, stoked at your pleasure; that's a hypocritical measure of the intolerance I can tolerate. I am the guiding compass of any moral barometer running on a broken speedometer. I am the king. I am the victor.

My mind accelerates at a particularly festive rate. My brain correlates any infatuated rivalry with a stick of dynamite and a tirade of animosity. My soul leaps like a bird snapped in the jaws of an angry leprechaun. Porcelain glass shatters my ass, battering the few remaining passive acts

I have. Misguided thoughts tumble like a tumbleweed and buzz like a bumblebee caught in a dandelion's seed.

I forge any soaring height with raw emotion, then split an atom to marvel at its corrosion. I fuse my fights with battery acid while I smack an ungrateful bitch with a packet of aspirin tablets. I spew flames and fire from a burning pit, and I release uneaten torture every time I spit. I encounter equestrians and strip their humanitarian badges when I catch them having sex again. I probably seem like a joke when I rumble and groan, but every time I sneeze a homeless person grows more lonely and cold. I may not make much sense, but that is only because I am senseless.

My words are speeding bullets that cause a wreckless amusement ride to turn into a reckless attraction. I am a maniac trapped in a tragic act. I am a lunatic stabbed during a lunar eclipse. I am a king, and this is my kingdom. Here is my conundrum.

If I am a king, where is my heritage? I am a lone survivor, misguided and unloved. I am a king trapped by walls and a fleeting hope to fly. I'm lacking a kingdom. I am a dream, and I dream within my dreams to prove nothing is as it seems. Falsehood and empty promises proceed to precede comments about any worthy deed. Torture and mental malnutrition split any chance I had at achieving my ambition. Lack of nuisance locked me in a noose from which I can't escape. My whole demeanor smashed when a worthless army slashed my back. I crashed between heated flashes and head gashes, but my new brain maintains. I am a king, and I am worthy.

I am the lead bullet in a knife fight where the lone ranger drew his gun in spite. I am the willow tree grazing your faithful ground, breaking any who seize my tattered mound. I am a rebellious act upheld by knives and needles, twisting like an accordion in the breeze. I am more than a breeze; I am a gusty wind. I am a human flustered with filibustering. I am the heir to the throne without a care in the world.

I am a king, and this is my heritage.

JUNE 5, 2016

I hate walking into the kitchen at night because I can see our new kitchen without any distractions. It is fancy and expensive, an extreme difference from our old kitchen. It confuses me. I enjoy having nice things, but I fucking hate it, too. In my mind, I still see our tiny, crowded kitchen. Nothing was fancy or elaborate in that old kitchen. We had no money, but now we have some money. I'm so confused.

I remember one time when I was ten years old. It only took ten dollars to make my day perfect. I was in fourth grade. It was early in the morning before one of my football games (I played football for one year just to try it, and I hated it). That morning, unbeknownst to me at the time, was special.

I used to play a game on the computer. The game itself held an emotional tie to me, but beyond that it didn't mean anything. I remember being frustrated because I couldn't advance in the game because I had to buy a premium membership. I was stuck. So, what did I do? I worked up the courage to ask my dad if he would be willing to spend ten dollars on my game.

Were my eyes hallucinating? Was it only a mirage? No. My dad sat next to me and pulled the magic plastic card from his money carrier. My eyes danced in an eager state of ecstasy. I couldn't believe what was happening. My dad, a man too tangled in the web of reality to explore a world of fantasy and imagination, spent ten dollars on my childish game. I felt complete and utter disbelief in that moment. Ten dollars made me so fucking happy, and maybe that's why my dad didn't have a problem spending it. The statement money can't buy happiness is absolute bullshit. Whoever came up with that ridiculous phrase never had this memory. My dad proved you can buy happiness. Happiness costs ten dollars. Ten dollars. That sounds like an unbelievably high price, but I know it was worth it. Ten dollars...

I went to my football game later that day, but the only part of me at the game was my physical body. My mind, whether I realized it or not, was at home, calmly sitting in my computer chair. It didn't matter. I sat on the bench the entire game, as I did for most of the season. Observing, listening, and staying silent: the three keys to being myself. Interestingly, that was the only game our team won that season. I received one win and ten dollars in the same day. It started raining after we won, but nothing could dampen my spirit.

After our victory I returned home, where my ecstatic mood remained. I played my computer game for the rest of the day. Lost in a world of fantasy and magic, I felt wonderful. An entire day was wasted in favor of an overly active imagination and a heated desire to escape reality.

Now, when I look back at that memory, I think about how my happiness was worth ten dollars. For most people, ten dollars is nothing. They spend more than that on individual items at the store. But, to me, ten dollars was a small fortune. I walk into our kitchen and everything I see has a dollar sign attached. Thousands and thousands of dollars, days and days of happiness, and for what? Hardwood floors? Quartz countertops? I am stepping and leaning on my happiness, but it doesn't squeak the way it used to. Instead, my happiness screams silently to hide its true agony. Money is a powerful essence in the greedy palms of humanity.

Typically, I avoid spending money. Besides the logical reasoning behind saving funds, I dislike forfeiting my physical happiness because it reminds me of the money my parents never had when I was young. It makes me think of ten dollars and the time my dad bought me days, and possibly weeks, of happiness. When I visit the real world, and spend more than ten dollars on items, I feel guilty. Fast food is the worst way to spend money. The food may satisfy my immediate hunger, but is it worth it? Am I making the most of my happiness by spending that ten dollars? I don't know.

I'm a relic of the past. In my mind, our family is living paycheck to paycheck, still struggling to feed and clothe ourselves while keeping up with the bills. Ten dollars? My dad gave me a fortune! Fuck it. My dad doesn't care about spending money as much as I do. He doesn't give a fuck because otherwise he would stress twice as much as me. When he goes shopping, he grabs what he needs and moves along in a hurry. When I go shopping, I grab the same items, but it hurts me because the products are translucent. I can see the price tags of every item, unlike my dad, unless he pretends not to notice the things that I notice.

I feel guilty for placing my parents under so much stress. My dad worries about sending me to college soon, and my reassurances are unnoticed in the ruins of my dad's comfort department. I try to tell him I plan on attending a community college, but I don't think he listens to me. Hopefully I get a job so I can pay for my own education and living arrangements.

That's another problem. I can't handle a job. Summer is here. I can already feel the questions brushing against my legs, climbing up my body, and nestling inside the distorted visions in my head.

"When are you going to get a job? Where are you going to work? What are you going to do with your life?" I hate being asked condescending questions like those. The world is a cruel, dangerous, and unloving place where fear tactics are the driving impulse. I feel like I would be physically and mentally incapable of holding a job. Unfortunately for my expectations, everyone around me already has a job. They make everything look so damn easy, and it puts an enormous load of pressure on me. I need to make more than ten dollars—that's for sure.

I dread getting my haircut because the cosmetologist asks too many questions. "How is school? Do you have a job yet? Did you go to prom?" No, no, and no. Please quit sticking magnifying glasses underneath my skin. Can you stop asking me questions for one moment? That's just another question for you, reader. Thanks.

Why do I hate being the center of attention, but I can't fathom being ignored? Why the fuck do I feel like that? Regardless, I despise mostly everything. I hate being ignored. I hate being noticed. I hate being pointed at and laughed at. I hate talking without hearing a response. I hate asking a question that nobody has the answer to. I hate tolerating the people around me. I hate faking smiles when I feel like dying. I hate telling lies about myself to seem more interesting. I hate being considered the smart and helpful kid. I hate when people give me reasons to shame myself. For example, if I complain about something that bothers me, someone will tell me how good my life is and that I am a spoiled brat. They give me anecdotes from shitty times in their lives to try and make me feel worse. That's called the shame game, and I'm the most valuable player; I'm the most shamed on and the most shameful.

Ten dollars. That's funny. The game I've been playing recently dented my pocket by ten dollars. I only paid ten dollars because I split the cost with my brother. Maybe it's just a coincidence, but, in the grand scheme of life, I like to think that it makes perfect sense. Happiness costs ten dollars. What about inflation? Again, I see our new kitchen and I think of my happiness inflating like a balloon. It's too much.

Money can't buy me happiness anymore. Nothing can.

JUNE 8, 2016

If I could swallow pills I know that I would be an addict. I'd snort a line of coke up in the attic, and smoke a little dope to release all my stressing. I would take a rope and stick it in my pocket, saving it for later when my hands are chalked and blackened. I retrieve the contents of my pocket, form a noose, and lock it around my throat like a locket. Shout out to the few who remain attracted, but fans mean nothing when your attitude is blackness. I jump off a balcony with the rope around my neck until it snaps my vertebrae and every thoracic. For the foes denying my life is tragic, here is another image of why I am traumatic.

My gene pool is more similar to an ocean; diving deep inside is an insane notion. The darkness dwells below and it devours everybody who dips inside. My heart attacks provoke therapeutic vibrations. Bad vibes are an extension of the damage, not to mention I erode faster than an artificial canyon. My mental state deteriorates at its finest state, but destruction is an inevitable mindset. I am surrounded by pictures and conversations of twenty pilots, one of those who may be dying. My words will mystify and mist your mind until you realize I am that remaining pilot. Slowly dying, this is my last attempt at trying to maintain the selflessness I used to bring. I'm driving nails through my skin and following suit with four and a quarter inch screws. Divers search the ocean and they cannot find me. I pretend I do not see them hunting in my shadows.

Everybody attacks me and I act like that is fine, but can I have a break to regenerate my trust? I've been searching empty palms for a while, and only now does it feel like the emptiness is definite. I'm stalking borders while I'm bored and I want to walk the borderline because I only pretend that I am boarded up normally. My protection is weak and I am feeble; walking lines is the only way to lift this helplessness. I'm walking a tightrope in the night sky while I'm trapped in an existential state of being, dangling like a modifier. I'm beginning to think my life is another projected image completely photoshopped to remove any signs of suffering. If suffering isn't enough punishment, I'll gladly bear witness to this dismemberment. Every time you see me smiling is probably a brief moment I forgot my life is photoshopped. I cropped the darkness out.

I malfunction and hallucinate birthday cakes raining down, bathing me in drips of scarlet pain. Every frame in my life is a painting. When you see me passing and I appear faint, it's because I am secretly fainting. The colors used to paint me are more fake than the words of a liquor-stricken father who claims he loves his son or daughter. I am faint and fading like the colors that made me who I am today. I'm eagerly waiting for someone else to try and paint me. My life is an endless portrait, and I am Mona Lisa, sitting silently and waiting to be tortured. I only pretend not to notice any stifling acts of paint that inebriate patients who seem to lose their patience. I lose my own patience as my voice is stifled and my mouth is placed in a muzzle. I cry for help, but nobody can hear me. My painting is a hidden treasure. Museums avoid me because they know I'd be stolen. Concealed and omitted from the public eye, I am a helpless act of selfless self-incrimination. I'm displaced by any reason to battle the demons that wait outside every place or predicament I face.

If my pool is an ocean, I know it would be inhabited by pirates who would seize my treasures and countless assets. They use it to their advantage, thwarting any schemes I conceive in schizophrenic dreams. I become a puppet on a string, but the string is made of unbreakable twine. Pirates puppet me until I feel about as real as the Muppets— Kermit would be pleased to know he is real. Pinocchio is a real boy, and I am a wooden puppet whose nose remains the same length for every lie told. If I told you how often I lie, my nose would grow longer than

America's financial crises. I tell people that I'm happy when I became a facet of these pirates, dropping anchors on beaches and plundering riches. I pretend they disappear, but when I hear my thoughts the pirates rush to collect their funds. My memories are a collective piggy bank to them, and I indiscreetly comply to their demands and provide my debt. I took out a mortgage to pay them back, and again I am reminded of the time my parents took a dip in the pool of debt.

I wouldn't go skinny dipping in my thoughts even if I was the only one around. I keep my clothes on even in my dreams to see if I can ward off any trauma that attempts to tear my armor and harm me. Are you telling me to relax? Give me another reason to perfect my fake persona. I relax until I master any plastered acts of plastic happiness. If being fake was a test, I know that I would pass it. I lie through my teeth, tongue, and cheek. My mind rolls faster than any other, and I bend these thoughts until they are more than tragic. Thoughts are traumatic, and my mind cannot contemplate any reason to forgive these tragedies. Instead of forgiving, which seems easy, my mind recalls tragedies to the present. I am trapped in a fated act of karma that stabs my heart like a hot curling iron dipped in an oil fryer.

Everybody around me is saying I should relax because they don't think my life is hard, but more than my eyes are rolling backward. Boulders roll off hills and crash into the ocean while fossil fuels burn holes in the ozone layer. Underwater geysers explode heated steam; everything bursts to the surface in a lucid dream. I am rolling down a hill and tumbling past Jack and Jill. I am a tumbleweed tumbling across the desert sand.

I am a rolling stone thrown in the ocean, sinking when I was expected to skip.

JUNE 10, 2016

My brain and my cranium are packed with panic and pandemonium. My mind is a biological zoo and a philosophical screw is loose, wedged in between a serpent's den, a spider web, and a bird's nest. I've defied the laws of nature ever since my premature birth unearthed an unearthly being. My body is an insult to evolution and a contending contestant for the most contribution to the Earth's pollution. I recycle in spite of this fact, but I spit saliva and piss on any poisonous plant I extract from the roots and womb of Mother Earth.

Lions and lynxes mix with other carnivores on the brink of extinction. A snow leopard leaps in next to a pack of wolves while a sheepskin fleet flocks to the closest cove. Cozy and comfortable animals produce more residue than if they were bloodthirsty cannibals. What is this, a circus act? I don't do drugs, but I know about Percocets performing twisted actions of splattered madness. Who am I, a fool? No, this is my circus act. I will direct any immeasurable message at the stiff and sterile audience. Welcome to the show.

Speaking of sterile, did anybody neuter or spay these brats and bitches yet? I don't need puppies or kittens dancing little jingles in my head while my brain heats like a soldering iron touched to black shingles. A gorilla growls at me, but if it gets too close to the glass I won't hesitate to bust a dart in its ass. Why not? I'll attach a batch of lead to its fucking head for interfering with my speech, and now it's speechless. Surprised?

Come on now, don't you watch the news? If not, please take notes of channel seven when it's on at two. Animal cruelty, is that a penalty I am affiliated with? No, I protect these snappy bastards in my house, home, and yard. Orangutans and monkeys sprout from trees like the dreams of a diseased mollusk. A penguin and a moose battle in the woods over who can forage more food. Why am I announcing this imaginary battle? Why do I sound like an angry and unstoppable man? Why am I a scientist buried beneath centuries of lies and dust distributed from the mouths of those who would lie to protect themselves?

In my ocean, there is an orca and a dolphin singing a song about how life begins. I conceive a million images of each of these animals. Camels munch cantaloupes while gazelles get chased by antelopes. The gazelles are pressured to elope with the camels and the antelopes. The rain forest is a jungle book with an innocent fish tied up in a mangled hook. Radioactive water decays any fish who swims in Chernobyl's aftermath, like alternative shopping for a sauna bath. Tigers and sabertooths gnaw on the skin of a middle aged Indian man seeking a job for animal management. How's that for a circus act?

I escalate any promiscuous promise to complete dominance of these poor mismanaged mammals. I cradle and save any Tweety that stumbles out of its nest. I calmly utter soothing whispers in the ear of a startled horse. I stumble at the sight of a bear, but that doesn't mean I don't care about it. I'll gladly feed it from afar, but I always roll the windows up if it gets near my car. I am a zookeeper keeping peace in the premises. This is my premises, and this is my circus act.

I throw peanuts in the crowd like the conductor of a grand show. I throw peanuts at an elephant baby so it stops chasing me. It's running me up a tree, and the bark is rubbing up and chafing me. I circumnavigate any whale's migration route to ensure its safety, safeguarding a treasured key to the animal kingdom. I promote the return of coral reefs for tiny fish and critters who deserve relief. Why do they need relief? Why do I need relief? We need relief from the passionately torturous actions of greed and grief.

Bugs and pests pester me, but I bash my own brains out on a quest to conquest misleading questions. Any questions? No? Good! I am a lunatic lit at the sight of a thousand Canadian Geese flocking to the heart of America's Midwest. Rats and rodents spur a conversation of bold opposition until my thoughts trap their miniscule heads in submission. In a position of power, I am a superior warlord smuggling drugs like a Trojan War horse. This circus is almost over.

Who is there? Who is behind that cage? Is that an animal hunched over that black and centered stage? Can I throw peanuts at it and hope it moves or flinches? Should I knock over its bed and rip the sheets off from over its head? Who is that figure, discombobulated and hobbling? Why are its eyes that color? Doesn't that thing have any friends to call its own? What happened to force that suffering animal to live such a sheltered life? Is it moving, or is it only breathing faintly? Should we call out to it and hope that it responds? How about we throw rocks at it and maybe it'll budge? Too bad there's no glass to block me from falling in its cage, right? Who would want to live in that confined space? How is that thing so frail and skinny? What is that animal, anyway?

I look out and stare back at their hungry faces, displacing my anger amongst them equally. One day I vow to break free, spread my wings like Icarus, and soar toward the sun. I may be an animal, but do not allow my predation to appear ominous. I am merely the result of a culture supported by sticky flesh and sketchy figures. Forever trapped and entwined in my jail, this is my safety net, my harness, and my circus net below the trapeze. That's what writing means to me.

I am that animal, and my life is a circus act.

JUNE 11, 2016

Researching various mental illnesses and personality disorders today, I discovered BPD, otherwise referred to as Borderline Personality Disorder. After browsing multiple articles and posts related to BPD, I noticed how many symptoms I seemingly have. Do I have BPD? I pondered the question, but does it really matter? One article claimed BPD is related to PTSD, which would increase my likelihood of having BPD, except I don't know if I have either or both illnesses. From my perspective, speculation is my only attribute. I have strong evidence to argue my speculations further, but why should I? It's not like I can diagnose myself with severe mental illnesses. On the other hand, when would anybody be able to diagnose me? I hide signs of weakness from my family, so of course I would hide my emotions and thoughts from a doctor. That last sentence was poorly written. Fuck it. I'm my own worst critic.

I wonder what other people think of me. What would they think if they read this journal? They would probably disregard my thoughts as insanity, and that's if they even bother to read it. Honestly, there are portions of this journal I dislike and would proudly edit or destroy, but I made a promise to myself. No censorship. No editing. I want an authentic, original representation of my thoughts at the current time of my writing, even if that means I dislike my previous writing. If I wish to disregard an entry, there is usually a percentage which can be salvaged. Typically, this method works to my benefit.

JUNE 12, 2016

The fear of being neglected or abandoned is powerful. I am grateful I have a few friends who are consistently capable of dealing with me. It makes me feel terrible. I stress my friends with my problems constantly, and I hate myself for it. What alternatives do I have?

I want to be loved, but who would love me? Who would put up with my problems? Who would love me for who I am, problems and all? Who would love me regardless of my insecurities? I crave love and compassion reciprocated to me, but I feel like I will be alone forever. I am addicted to love, but I have an allergy. What am I supposed to do?

What the fuck am I doing? I feel like my life is falling apart, and it doesn't matter how hard I try to keep myself together. I can't stop myself from blowing my composure. My life is an unfathomably complex puzzle, and another piece falls off every time I try to keep the pieces together. I can't hold every piece at once. I can't do this by myself. I need help, but nobody is going to help me. My arms will become exhausted and I will drop the remaining pieces of this complicated jigsaw puzzle. The pieces of my life are falling apart, and I will collapse with them. What happens when every piece crumbles? Am I dying?

One time I spent the night at my friend's house and we had a lengthy conversation about depression. Soon enough, we veered toward the topic of suicide, and I let him do the talking. I didn't say anything, but I'll never forget what he told me.

"Suicide is so dumb. Why would anyone do that? It's stupid." He laughed, sucking beautiful summer air into his healthy lungs. I couldn't believe what he had said. He didn't understand at all. He doesn't have the foggiest idea what it is like to hate yourself or your life so much that you want to die. He doesn't have a fucking clue.

JUNE 17, 2016

If Satan was a person, I'd be his friend so I'd have someone to relate to my discrimination, and I'd relate to his. He is portrayed as the manifestation of hatred, sin, and evil, but how do you know until you get to know him? I'd show him kindness, respect, and morality in the hope that he would reciprocate my actions. We'd exchange stories and voice our discrimination without fear of providing incriminating evidence to a witness. Satan isn't real, and neither is God, but, if they were real, I know at least one of them would be a liar. Should I draw an image in the blank space you call your head? Sit down, and let me tell you a story.

God and Satan are representatives of a more well-known demographic: humans, people. Without saying which is which or who is who, I'll present my target imagery. In school, there are different types of kids, and there is nothing wrong with that. Problems materialize when bullies strike, usually attacking another student who appears weaker. Bullies attempt to achieve a morbid sense of egocentric stamina and stability. Bullies, although disgusting abominations from the inside out, are feared by the entire school. Using this fear to their advantage, bullies obtain a status of popularity and power. Over time, bullies may even gain a snickering fan base of volatile followers, even if those followers are too preoccupied to notice their own distorted behavior. In fact, given enough time, these bullies may even be embraced, loved, celebrated, or idolized. Why would a bully receive such positive criticism? Well, bullies single out others and feed off their perceived flaws like a blood-sucking mosquito. Although the people being bullied may be completely normal humans, they are viciously humiliated by bullies and a barrage of the bullies' followers, a deadly swarm of locusts. People who are bullied are visualized as weak, unworthy, and abnormally different, even if none of those statements are true. It doesn't matter if those statements are true or fake because sooner or later those people will believe their bullies' taunts and accusations. They believe their identities revolve around those accusations until they slowly morph into the accusations themselves. The bullies stampede and parade their victory, and the freakish person being bullied secedes into his or her loathing misery.

Does this sound familiar? God is a bully, whether you realize it or not, and Satan is a victim of God's brutal wrath. These stories are fake, but the overall message is hopefully received. Satan and God are not real, but that doesn't mean their existence is forgotten. There are Satans and Gods everywhere. Stop worshipping false deities, open your eyes, and digest the world. God is present in every terrorist. Why else do you suppose they yell and shout the words "God is great!" before committing their horrific tragedies? God is present in every rapist, slipping tiny pills in drinks at the bar, or forcing someone into a soundproof bedroom. God is present in every abusive father, mother, husband, and wife, ignoring the desperation of the families at stake. God is present in every bully, stealing lunch money and shoving scrawny runts into lockers. For everywhere God is present, there is a Satan. Satan is present in the victims of terrorism, pleading to be excused from a chaotic death. Satan is present in every rape victim, silently forced into an unloving attraction. Satan is present in every child of an abusive parent, with the child witnessing the destruction of a family. Satan is present in every kid who is bullied, crying alongside those who are too dehumanized to think properly.

That is why I would choose to be friends with Satan; I do not support a friendship with God, a bully. Forget your feelings, reader. You have been desensitized into believing Satan is an evil entity, and you have been tricked by tales of a good and loving God. God is a bully, and if you blindly follow in his path you will most likely become a bully, as well. For once, seek a relationship with the unloved Satan, for he could surely use it. I watched him cry, and I felt pity for him. I felt empathy for him because I know what it is like to feel worthless. I took his hand, and I placed myself as a barrier between two opposing forces, God and Satan. No longer shall bullying be tolerated. I understand the discrimination at play, and I am appalled. Satan is the friend you never knew you had because you were too busy living in your own world. You were too busy allowing others to suffer.

That's the feeling you get when you don't give a shit about all the nonsense flaunted by the media. Shootings, gun controls, uncontrolled violence, rampages, accidents, and riots. Civil inequalities, blatant racism, sexual identities, marriage certificates, and bathroom privileges are more examples of toxic nonsense. Religion, terrorism, hatred, political sways, corruption, and tax evasion are common in the news, but what does it all really mean? It's a common conscience paving way for consequences.

I'm sick of hearing bombers bombing cities, marathons, airports, and blowing off car doors. Why do we support this? Why are we still talking about this? Why aren't we doing more to prevent bullies and their consequent problems? No, instead we have marijuana smokers, cocaine addicts, and heroin shooters being thrown in prison for possession of illegal substances. Decriminalize drugs and set people free. Why is this even a problem? Why are we allowing bullies to dominate the globe and dehumanize ourselves? I'm sick of nagging reporters bitching about these frivolous problems.

Timmy got his bike stole? His house got blown off by a massive cyclone? His parents died in a car crash and his relatives emigrated home? Timmy looks around and sees his life is worthless; it's nothing but broken pieces incoherently strewn in the wind. Timmy reads his superhero comics and it sends him to a world where problems are averted, crimes are prevented, and decent humanity is a common sentence. Why is Timmy still sad? Doesn't he like reading about Superman being a hero with a bright red cape? Does he not like how Superman is scared of green rocks? Unfortunately not. Timmy knows it's fake.

I was never involved in comic books, but I know Timmy's pain. I never had a passion for superheroes saving endangered citizens, but that was before I craved a new superhero. I can hear the questions now.

"What superhero is it?" The only superhero I know is a man whose initials are SM. "Is it Superman?" No, Superman couldn't last a day in my shoes. Superman is fake, but my superhero is real. My superhero makes Superman look like a pathetic role model with an atrocious image of success, but that's not the reason I need my superhero. I need him because he saved my life more times than I can count. My superhero is Suicideman.

Suicideman is the most loved and respected superhero. "Why? Who is he? What does he do? Does he have any powers? Why is his name so intimidating?" Relax. Enough with the questions. Suicideman is a hero who talks to people before they attempt suicide. His powers consist of the elements his patients lack in their lives: love, compassion, courage, hope, and strength. He spreads his power through words, using his mouth as a weapon much like a firefighter uses a hose as a weapon to battle flames. My superhero's name may sound intimidating, but he speaks the truth. He deals with people who suffer, and he named himself in order to reflect the seriousness of his patients' suffering. His words are healing powers, and they tend to more than broken limbs. He provides psychological comfort and understanding. He empathizes with his patients, listening to their confused emotions. He promotes sympathy and compassion, spreading his message through the power of heartfelt communication. He is a superhero.

My mind forfeits my body and my thoughts darken and crash. Suicideman is not a real superhero; he is only a figment of my highly deluded imagination, an endless realm of aggressive fantasies. An epiphany hits me over the head until a welt develops and cultivates my skin.

I am Suicideman, but the only person I've claimed to save is myself.

JUNE 18, 2016

How was my day? Did it seem perfect, or was I only flirting with failure? All it takes is one sentence to set me off like a bottle rocket until I crash and burn in the ash and rubble. What the fuck does the world want from me? Why do you care so much? And you, why do you not care at all? Why does everything always bother me? The truth is, I don't have answers for any of these questions. I'm an unreliable narrator telling the tale of my life through lies and illusions.

It's the day before Father's Day, but do you think my father gives a fuck about a holiday? I tried talking to my dad today and his responses were short and insulting. One particular statement nearly left me in tears, but you know damn well that I didn't show it. I cried later in the bathroom, gazing at the shattered glass I call my reflection.

"What'd you do, play games all day?"

My dad insulted me without the blink of an eye. Did he realize the implications of his statement? No, he didn't. He didn't care. He knows one of the reasons I play video games, but he probably doesn't even care enough to remember. This is difficult to write. I'm tearing up. I can't do this. I can't fucking write, but I have to. You have to, you have to, you have to. I've heard those heavy words too many times, pounding my head like a wave of impenetrable hail.

I started playing video games because of my dad. He possessed, in my young, adolescent mind, an unlimited selection of games. My dad would spend countless hours playing video games late into the night with my uncle. It seems irresponsible for functioning adults, but I know why they did it. My dad played video games to gain a satisfaction that was never provided in his childhood: an unflinching passion and an undying love to savor a moment of fun and happiness. My uncle was unemployed and spent many months living in our house, sleeping on the couch in our living room. They played their games together, and I loved watching them play. I admired them.

I played video games because I wanted to be like my dad, and I wanted my dad to play with me. From an early age, I discovered the only way my dad would play with me was during video game sessions. Specifically, I had to play games he liked; he refused to play certain games, even if I enjoyed those games. That concept was true then, and it is true today. It's the only time I have a chance to bond with my dad in a healthy fashion. My dad loves video games, whether he cares enough to admit it or deny it. Games were difficult to afford when he was a kid, but what was the first thing he bought with his money when he got a job? He bought a Nintendo Entertainment System (NES). To this day, my dad has an addiction to Candy Crush. He plays video games, and I adopted myself to fit that image. That's how it has always been.

How does he have the audacity to insult me for playing video games? How does he have the nerve to tease me in that cruel and unforgiving fashion? Yes, I played video games all day. Didn't you see me, dad? Don't you want to play with me? I'm right here, waiting for you to play with me, dad. Why won't you play with me? Why are you walking away? I'm not six years old anymore, dad. I just want to play with you, dad. I just want to play a game...

I couldn't even write that last paragraph. Halfway through, I started sobbing uncontrollably and I had to bury my head in a pillow to muffle my wailing cries. His words refuse to exit my mind. It was more than the words; it was his spiteful tone. He didn't ask me a question. He accused me. He didn't accuse me, though. He interrogated me. Are video games bad? Is that the problem? Or am I a bad person because I play video games? Huh? Answer me, somebody! I'm sick and fucking tired of hearing the resounding emptiness in my words. I could knock on my words and hear an echo; that's how hollow they are. Words are empty shells, devoid of emotion and lacking remorse.

My dad was playing Mario Kart with my little sister when he insulted me. Can I call him a hypocrite? I don't know. I'm arguably a hypocrite myself, so I believe it to be unfair to label my dad as hypocritical. But can I be upset that he was playing a game with my sister? Where is my game? He plays with her almost every day. How come he never did that for me? Was I not good enough? Was I not the pride and joy he had hoped for in a son? Is it too late to grab the receipt for my life, send myself back to the hospital, and euthanize me?

I fucking despise myself. Am I not good enough for the rest of the world? Is that what this is about? I can stand in front of a mirror and tell myself how strong I am, or at least I can before someone comes along and tells me how wrong I am. My mom bitches and nags at me to quit slouching, but she'd be slouching too if she felt as low as I do. I want to slouch so low my back disconnects from my spinal column and my torso slumps to the floor like a sack of potatoes. What the fuck do you want from me? I just wanted to play a game.

I keep my dad's old NES hooked up in case he ever wants to play with me. Surprisingly, that outdated, dusty box still works after thirty years. I love that shitty box, even if it can be annoying at times. But, despite my best efforts, he doesn't want to play with me, and he probably never will. Instead of playing games with me, he would rather insult me for not working. In his eyes, I am below required expectations. According to him, I am an absolutely lazy, worthless piece of shit. I destroy everything I touch. Fuck. I think I'm going to start crying again.

If you've never seen me cry, it is probably the saddest thing you can possibly imagine. I am trapped in an inescapable childhood, surrounded by my worst nightmares and my most toxic realities. I am an inch from death, hanging by a lonesome thread. If my life were a recipe, this is the part where Rachael Ray or Betty Crocker would bark out passive-aggressive instructions.

"Add tears with a touch of uncontrollable sadness and an inexplicable urge to launch yourself into an oblivion. Mix thoroughly until the weeping is constant; heaving sobs shake the entire body, as you can see. If your mixture isn't crying like that, it may often be cooked raw. Allow individual tears to flow down your face. And that's it! The recipe for crying is complete."

It's too depressing. My dad hasn't cried since he was a young teenager. He was playing football with his friends and he broke his pinkie finger. He snapped it clear to his wrist, and now his finger is bent at a downward angle. That was the last time he cried. I've never seen a single tear fall from his eyes—not even a shiny remnant beaming at the surface. One time, I mustered the courage to ask him why he never cries.

"Crying doesn't solve problems."

I always believed he was right. Why do I even cry? He's right. Crying doesn't solve any of my problems. What's the point of crying? My dad hates it when kids cry, or at least he hates it when I cry. He thinks that crying is for babies; it's a sign of weakness. If I cry, it only upsets him further. I have many memories of myself sitting on the couch after my father's rage forced me there. I would wait for my hectic breathing to return to normalcy. My chest swayed up and down sporadically, and I sniffled during the entire ordeal. I hated it. I felt terrible. I still feel terrible. Crying, I'm always crying. I'm still crying.

I have to help my dad set up a fence in our garden tomorrow. We have to work on Father's Day, unfortunately. It's not like my dad cares. Every day is a work day. No excuses. Last year, I helped him set up the same exact fence, and I messed up. I made a mistake rolling out the fence, and he yelled at me. I don't remember exactly what he snapped at me, but I remember his words slapped me across the face. I cried later in the day, a time when he would be unable to witness my despair. I try my best to help him, but it doesn't matter. I always end with the same result: disappointing him and myself, no matter how high or low my expectations. Remember the day I never put down the shovel? Was that exceeding expectations? I shattered the fucking expectations, but it didn't matter the next day. There was more work for me to do the next day. I cannot stress enough that every day is a work day.

Yes, it is true I played games all day. It's summer. I am reasonably trying to salvage my childhood before adulthood murders me and rips me to tiny pieces. Don't I deserve some happiness? No, Justin. You do not deserve anything, you worthless scum. You are fucking despicable. You are the mud I scrape from my sneakers. You are an abomination to the pinnacle of human existence. You are a valley between the insurmountable peaks of surrounding mountains. You are trash that is thrown in a dumpster and dragged to an equally disgusting landfill. You are a child.

What'd you do, play games all day? He said that. I can't digest the words. How could he say that to me? Is that the same father that once played a racing game on bumper cam until three in the morning, drove to work at eighty miles per hour, and kept wondering why his car was moving so slow? What happened? Did nothing happen? Are my memories distorted? I don't know anything. Maybe I should leave the games to other people.

My life is a game, and maybe it's time I stop playing.

JUNE 20, 2016

My mind debuted on the same day I came out my mother's vagina, covered in blood and stuck to a placenta meat larger than China. Do I disgust you? My goal is to throw caution to the wind, snip a trinket of police caution tape, and duct tape it to a tree so it flutters in the wind. Was that sentence more soothing? Am I smoothing out these edges? My content is the most explicit, most permitting, and most fitting example of how to capture the attention of ten pedantic Neanderthals. I say my mind debuted, and now you bear witness; colder than a bare waitress at a nudist bar.

I stand on a platform with my feet plastered to the floor of the stage. Who placed me upon this pedestal and watched me erect pillars of knowledge cramped tighter than thin-ass paper stacks? This page is my pedestal, and my words are a booming voice redirected at the avoided messes I call my audience. They don't get this message every time I message them because their brain speed is fixated on maintaining a pathetic performance. Is that an interrogative? No, it's a declarative statement. This is imperative. Listen, I have one chance to break the world record for delivering mental incarceration in a counterintuitive span of time. Did you get that message, or were you too hyped in the cesspool? It's a mess because nobody hears my message.

For those of you applauding me, I am appalled at your competitive rivalry. Who can clap the loudest? Who can scream the longest? Who can smack a capsule of Tylenol in the Adam's apple of a possessive rodent who splurged on medicinal tablets? What's the matter? Why are you looking at me like that? Hasn't anybody said those words before? Am I more original than a witty line repeated six times beforehand? Is that a consequence of being rich in entertainment, void of the constant constraints plaguing middle class patrons? I'm stringing together drunken words into a crocheted case of alcohol poisoning for your brain to sip as poison. Would it be more appropriate to procreate at an extensive rate and exterminate our future generations? Fuck you. You're an abomination, an abominable snowman in a whorehouse with the lights dimmed, giving rim to the first person to drop their pants. Applaud me, fools! Stop staring at my genitals and start focusing on my fapping lisp! Whoops! Didn't I mean flapping lips? That's a Freudian slip, isn't it? Ah, fuck it, you'll applaud anyone, won't you?

My head is heavier than a heavyweight boxing champion stomped to the ground. I've got blood squirting from both of my eyes until I look like a Toaster Strudel pastry glazing. No, that doesn't mean I'm crazy. What is craziness, anyway? Is craziness opening the same unhealed wound sixteen times because it's stainless? Not steel, but my mind warps time at the speed of thought. I spark a candle wick with lighter fluid and watch as it sends my house up in flames. Is that crazy? My brain melts at the sight of foreign flesh because I'm a depressed mess with a broken wire mesh to protect my skinny head. Did the candlestick fire melt me? Or was it possibly the impressive combination of admiration displaced among various artists? I take pride in the fact that I was raised to admire and idolize, otherwise I'd probably run rampant and scream for a place to divert my mind. Lead weights are tied to my brain-dead head as I'm thrown overboard into the ocean. Life is an internal mutiny.

Do people idolize me? Do they get jealous when they see me spewing words at an incomprehensible rate? Could you comprehend what is considered common sense? My words are remotely untouchable, disguised in the fact that they appear to be erasable, or biodegradable. Is this another way to bother a romantic who knows that failed antics are more likely to repeat an unstable relationship? I could spend an eternity annotating my words, and then write another book about those same annotations. Is that too complex? Am I too reliable? Would it be thrown out of context if I smashed words together every time I lost a contest? Inside my head there are Spanish Conquistadors repeating their tethered actions of homicidal genocide. Armored horses purge a forest consisting of several forces; those forces are natives and torturers, nature and nurture. Swelling battles ensue, crippling my mind with their zealous onslaught.

My life isn't a play, but, if I'm stuck in the center of this stage, I might as well stay. If Ebenezer Scrooge had a screw loose, I must be a bucket of bolts because I'm nuts. I'm spraying words from my mouth, giving readers' imaginations a verbal abrasion. I have my own style derived from social pleasures. I regurgitate recurring hatred for the sake of pleasure, but I'm not social at all. I don't remember the next line for you to carelessly decipher. I am a complication, an underestimation of the human mind. Would you blindly follow me if I told you I never told a lie? Don't follow blindly; shove a light up the ass crack of the person you're behind. Get it, behind? Shit, I bet my wordplay seems like a joke to you, but it swerves under your feet like the aftermath of an earthquake. These vibrations and tendencies tend to eliminate a sense of deliberate hatred for people who deserve a plate of greatness. My life is a bowling strike, but the pins keep resetting.

Women are all dirty sluts who would suck a dick without a second thought. Men are massaging the misogynist gene hypocritically as they get their dicks sucked. Those two sentences create more disturbance than an airplane experiencing turbulence. Of course, I don't truly think that, but I thought it anyway, didn't I? My life is comic relief for someone else's main gig; it probably starts in less than a week. I supply so much wit that you should bring a life preserver when you read these words or you might drown in it. I'll get cited for jealousy plagiarism by producing more original content than the rest of the world combined. I'm taking every word in the written language, mixing them together, and dispersing a written testimony for the crimes against humanity. How do you use every word in this language without displeasing a member of the opposite understanding? My words create disturbances in the upper atmosphere. My words are electromagnetic pulses that irradiate your cell phone battery. I'm climbing out of a labyrinth with words dangling from my sides like a corrosive keychain. Fuck a hospital accident. There is no such thing as an accident, as they say. Switched at birth? I was supposed to go to some other poor-ass-white-privileged-family. I don't think you know the truth. How else am I supposed to persevere this comatose? Fuck a compromise. Death is blindly grabbing for my scrotum, but I stab Him back in the septum. Are you still skeptical? Are you susceptible in suspecting my mind is dripping hot candle wax? I fuel this fire with or without you. I don't need your help.

Am I destined for greatness, or am I only paving the way for increased devastation? An application of skill is an unfulfilled action I haven't mastered. Am I a storyteller, or are my stories coarse and horrid? Is my voice strong and influencing, or is it hoarse and embarrassing? Is there even a correlation between my mind and my emotions? Am I even telling a story, or was the book never opened? Did you judge me by my cover?

Intermission, and then the story continues. Go home for now, folks. Return to your mediocrity while I stack my mind for the next show. Thank you for being a patient audience. Goodnight, and remember to return for the next show!

JUNE 25, 2016

My style is erratic, worn threads with tattered edges. I torture myself using illusions provided to me by the people I love and hate the most. I'm waterboarding my mind with an impassionate smack, stripping my consciousness of its conscience. What does that last line mean? I believe I'm referring to the fact that I may be lacking a conscience suitable for handling the proper consequences I'll receive for writing these words. Crucify me and drill nails through my skin. Who the fuck is Jesus? Who claims that asshole died for me? If He died, He probably died so He never had to take my pain. He couldn't fucking handle it. Stretch out my intestines on a rack and proceed to melt hot iron on my chest. What do any of these lines mean? I am merely visualizing independent scenes of my torture gallery. Do I carry a burden, or am I the burden?

I'm taking a dull knife and cutting jagged lines in your fertile skin. How do you fucking feel? Does that fucking hurt? That's the pain I feel when you're not looking, but it feels twice as bad when you are looking. Fuck being ignored. You say I'm a zombie, mindlessly gazing into space with a look of indifference glued to my face? You're lucky I'm not a zombie, otherwise I'd gnaw on your juicy flesh and suck your brain out of your thick skull like I'm drinking a milkshake through a straw. Fuck you. I'll absorb your knowledge until you acknowledge my presence and admit to my persecution, but it doesn't matter because I'll still submit you to a verbal execution. Was that sentence too complicated for you now that you're missing a brain?

I am a diabolical fireball exploding in people's faces at a crowded mall during the Fourth of July. I burn courage with the annunciation of words. Literary devices are instruments of torture; they're strapping cords around my body and throwing me in a corner. Somehow, I manage to slam the door in my face. Smack! Did you catch that onomatopoeia? That's another torture device commonly used to fill a reader's corneas with the sounds of a word. Does that make sense to you? Fuck it. Do I have to explain everything I say in order to properly deliver my message? Should I wait for somebody to decipher this code and ensure my devices don't go to waste? While I'm at it, I said corneas because you use your eyes to read words off the page. Why do I have to explain myself to an extent I probably shouldn't? Is it because nobody ever listened to me? Or is it because I'm sick of being dissed for the sake of personality?

My mind delivers fucked up thoughts to disperse on a world that wouldn't hesitate to criticize me. Does being criticized mean people give a fuck about me? I don't know how to determine who cares and who pretends. I do know I want to steal transfusion blood from hospital rooms, seal it up in fake ketchup packets, and sell the packets in the cafeteria. I might as well take a shit, melt it over a fire, and lace it with chocolate in your kids' Halloween candy. What the fuck do these thoughts mean to you? How do you perceive the brute without first knowing the excuse? My excuse is I lack common sense and the common decency to see a will to live. If I die, someone would resurrect me so they can keep using the carpool lane for their morning commute. That really shows you how much people care about me, doesn't it?

What is an identity? An identity is a term used to shade a broken entity. How do you hide an identity? I could sit in a sea anemone until I can't see my enemies, but is that a fucking remedy? My desk is an anemone, and I feel as trapped as Nemo. Did you catch that reference, or did it fly over your head like September eleventh? I'm throwing out references like advertisements in a reference book. Did you understand that line? Am I even clever? Nobody comments on my references. Do they even understand them? Should I annotate these words with an entire paragraph each and sell another book to mooch off the profits of the first?

I'm a disastrous bastard who is giving trouble's ass a kiss. That's called ass kissing, and that makes me an ass kisser. What's a teacher's pet? First grade teacher, come again? Call me a nervous wreck instead. Fuck a knife; slice me with scissors until my arms are covered in nine-inch slivers. Where is this conversation heading? Is this even a conversation, or am I spewing thoughts at a fixed rate to a dumbfounded audience? Are you still listening? Are you tuned in to my radio station, playing my jam until your legs turn to jelly and your face caves in?

He's masked and transparent, a frequent visitor of the Earth who gobbles up victims like an everlasting banquet. Invisible to the passing eye, but, if you stare deeper inside, you'll find a reason to believe in constant misery. There's a lapse in time elapsed over the course of time, and that's called my history. My mind is a leech, sucking on my thoughts as sustenance. I am abhorrent, but that doesn't mean I lack morality. I'm referred as a Destroyer of Worlds, but the only world I've destroyed is my own. I'm reliable enough when it comes to self-destruction. In this aspect, I exceed expectations. Fuck report cards. I'm through with grades and labels. I'm sick of life beating me up after it's through nagging at me. What thought am I attempting to accomplish? What line do I feel is most important? What will be my lingering line? Is this my cliffhanger, body dangling off the side of a cliff with the rope tied around my neck and the other end tied to a tree?

I didn't become Death. I am Death.

JUNE 28, 2016

Today was interesting. I guess that's a blessing and a curse. My mom, brother, sister, and I went to see a movie at the mall; the movie was Finding Dory, the sequel to Finding Nemo. We also made plans to stop by Mama Darla and Papa Charlie's house after the movie. It sounds like a trivial set of affairs taking place in a normal day, but let's not forget about me. Let's dive in this shallow pool, shall we?

I woke up and went about my morning routine as usual. Nothing out of the ordinary in that aspect. Except something seemed wrong, and I tasked my brain to solve the puzzle bunkered in my head. Why was something wrong? No idea, next question. What was wrong? Well, something was disrupting my routine, and I was unable to figure out what was being deflected against my protective shield. What were we doing today? Shit! I almost forgot. That was the fucking problem. We were going to go see Finding Dory at the mall, which features an enormous cinema section, including multiple theaters.

Now, I never felt too interested in seeing this movie. I watched the trailer months ago and I was unperturbed. It doesn't matter what I think, though. No, it never matters what I think. That's why I keep to myself most of the time. My mom doesn't give a shit if I like the movie or not. We were going to watch it, and nothing would change that. That's how it has always been.

There is no such thing as an argument with my parents. My words mean nothing to them, and I'm sure these words would be the same. Maybe that's why I have a knack for debating and arguing; I always try to win arguments with other people. I never win arguments with my parents, but maybe I can win an argument with someone else. People don't like me when I argue with them, and I don't blame them. My only wish is for them to forgive me. They can't see my perspective of the argument. They may be angry with me for arguing, but their rage is nothing compared to my own. I don't direct the majority of my rage at others; I direct it at myself.

Anyway, we drove up to the mall without any problems. We waited in line for our tickets, and that was where I realized we had a situation. My radar detected an array of problems, but my mom wasn't listening to me. The line to enter the theater was filled with close to a hundred people. Lines for popcorn and beverages were not nearly as long, but people were everywhere. Shit. I knew we were never going to be able to get in the theater. Screw popcorn and drinks. I was more concerned with finding a seat.

Together, we made it up to the ticket counter, where my mom flawlessly executed a few short, quick lines of dialogue. She asked for tickets, and the man behind the counter responded kindly, although I sensed the truth behind his words. My heart plummeted into my stomach, and it was thoroughly devoured by a collective wave of gastric acids.

He told us the only seats available would most likely be directly in front of the screen, if we could even find seats together. My mom was pissed, but she had to make a decision. Was it worth the risk, or should we bail? For what seemed like an eternity, she pondered this perilous question. Too long, too long! She was taking too long. I could feel the impatience of the people behind us stabbing jagged daggers in my fleshy sides.

How long did she wait to answer? It couldn't have been that long, could it? I can't remember. The memory moves in slow motion, and the fast forward option is broken. I don't know how long it took for my mom to answer, but she managed to tell the man that we needed a refund because we were leaving. Before I knew it, we started walking away, beyond the stares of disappointment and disapproval from people in line. Passing under the black rope of failure, we receded from the cinema area. It was over.

After snapping out of my own sense of disillusionment, I returned to reality. The slow motion was over, and I could no longer feel daggers in my easily penetrable skin. That's when I noticed my sister started crying. I watched her happy smile fade just as quickly as it had appeared. It was replaced by puffy red cheeks and teary eyes. A depressing cry escaped her pouting lips. She was so excited to watch that movie, and now she realized we weren't going to watch it. She was broken, but she wasn't the only one.

I looked at my sister and I felt an overwhelming sadness. I could easily replace a younger version of myself in my sister's feet. I was a happy child shadowed by a dark and depressing series of failures and disappointments. Is that what my childhood was like? If it was, I don't want my sister to experience that. She is so precious, so innocent, and so pure. Nothing should destroy a child's happiness, but life doesn't care about children. Life doesn't care about people. Life doesn't care about fair or unfair. Life doesn't care about right or wrong. Life doesn't care about morals or laws. Life doesn't care about murder or rape. Life doesn't care about crime. Life doesn't care about equality, liberty, or freedom. Life doesn't care about happiness or sadness, feelings or emotions. Life doesn't care about you. Life doesn't care about my little sister, and it certainly doesn't care about someone like me. But I guess that's life. Sometimes you have to take the wrongs and shape them into something right.

Examining this memory, and this exact moment, I feel extremely upset. I know exactly what this memory is. This is another example of how our family experiences incredible displays of misfortune. We were half an hour early to the movie theater and we still couldn't win. The theater was already packed, crammed row to row like a package of sardines. Why did these people decide to go to the theaters on the same day as us? Why couldn't they just stay home for once? Why can't our family have a moment to enjoy for ourselves? What the fuck is the problem? Why are we not allowed to have anything nice? Why is everything a problem for us? Why is everything pitted against us? Why, why, why?

I'm shedding tears trying to write these words because I know nobody is going to answer these questions. Nobody cares, and that's been hard for me to realize. I'm completely alone now, and maybe I've always been alone. Maybe I'll always be alone. Life is done dealing with me and my problems. Life won't answer my questions. Nobody will answer me. Nobody, nobody, nobody. I use that word too much, but I don't fucking care. The truth is that nobody cares. Not even the truth cares about me. Nobody.

Snapping from my trance, and getting back to the story, I listened to my mom trying to soothe my sister. I could tell she felt bad for ditching the movie, and she wanted to replace my sister's broken, liquid sadness with laughter and smiles.

"Katie, do you want to walk around the mall?" My mom gently held my sister's hand. A mother's tender touch works miracles. One such miracle was witnessed before my eyes as I watched my sister slowly nod her head in agreement to my mom's question.

We walked around the mall for a few minutes, and we passed stores, shops, cars, and chatty vendors. Eventually, we approached a group of kiddie rides offering cheap entertainment. Cars, trucks, and boats slowly rocked back and forth after swallowing a few quarters. Usually, or at least where I live, you can find these types of attractions next to gumball dispensers and impossible claw machines at local grocery stores.

My sister's face lit up in happiness, and she dashed off to an ice cream truck. My mom handed me three quarters—while whispering in an exasperated tone about how expensive these shitty ripoffs are—and I carefully pushed them through the coin slots for my little sister. Thunderous smiles boomed from my sister's face as she pressed the start button. The machine, an adventure for any child, creaked and groaned as it rocked back and forth. It didn't last long, but it did its job. My sister was smiling again.

My mom searched on her phone and discovered Finding Dory would be playing at our local theater at seven o'clock, later in the evening. Excited to bear good news, she dropped the bomb as we walked back across the mall toward the parking lot.

"Katie, we are going to see Finding Dory later tonight, but it will be at the tiny theater near our house." She paused, as if for dramatic effect to add to the suspense of such a statement, and then continued. "How does that sound?"

My sister's face was the definition of ecstasy. She displayed pure happiness, showing no signs of how she nearly cried a bucket of tears only ten minutes earlier. That cracked a smile out of me. I loved seeing her eyes flare up in excitement. What an interesting day, and what a turn of events! It was only half past one. That's when I remembered we still had to visit Charlie and Darla. Shit! Just when I thought the day was over, right?

Half an hour later we were at their front door, awaiting Charlie's welcoming remarks: a chorus of ill-tempered, probably drunken statements regarding the deteriorating condition of our grandma, Darla. The bitching and complaining between those two never ends. Neither one of them knows when to shut the fuck up, but at least it is amusing. Charlie is a real character. I'm lucky to not be related to him through blood, but I am gratefully able to observe his shenanigans. Everyone has a story to tell about Charlie. I could tell quite a few stories about him, and I'm sure I will, eventually. Maybe when he dies I'll dedicate that day to celebrate his life. That sounds rude, but, in all honesty, I'm amazed he is still alive. He's been smoking and drinking his entire life, and he survived a nasty case of Lyme disease that left him hospitalized. Somehow, he evaded lung and liver cancer. He's a lucky fucking bastard, in my opinion.

I wrote about Charlie and Darla in one of my first journal entries because I thought it was a perfect icebreaker. What better way to begin a journal than with a humorous scene? It's comic relief from my life, if I may call it that. Originally, I planned to write more about other people than I ended up doing. I wanted a diverse cast of characters to represent my life, but that idea faded from existence quickly. Charlie could have been the centerpiece of this crazy circus. That would have been an interesting journal, wouldn't it?

It would take years to describe a couple of hours with Charlie and Darla. The only way to truly experience their characters is to stand in their presence. I have done that too many times, unfortunately. Today was another day where I was unwillingly dragged into their bickering. But, as I've learned, every family has a Charlie or Darla, or both.

Strangely enough, they refrained from bashing each other today. Darla, overweight and elderly, experienced severe pain in her knees. She placed the blame on her arthritis, and that is bad news for me. Genetics is an awfully great example of my future. I can almost guarantee I'll have arthritis; it will probably be in my wrist. Wonderful.

Anyway, Charlie fiddled with an AT&T "high speed" cable box while the rest of us sat in the living room. By fiddling, I mean he was attempting to fix it while uttering a string of barely coherent swears and other such derogatory pleasantries. It was extremely amusing, and I had to restrain myself from laughing. He is too fucking funny.

After a few hours of listening to Charlie whine and complain, we finally went home. We ate dinner and then got ready to go to the movie theater—two different theaters in the same day. Before I knew it, we were walking up to the booth to buy tickets.

As we walked into the theater, I noticed and recognized my friend Jason and his dad. We struck up a conversation because we hadn't talked since school let out in May. I was surprised to meet him in public, and I'm sure he was just as surprised to meet me. I asked him about his summer, and he told me he spent the previous four days at a big university for a wrestling and leadership camp. While I was happy and proud for my friend, I couldn't help thinking about how I have done nothing in comparison.

What have I done this summer? Does writing in my journal count as using my time productively? I never mention my writing to anyone. In eighth grade, I shared my writing once. It was a horrible mistake, but I'm not going to talk about it now. Maybe another day. Or, slightly more likely, I will never talk about because I don't want to scare myself into a frenzy of writing anxiety.

I need to end this entry on a positive note. We watched the movie without any further problems. The movie was decent, but it didn't hold the same emotional impact that Finding Nemo had. I'm tired. I can't write anything else today.

JULY 3, 2016

I had a crazy fucking dream. I guess I've been thinking a lot about my journal because that was the topic of my dream. I'm not sure where my dream took place. If I had to guess, it took place at my school, except my school received a major visual upgrade and a new expansion pack of area to explore. Here is a simplified rundown of this insane dream:

Basically, my former chemistry teacher, a sarcastic asshole at times, somehow found my journal. I think she stole it, but I can't remember. Either way, she had my most valuable possession. Using her savvy knowledge of chemistry, she did some Breaking-Bad-Level chemistry shit to my journal. Suddenly, the journal produced magic powers and started glowing a light blue, luminescent light. My chemistry teacher pulled off some dark sorcery shit and turned the words from my journal into a blue liquid. Never missing a beat, she bottled up the liquid in vials, which she placed strategically around the school.

She saved most of the liquid for herself and named it Essence. In her classroom, she stored a monstrous pool of Essence. Wading through the pool, she gained superpowers and an ability to memorize every word in my journal. Mad with power, she became ruler of the school, and the antagonist of my dream. So, where do I come in?

Well, I found out my chemistry teacher stole my journal, but it was too late. She had turned the school into a totalitarian system in which she was the ultimate dictator. At that point, I was powerless against her.

I couldn't leave the school, and neither could anyone else, although my classmates were not bothered by anything. Everyone except me was brainwashed by her. She forced her students to drink vials of Essence, and it gave them super strength. She fueled her students to fight and torment me. My own friends and classmates were blindly beating me through a series of karate chops and mixed martial arts. This wasn't a dream—it was a nightmare.

Luckily, I found a hole in her sinister plot. I realized the Essence was her source of power, and I decided to find and drink a vial. Immediately, my energy soared. The power of an atomic fusion bubbled in my core. Using my fresh power, fighting tactics, and a raw mixture of luck, skill, and adrenaline, I managed to fight back against my classmates. After fighting and winning, I drained their Essence and used it to strengthen myself. I felt like I was in a video game.

Anyway, my chemistry teacher roamed around the school, nonchalantly taunting me. She would walk around the school and quote lines from my journal. Since she stole my Essence, I couldn't remember anything. Thankfully, every time I stole and drank some Essence I'd remember more excerpts and pieces from my journal. Slowly, I battled my friends, snapped them out of their brainwashed states, and replenished my memory. Her pyramid scheme was collapsing.

Even though I saw her often, I couldn't attack her. She was practically superhuman. You wouldn't be able to tell by looking at her, but she could have destroyed me. Basically, she tortured me by keeping me in an inescapable prison where people attacked on command.

Overall, that shit was crazy. I was in the middle of a fight scene when my sister woke me up. I was slowly accumulating Essence, and I believe my next move would have been to destroy her pool of Essence; it was her source of power. After that, I probably would have prepared for an epic showdown with my chemistry teacher.

JULY 4, 2016

Today went better than I thought it would, but this shit still sucks. I go back to school in six weeks, and there is still so much left to do. I don't have enough time. My summer is more than halfway over.

I want to write about today, but I can't because I don't have the time or space. The Fourth of July is such a shitty holiday. I mean, don't take this out of context. I love celebrating freedom, and I am extremely grateful for people who died to protect my freedom and my country. I have incredible respect for active and retired members of the military. That stuff doesn't bother me. The fireworks and celebrations kill me.

I am terrified of fireworks, without a doubt. I guess they aren't that bad if you watch from a distance, but it's going to be worse next year. My dad was talking to one of his buddies from work about doing The Show again. The Show is a group effort to buy fireworks, thousands of dollars' worth of fireworks. My dad used to do that shit, and we had huge parties at our house when I was little. That's what caused the memory, one of the worst memories I have. Fuck. I don't know how I can even begin writing about that memory.

When you're little, helpless, terrified, and immobile, not to mention the present fear of dying in a blazing inferno, it doesn't leave a good impression. I can't believe my dad talked nonchalantly about buying fireworks. Does he not remember what happened? How could he possibly forget? My mom didn't say anything either, even though she went ballistic at my dad for his fireworks shenanigans. She was furious with him, and she had a reason to be. When she came home, there was smoke billowing out the windows in that memory. To put it simply, she was fucking pissed. Ultimately, that day ended my dad's brigade of firework specialties. Fuck. How am I supposed to write about that? Where do I even fucking start?

This is fucking killing me. I have so much to do still, and not enough time. I need to finish my journal, read two books, then read two more books about math because I don't remember anything useful and I'm going to fail all my math classes, then read a book for English, write an essay about the book, prepare a poster based on the book and essay, and present my poster on the first day of school. Everything previously mentioned is required for my success. I also wish to start memorizing words in the dictionary by practicing a page a day in my spare time. I bought a ton of games that I have been dying to play for years, and I desperately want to finish them. My friends and family are pestering me to spend time with them. Also, I might as well cross off days that involve going places or doing hours of mind-numbing chores. You better fucking know that it'll take up the majority of my time. Fuck. I don't even have enough time to sleep. My nights are filled with shitty sleeping, imaginative dreams, and vividly real nightmares. By the time I wake up, I feel awful. I bravely walk out of my dungeon and into the bright yellow light, trudge upstairs, and receive a round of insults from everyone in my family; they tell me I look like shit, as if I didn't already know.

Does the entire fucking world hate me or something? Is there a sign taped to my back saying, "Torment Me!" that I don't know about? I feel so pissed. I'm waiting for it. I'm waiting for someone to tell me that since I hate everything so much, why don't I just kill myself and leave this planet and stop complaining and stop making excuses and stop procrastinating and stop being lazy and stop working too much and stop getting good grades and stop getting bad grades and stop going to school and stop playing sports and stop enjoying hobbies and stop writing and stop fucking living. Why not? But nobody will say that to me because I have good days. I still have happy times and memories. I'm drowning, and good days are me reaching the surface of the water for a gasp of air before I plunge beneath the icy surf again.

I can't get a job. Without a job now, I'm already under enough stress. I can't maintain a relationship, or a friendship, for that matter. The ships are sinking, and why would I bother trying to stop them? I'm close to feeling desperate again, and desperation leads to poor decision making. I might stop doing my homework. Fuck summer projects, anyway. If people don't want to listen to me, I don't want to live anymore. I'm anxious because I know there is going to be a day where I open myself up to the world. When I do, I'll say:

"This is me. This is who I am. Like me or not, this is my life. I require your attention. I ask for your respect. I will do my best to earn your support. This is me. I am this person."

I think an alternate option before killing myself is a "fuck everything" approach. I think about this a lot; I think too much, as I've been told. Unless something happens, that's the route I'm heading. That's why I need time. I sound so damn needy, and maybe I am needy. I've had such an emptiness of needs and wants, and now that is the only thing I can think about. I don't have a fucking clue. It's like Watson trying to follow Sherlock's thought process.

I hate myself most of all. How is that even possible? How can I possibly hate myself more than anything else I claim to hate? I would get into a fight with myself if I could. Damn, I even hate myself for writing these words. It's like an endless loop of pure hatred. But, there are times where I love myself, too. Sometimes I write and create beautiful words. I love those words. Then, something happens to me. I realize other people might not love my words as much as I do. How? How could anyone not appreciate these words? How stupid and naïve must I be for even thinking people might like my words?

"Ha! You're so fucking dumb! Fucking stupid, you stupid fucking fuck. Boo-hoo! Why don't you cry more? That's the only thing you're good at: crying."

I'm waiting for the day I fail so hard that Plan B goes into action. I'll say fuck everything, and I'll block all contact on social media. I'll go through school not giving a single, solitary fuck, and I'll get into as much trouble as possible. My parents will be pissed at me because they don't tolerate troublemaking or talking back. I'm going to talk back until people's backs leave an indent in the wall. My dad would beat my ass for causing trouble, but I don't care. I'd keep fucking doing it. I'll keep saying fuck everything in the hope to see my life unravel. I'll present my grand finale, all eyes will be turned toward me, and I'll be ready. I'll die, and it'll be over. At least, that is one possibility.

JULY 7, 2016

I should be upset right now, but, honestly, I'm only disappointed. I think the real emotions will kick in later, so I guess I'm fine for now. I'm getting tired of all these setbacks, you know? No, you wouldn't know. That's my bad. Let me explain.

I was eating dinner and my dad interrupted me with a verbal testicle puncture. "Yep, got some work for you on Saturday," he said.

At first, I was fucking terrified. I thought he signed me up for a job interview without consulting with me. Lately, he's been nudging me toward applying for a job at his training site because they recently hired some college aged kids there. In my dad's vision, I would be a perfect option to fill the position of a college kid or two. See, my dad is well respected as a worker, and I know everyone else will expect me to be as exceptionally gifted as he is. More than anyone, I know my dad will hold me to the highest expectations. That's not even mentioning I don't have a fucking clue about cranes, trucks, cables, or any other shit my dad deals with.

Originally, I thought he signed me up for that nightmare-inducing sequence of shit, and I was slightly relieved when he told me I had to go help Charlie clean out his trailer at the campground. Why did I have to help my asshole grandpa? Well, he is selling his trailer because he never stays there anymore. Charlie and Darla are close to seventy years old. Although they won't admit it, they have difficulty moving around. So, now I have to wake up early Saturday morning, nervously drive to the campground, and help Charlie clear out all of his garbage and useless shit.

Charlie by himself is fucking ridiculous, but I can't even imagine how many drunken slurs he throws at his feet while he works. For Charlie, everything is an inconvenient ordeal. For example, and to prove my statement of how ridiculous he is, I'll describe his shopping method. He lives in a city, which means he is never more than a few miles from a grocery store. Yet, even in the winter he keeps a cooler in the back of his truck for cold items (usually beer) he buys at the store. What the fuck? He's only five minutes from the store. In comparison, my mom and I drive twenty minutes to do our shopping, and we don't even bring coolers during the summer, although we do crank up the AC.

Honestly, I'm not upset about any of that shit I just talked about. See, I'm bugged because my dad signed me up for this task without telling me. I didn't have a choice anyway, did I? What am I supposed to say?

"No, I don't want to help you, or anyone. I'm the one who needs help. Can't you leave me alone? Quit bothering me. Get the fuck away!"

No, I'm not allowed to say those spiteful words. Declining a plea for assistance is not socially acceptable. I guess that's why it isn't called socially declinable. Anyway, I asked my dad about helping Charlie, and his answer pissed me off even more than I already was.

"I was supposed to go, too, but I have to work," he said.

Are you fucking serious? Why didn't he ask Charlie to change to another day? Charlie is retired, and he rarely leaves the house. He can afford to miss one opportunity. I don't even fucking care at this point. I guess I'm alone. Again.

My mom didn't say anything, either. Thanks for sticking up for my perspective! Lately, I've been getting increasingly pissed at both of my parents. I'm so tired, weak, frail, and fifty more redundant synonyms. You know what else sucks? I could work my ass off until it sails to the moon, but my parents will still say I'm lazy. Damn, I could be in Stephen-King-Workaholic-Mode and still win the honor of laziest, worthless waste of a First World child. I can't escape. Thinking of an analogy, I am a struggling student. I need extra help, additional attention, and massive support. Maybe the pace of the lessons needs to be slowed, or maybe I could use a friend or two. No, life doesn't work like that. Instead, the teacher speeds up faster and faster with every lesson, fully expecting the student to keep up.

In the meantime, I'll keep myself together. Fuck. I'm not sure how much longer I can hold my composure. I can only tolerate so much before I break. Trust me, I tolerate more than you think. Honestly, tolerance is knowing the glass is half-empty, thinking of filling it, and remembering you're out of milk. Thinking back to a time in health class where I sat by annoying people, I remember tolerance. Let me explain myself. I knew those people were bad (glass is half-empty), I wanted to move to a different seat (thinking of filling it), but I couldn't move anywhere else because nobody wanted to trade seats with me (remembering you're out of milk). That's how I view tolerance. You have to learn to tolerate your surroundings. Repeat those thoughts, and you've built the chassis of my life.

Midnight, same day. Finally, I finished the book! My productivity is cause for celebration, but I have nobody to celebrate with. Well, I guess I'll pat myself on the back, tell myself I am proud, and move on. No need to dwell on past achievements, right?

So, what book did I read, and why is it important? I finished reading *Big-Enough* by Will James. It was an incredibly engaging tale. The book is nearly one hundred years old, but its contents transcend the passage of time. *Big-Enough* is a piece of history in my family, as evidenced by the cursive message scrawled inside the cover. The message was written by my great-grandfather, John. In the message, he addresses the first time he read the book, and then continues by passing on the book to my grandpa (his son, who was eight years old at the time), Don. This book was my grandpa's Christmas present. When my dad was old enough he read this book, and now it is my turn. For such a dysfunctional family, this is the only tradition we have. I don't know much about who I am, but I have this book.

How was the book? Honestly, I'm still processing how I feel about *Big-Enough*. I think, given enough time, it'll be one of my favorite books. Personally, the book is my favorite because it holds an emotional connection. The story was decent, although it was unlike any text I'm used to reading.

Here's a basic rundown of the plot: a boy and a colt are born on the same day, and they immediately become lifelong companions. The story follows these two characters and their struggles as they embark on their biggest adventure—leaving home. Now, that is an extremely simplified rundown, but you get the picture. Oh, and I should also mention that I am thankful the author explains cowboy slang.

The first fifty pages were the hardest for me to read. Basically, the entire introduction was difficult. Why? Well, the boy, William, called Billy, grows up alongside his horse, named Big-Enough. The horse is named Big-Enough because it titles him perfectly. He's big enough to be Billy's horse, and the boy is big enough to ride him.

Billy grows up watching his father herd cattle, buck horses, and be a man, and Billy is big enough to be like his dad. Billy's dream is to own land and be a cowboy, same as his dad. Despite Billy's wishes, his parents send him to school because they want Billy to be educated. When Billy enters adulthood, he hops on Big-Enough and rides away from home. He leaves a note for his parents, promising he'll come back someday.

While Billy is away from home, he seeks to prove he is capable of being successful at the way of life he prefers: riding horses. The rest of the book details his rise as a determined boy destined to be a cowhand. Then, as a man, Bill returns home at the end of the book, still riding his trusted companion, Big-Enough. His parents, more than ecstatic at the sight of their estranged son, eagerly greet his return. The book concludes with this family reunification, and Bill's parents realize their son doesn't need to have an education. Bill was happy because he followed his own path and didn't let anyone dissuade him. It was a chillingly realistic ending to a beautifully crafted work of fiction.

As I previously stated, this book, and specifically the beginning and resolution, emotionally slayed me. I cried multiple times before I finished. My dad has told me for years that he wants me to read *Big-Enough*. I think this book attached to him even more than it did to me, which is a gravitating statement. He grew up in an arguably similar fashion as Billy. My dad, same as Billy, was always too focused doing work on the farm to care about homework or school. He had to get a job at twelve years old so he could help feed his family, or at least to pay for clothes. He left his parent's house when he was eighteen years old. His life, or his childhood, bears a striking resemblance to Billy's childhood. My dad told his parents he'd visit them someday, and he fulfilled his promise. He's been back quite a few times, actually. I understand the value my dad has placed on this book, and I have my own value to bestow.

Whether my dad realizes this or not, some of the countless things my dad has said or done over the years are eerily similar to the words in *Big-Enough*. I'm positive he has used the term "Big-Enough" to describe me more than once. He probably told my mom I'm big enough to ride a bike, or help him work. Well, he might have been like Billy when he was younger, but now he acts like Lem (Billy's dad in the story). When I was younger, the only thing I ever wanted to do was mimic my dad. I wanted to be a mechanic—just like my dad. In the story, Billy is the exact same as me, always following in his dad's footsteps. But life is a story, and that means there are twists, turns, and bends in the plot. My dad went bankrupt, was forced to sell his auto shop, and he got a different job. Suddenly, my only passion diminished. In *Big-Enough*, Billy's parents make him go to school, which means he was separated from his horse.

The only noticeable difference between the book and my life is that Billy never strays from his dream of resembling his father. He wants to be like his father, whereas his father wishes for him to become educated. Although, it is later revealed that Lem secretly approves of his son's decisions. I no longer want to follow in my dad's footsteps, unlike Billy. This is where I believe my dad has emotional ties to the book—stronger bonds than I conceived while reading. He's still pushing me to follow in his footsteps. At least, that's what I got out of the book.

I didn't tell my dad I read *Big-Enough*, and I'm not sure why. Funnily enough, he wants my brother to read it, too. There is no fucking way my brother will have such an emotion-fueled interpretation. I doubt he'd even like the book. That kid is a fucking antisocial, bipolar, aggressive, Red-Hulk piece of shit. He doesn't care about anything that doesn't directly concern him or his computer. If I could, I would demolish his computer; my frustrations are fueled by his own careless nature. Every day, he tells me he doesn't care about anything I try to talk to him about.

Fucking asshole says he doesn't care about me, but then turns around and asks me to watch a video, look at an image, or examine his new animation projects. He's not a brother; he's an embarrassment to the definition of a harmless little brother I'm supposed to protect at any cost. I trust some strangers more than I trust him. He's the only person capable of making me physically violent, and he reciprocates my actions. Honestly, he always hits me first, so he deserves to be pushed around. I despise his lazy, hypocritical, selfish, scummy, fat ass. Am I irrational for my implacable hatred? I'd abdicate my perpetual blood-boiling, emotional rampage if my brother proves he loves me. Lucky me, never going to happen. My brother isn't me, and his interpretation of the story is even more meaningless because he has nothing in common with Billy.

Do you know what is fascinatingly creepy? My dad, whether he realizes it or not, often quotes Lem Roper's words while talking to me. He tells me that he wants to give me the education he never had, and the opportunities he was never presented. So, what's so scary about that? His words were nearly quote for quote in the book, which freaked me the fuck out when I was reading. I can't help but feel like shit though. I'm in no way living up to my dad's expectations.

I'm supposed to be Bill, but I'm still Billy.

ACT II

JULY 13, 2016

I want to talk, but I don't know what to say. I want to speak, but I'm having trouble finding my voice. I want to write, but I can't find the right words to describe how I feel. Is it normal to feel this way? Am I insane? Why can't I write? The finish line is in reach, but I'm running out of gas. The tank isn't half full; it's fully empty. Look, there's the tape I have to cross to win the race. Why is my breathing so labored? My lungs are collapsing under the pressure. Why is my head spinning? My vision is blurry, and my head is dizzy. Which direction am I supposed to go? Drunkenly blurred, I lose sight of any familiar scenery. What is that sound? Why do I hear footsteps? Oh, those are the other racers. They finally caught up to me because I stopped moving. I thought I was the steady tortoise, but I guess I've always been the hare. What happened to their footsteps? They must have passed me and finished the race. Well, I lost again, but it's not a problem. I'm used to losing by now. I'm already a loser.

Why can't I fucking write? You know, my dad made some foreboding comments about me in public the other day. When he talks to friends and acquaintances I am a common topic, apparently. Do you know what he says about me?

"Oh, your son got a job? Your son is hanging out with his friends and enjoying his summer? Your son is living a wonderful life? You want to know about Justin? He sits in the basement and plays games all day. He doesn't have a job. He's lazy."

How come nobody ever fucking notices anything good about me? Am I fucking invisible or something? Is this a long running joke that the entire world is involved in? Is everyone in cohorts to humiliate me? I'm waiting for the day I wake up and someone yells "Got ya!" because the world pulled off the most infamous prank in history. Do I even exist? When did I become this hollow shell of a person? Am I a ghost? I'm sick of being a sponge of humility. I despise providing someone else with a supply of infinite humor. Once again, does anyone notice my good aspects? Is there anything good about me? Where are my attributes? Quick, I need an excuse for my poor behavior! Who stole my accolades and accomplishments? Come on, where is an optimist? Hey dad, how come you don't tell people something positive about me? Hey mom, how come you won't stop teasing me? Hey brother, how come you won't focus on my helpfulness? Fuck them. I do everything I'm told to do. I always listen to them. I get good grades. I don't do drugs. I have decent manners. I'm respectful to others. I never hear about that, though. Who would dare say anything positive about Justin? Fuck. I can't even look at my own name anymore. That's how much I hate myself. Writing each individual letter in my name is painful. Maybe that's why my signature is sloppy, and why my cursive is barely legible. I never practiced my signature because I hate writing my name. Then, my thought goes full circle. I hate writing my name because I hate my name. I hate my name because I hate myself. Teenage angst makes even the safest sanctuary scary.

Please take a seat as you, intrigued and impatient, await my woeful story. Dear reader, I beg of you not to lick your action-craving lips. Why not relax for a spell? Care for a *Cask of Amontillado*? Jokes aside, I'll take a moment to address my audience. You, sweet and innocent Capulet, have no reason to fear me, even if my flesh and blood were birthed as Montague as Romeo. Indeed, I appear threatening, as you've likely noted, but my presence bodes neither ill nor demeaning. I am nothing more than an arranged pile of skin and bones, weaved together as nature's proudest spider web. My appearance in your naked eye is amongst the smoothest of elemental silks. Truth be told, my squishy shell is nothing short of a mirage, projection, or hologram. I am human, but I occasionally transcend the limitations of my fellow mortals.

May this truth be spoken of all humans, or am I an exceptional exception? Humans are despicable beasts capable of horrendous destruction, and, for this reason, I forgive myself and my pitiable counterparts. Despite this, I believe these words, these thoughts, and these extraterrestrial images deserve a more suitable fate than man or woman. In this journal, I am an immortal soul worshipped by few, highly regarded by some, and feared by most. By physical standards I am a measly mortal, deemed a parasitic worm of existence. My words are immortality's breath, and these pages are faithful lungs. My writing is the essence of life, but I shun the mere idea of a Fountain of Youth. Truthfully, I'm an alien who utilizes a human name and body as an alias. This journal is my pseudonym. This journal is proof of my omnipotence, strategically spoken to prove I'm also omniscient. Turn the page, guess who's there? I'm always able to walk these pages as an omnipresent being. I'm not omnibenevolent because I'm considered a terrible person who is known for reversing people's positive perks. You unworthy humans sicken me. How could you be so ungrateful and unloving? Is it possible to be more unappreciative? Humanity is a term to describe Mother Nature's fecal matter. You filthy bastards are disgusting creatures in desperate need of a mass extinction. That's not even a threat, in case your barely functioning brain was wondering. I'd destroy you worthless runts myself, but I'd be embarrassed to bother. Why should I destroy you if you're already destroying yourself? I'll gladly preserve my energy for better consumption.

Earthlings, enjoy your stay in endless purgatory as I cruise the galaxy on a chaotic expedition known as life. I may be Martian to you, but I'm considered normal by other Martians. In fact, they admire me and praise me as a hero. They hand me a crown of pop tabs and bottle caps, but I gladly wear it as if it is made of jewel-encrusted diamonds. I don't need accessories of expensive fashion to display my massive wealth. My fellow Martians consider me their leader, and I do my best to guide them through the unsolved mysteries of the universe. Each passage into the unknown vicinity is as vivid as a strip of acid. I do not require a guide or escort as I walk in the shadow of the valley of death.

I walketh black pastures, and I maketh you lie down beneath my feet. These pages, white as they may appear, are truly dark and sickening.

Am I becoming stronger, or am I growing weary? I want this journal to be the epitome of my existence, but I find myself struggling. I may not look like a leader to you, but do not doubt my abilities. Even the mightiest, sturdiest oaks were once saplings rooted snugly to the Earth itself. But which am I? Am I the tallest tree in the forest, towering above my lowly companions? Or, rather, am I a soft, stick figure sprouting from below, whimpering as I stare up at the ghastly canopy overshadowing my world? Spoken honestly, I am both, for I am the whim of destruction and the bane of life. I am a person, and I ask you to listen to my worrisome story.

JULY 15, 2016

Today was hardly exciting. Honestly, I found little to no enthusiasm throughout the day. Today was exhausting, both physically and mentally demanding, and yet I still found my day to be slightly happy. Is that even possible?

You're probably wondering what I even did today because I'm an egocentric asshole who won't explain anything. Today, my dad decided to take our family to a beautiful state park. Overall, the trip was rather interesting, but it didn't begin with the same level of enthusiasm it ended with.

When we were driving on the interstate, on our way to the state park, we slowed to a standstill. A throng of traffic, including us, delayed our trip's arrival by over an hour. Although this was annoying, it hardly felt important at the time. No, I was not bothered at all. I was far too preoccupied with my emotions to be bothered by a trivial and earthly problem like traffic. Conflicted, I battled an onslaught of emotions and thoughts while my family complained about traffic, congestion, other people, overpopulation, and highway construction. My parents were trying to give my sister, my brother, and I a positive memory outside of the house. My dad took a day off to provide us with this valuable opportunity. It's a rare occurrence in our household when my dad willingly takes a day off. He doesn't even ask for holidays or birthdays off. My dad is truly a workaholic in denial, but he found the strength to ask for today off. My mom's back has been troubling her for years, but the birth of my sister must have knocked her nervous system out of whack. She has had debilitating back problems for the past six years. Both of my parents put aside their most intrusive problems to deliver us a memorable day outside of the house. You know, that actually means a lot to me.

I remember the first day of school in sixth grade. I was in my tenth period, the last class of the day. Fortunately, it was a keyboard class, and I type extremely fast. Our teacher devised an activity for the students to introduce themselves one by one. He decided to ask each student to tell the rest of the class an important moment from the summer. Doesn't seem too troublesome, right? You'd be wrong in assuming it was easy. Honestly, I felt terrified. I had a problem: I couldn't think of anything to say. We never left the house on vacation that summer, or at least I couldn't remember if we had. Meanwhile, my classmates were talking about visiting Disneyland or Disneyworld or going on cruises or traveling to different states and countries. My turn to present quickly approached, and I frantically traced the events of the summer. Thanking my memory, I remembered we went to Six Flags once that summer. Yes! I had my answer, and I proudly introduced myself and told the audience about my glorious trip to Six Flags. I didn't feel ashamed, as I had originally expected. Why should I have been? After all, I had an answer.

Thinking back on that memory, I can't help but feel slightly embarrassed. How could I not think of more than one interesting moment during my vacation? That's depressing, and it only perpetuates the idea of how pathetic and undeserving I am. Now, today, I should have felt exuberant for this new opportunity to explore a natural wonder of nature. But I didn't feel anything. I wanted to go home, honestly. My parents asked me a question and I didn't respond. My mom, who was sitting in the passenger seat, turned around to look at me. She smiled, and I had to smile back. Smiling felt strange to me. I wasn't happy or excited, yet I returned her appreciative offering to seal my image of happiness. Maybe I can't make myself happy, sure. I shouldn't let that stop me from making others happy, right? My parents probably think they did me a favor, a selfless deed, by taking me on a wilderness adventure or some bullshit phrase like that. I'm glad they think that. Truth is, I didn't care whether I traveled or not. Why would visiting a foreign, exotic environment benefit me in any form? If anything, that's fucking scary. Floating in an emotionless space, devoid of feeling, I swung my arms wildly without fear of contact. That's how the drive to the state park felt. Nothing.

Later in the day, after a few hours of walking, climbing stairs, staring at large rocks, watching water, and maintaining my iron curtain of happiness, I think I fried a piece of my brain into feeling again. Considering the sun was staring at me all afternoon, I probably did fry more than a few brain cells. My emotions stirred, and I was finally able to return to reality for a short span. I felt disconnected from my body during a few crucial moments, which was strange. It was probably only stress, dehydration, and constant thinking, but it was incredibly surreal.

Now it would probably benefit me as a narrator to write a summary of the day, but, damn, that would be boring. Who fucking cares? I was too preoccupied with my thoughts to fully appreciate the scenery I was presented. What did I do today? Well, I explored the park with my family. We viewed scenic overlooks, canyons, and small waterfalls. After a few hours, we drove a couple of miles down the road and ate dinner at a restaurant located inside an indoor amusement park. We ordered a delectable pizza, covered in thick, greasy layers of cheese. It was a good day.

With this, I conclude my illusion.

JULY 17, 2016

My mom, dad, sister, and I went to Dairy Queen to get some ice cream. My brother didn't want to come with us because he's boring and unsocial. That was fine by me; I didn't want to be associated with him. Contrary to my typical thought process and emotional disposition, I was excited to spend quality time with my family. Plus, my dad was paying. Free ice cream, quality family interactions, and happy thoughts. What could go wrong?

The Dairy Queen is located directly across from our high school. Being one of the only restaurants in our miniature town, as well as the only ice cream hotspot, it is a fairly popular spot. Most of the employees and customers are students at my school (other customers include kids from the middle school, which is connected to our high school). I know most of the employees, which is strange when I walk in with my family. Ordering food from your classmates is unnerving. Toss in the anxiety of being in public and you've created a simmering recipe for destruction.

Anyway, I felt fine until we sat down to eat our ice cream. I always order a Mint Oreo Blizzard, and I love excavating to the bottom of the cup with my trusty red spoon. The allure of my delicious ice cream was overpowering. Its sweet essence distracted my mind from the critical task of operating my body in public. My brain operated on standby, and a nuclear crisis was imminent. What was the catch to this tasty, white and green luxury? What was my reasoning for being at Dairy Queen?

"You should work here."

Have you heard of the elephant in the room? I think I stumbled upon a safari. My dad pressed the nuclear launch button. Panic mode: ensue.

"Yeah, this would be a good place to work," my mom chimed in.

What the fuck? Can't I have one damn minute to enjoy for myself? Am I not even allowed to eat ice cream without being reprimanded? Should I tell them the truth and say I am mortified by the idea of getting a job? How poorly do you think that would go? If I had my opinion, I would never have a summer job. Honestly, I don't even think I would be hired. If, by some horrific misfortune, I was hired, I highly doubt I can handle a job. What's more stressful than work? Try school, a job, and battling yourself every day.

I tried to explain to my parents why I would never land a job at DQ. First of all, they aren't looking for new employees. They have a full staff, not to mention a mile of untouched applications. Second, I would need a recommendation from an employee, but I doubt anyone would recommend me. Secretly, I feel like I'm not meant to hold an occupation. Most days I feel as if I'm unfit to be a human. Why would I be worrying about something as simple as a minimum wage job at a fast food restaurant? Honestly, these words should explain myself and my persona more than any description or definition.

"Yeah, you're right," my dad said. "I don't want you to work here, anyway."

What? Didn't he just finish telling me that I should work at DQ? I was confused, but I let him explain his contradiction.

"I want you to work somewhere that gives you a skill," he said.

"What does that mean?" I asked.

"Serving ice cream isn't a skill you'll ever use. I was thinking of getting you a job at the shop, actually."

Wonderful. The "shop" he was referring to is a home base for operators (my dad is a crane operator). Sounds like a sweet deal, right? No, it's not. My dad always talks about the college kids that work at the shop. He tells me about how, according to him, the kids are lazy sacks of trash that sit around all day doing nothing. They are lazy, incompetent moochers who would rather pass off work to someone else instead of doing it themselves. I guess my dad expects me to be a better worker than those disruptive slackers.

What if I'm not better than them? What if I turn out to be an even worse worker than those unmotivated stains of shit? My only perks are my dad's recommendation and my strong work ethic. Are those truly benefits or am I imagining my own traits? Do I have a strong work ethic? I've never had a job. I rarely participate in community service events. I avoid work because it is an open invitation for stress and anxiety. How could I possibly be a better employee? Also, I am unfamiliar with my dad's form of work. I don't know how to tie knots or run forklifts or load trucks or organize rigging.

"But I don't know if I want you to do that because the operators tease the shop kids pretty bad," my dad said.

Thanks for that foreboding and ominous warning. So, if I work there I will be subjected to a multitude of derogatory and shameful comments from my superiors. Thanks for asking me how I felt about being unwillingly tossed into a rumbling ring of expectations. Pushed haphazardly against the ropes, I must now swing in defense. Thanks for asking my opinion on the situation. What? Justin has an opinion of his own? This is not permissible! We must suffocate his opinion until he is afraid to speak!

Luckily, my dad agreed that I don't need a job this summer. I convinced him that junior year is impossibly difficult and the additional stress of a job would not suffice. However, I didn't tell him that I would have a mental collapse if I had to work. Why should I? Obviously, the solution is to work harder. Apparently, I do not work hard enough as it is. Correct?

Next summer, even my slithery scales will not allow me to wiggle out of a job. Stress seems inevitable for my future.

AUGUST 1, 2016

Today I received my school schedule online. Naturally, I checked my classes for this year. I was immediately disappointed by how dull and abysmal my classes seemed to be. I didn't get a single dual credit class, which offers both high school and junior college credits upon completion. I initially signed up for four classes, expecting to receive at least two. I was awarded zero classes. As if that wasn't bad enough, the only class I managed to get was my third alternative, Computer Aided Design (CAD). CAD is a pre-engineering course, which would not be of any benefit to me because I'm not training to become an engineer. The guidance counselors fucked up my schedule. Again.

Guidance counselors should be called hindrance counselors because all they do is hinder me. This is the third time my schedule has been obliterated by their incompetence. Those two dumb assholes also messed up my freshman and sophomore schedules. But this year is going to be different. The manipulation of my classes is unacceptable. This year I'm going to march in their office and demand that my schedule be changed. I'm sick and tired of getting screwed out of everything.

Before freshman year began, we had a freshman orientation. During the orientation, which was more or less a bombardment of fear and propaganda, our school's guidance counselors handed out packets containing information about high school classes. After they passed out their packets, they gave a lengthy, verbose speech about picking high school classes. Basically, they stated that the classes we choose will determine our future. They ranted about this topic for more than half an hour while our conceited, snobby principal applauded their shenanigans. The entire night was a charade of bullshit.

Well, I followed my guidance counselor's advice. Guess what? I didn't get the classes I chose. What kind of institution are these crackheads administering? Seriously? Why in the fuck do I even bother picking my classes? I picked the classes I wanted—the same classes that would determine my future, supposedly—and they didn't give them to me. They didn't hold up their end of the bargain. Why do I bother trying? Why do I bother voicing my interests? Why do I bother accumulating and recording this information? Why do I bother writing in this journal? Why do I bother breathing the polluted air of indifference?

Could I possibly be any more vulnerable? After a treacherous summer stacked to the sky with massive obstacles, I yearned for an enlightening moment from school. To my utmost dismay, I was left crushed and disappointed. A moist, bloodcurdling rage seeped into every blood vessel, even the thin networks of capillaries. My school year hasn't even started yet and it is already causing problems. Is that even possible? Of course, it's possible, yes. It's happening to me. Once more, the world collapses around me, unknowing of the body that lies mangled and distorted beneath the rubble.

Those two stupid bitches that call themselves guidance counselors better wipe the smug grins off their robotic, unflinching faces. I'm sick of their manipulation. I'm exasperated with the constant combat of the war called life. You know, when I was dedicated to the idea of suicide, I wanted to tell people that my death was a homicide. I wanted to say that everyone, the collective mass of humans on this planet, murdered me. I would deal the ultimate blow, but people were accomplices. Those two guidance counselors were accomplices in my suicide plan. Every person, whether young, old, ignorant, smart, deaf, blind, diseased, dying, or anything else, held equal liability in my death. I wanted to call them out for their crimes and, subsequently, make them feel like absolute and unperturbed piles of shit. I wanted to drop my arms to my side, allow my lifeless body to crumble to the ground, and sob uncontrollably.

"Look at what you've done to me," I'd tell them. "Look at how you reduced me to this."

While I may hold partial blame in this scenario, I decided that my guilt is not a single entity. Instead, I chose to force others to recognize my pain. I wanted them to feel humiliated and guilty. I wanted them to feel like they drove me to suicide. Maybe if they felt guilty for their actions they would start caring for people other than their own conceited selves.

If my guidance counselors deny a change in my schedule, I will knock over their pointless computers, flip them off, and angrily stumble into the office to await an inevitable punishment; this will most likely be insubordination or destruction of property. This premeditated act is the only salvageable thought from the clusterfuck spawned by my guidance counselors' errant and, apparently, purposeful actions.

AUGUST 3, 2016

My dad wants to take my brother and I to the movie theater this weekend to watch *Suicide Squad*. Going out to watch a movie is a rare occurrence in our family, so I was slightly surprised by my dad's proposition. Naturally, I decided to talk to him about this ambitious plan.

I approached him after dinner expecting him to be in a talkative mood, as he usually is after gorging himself. Unfortunately, he most certainly was not in any mood to talk. He must have had a bad day at work or something because he was acting suspicious. After talking to him a few minutes, he looked over at the dishwasher.

"Yes, we can go see *Suicide Squad*. Only if you behave, though." He was deadpanning me with that laser-eyed gaze. What the fuck? What did I do wrong this time? Apparently, I am supposed to be a perfect person who never makes a mistake. I almost started laughing because I thought he was joking. Almost, until I saw that undeniably serious face he gave me.

"I shouldn't have to get my dishes out of the dishwasher. Put the dishes away."

Why does something so simple, such as putting away dishes, have to be a struggle? My dad is threatening to not take me to a movie that I didn't want to see in the first place. He is threatening me because I didn't do a chore, one that I do every other day, before he got home from work.

I can't deal with this shit. How am I supposed to handle a job? How am I going to juggle school, a job, and my writing? How am I supposed to manage my life like this? What in the fuck is happening to me?

I listened to him and started putting the dishes away, halfheartedly. Unheartedly seems to be a more suitable word. Halfheartedly cannot accurately describe how awful I felt as I put plates, spoons, forks, bowls, cups, pots, pans, and Tupperware away. Honestly, I can't even do that correctly. I always put stuff in the wrong order or in the wrong place or I drop something. My hands shake the entire time as my dad watches me mess up over and over, over and over until the cycle seems painfully monotonous. The amount of stress put on my shoulders to do a simple chore is barely believable. Why is something that is so easy for other people so difficult for me? What the fuck is wrong with me? Why can't I just be normal and do things right?

AUGUST 6, 2016

Today was an incredibly amazing and fantastical day. I'm still buzzing with an ecstatic mood from everything that happened. Why am I so happy? Well, that's a lot to explain at once, but I'll try my best. Where do I begin? I guess I should start at the beginning of my day and slowly build up to my favorite moments. That would probably make the most sense, right?

I should start by saying that yesterday I saw *Suicide Squad*. The movie itself was atrocious, but the experience and atmosphere was worth the price of admission. I was momentarily lifted out of my depression for an exciting evening with my family, and that's what mattered to me. I didn't care about superheroes or villains or actors or actresses or movies or scripts or dialogue or credits or plots or anything else. Instead, I cared about having a great night. Everything was wonderful except when we were driving home afterwards. My internal rhythm of sadness returned instantly upon being seated in the car. My dad started driving home, and I felt depressed again.

My dad talked to my brother and I about having a movie night every weekend. It sounds like a good idea until you realize he's never home to have a movie weekend. That idea is just another one of my dad's ambitious dreams that will most likely never be fulfilled. One time, he told us he wanted to build a pool behind the garage. That sounds normal enough, right? Well, he also wanted to build a changing room.

A changing room! What the hell do we need a changing room for? My dad seemed confident in his idea until my mom dismissed it with a few quick sentences shot like a dart to pop his thought bubble. His idea was destroyed, but he fiercely held onto the remnants.

Last night was nice, but today was one of the best days I've had in months. For starters, my dad and I got new phones. We had to wait inside the store for over an hour, but it was well worth the wait. I was in desperate need for a new phone because my old phone's battery was obliterated, probably due to me constantly being on it. Toward the end of the battery life it would drop ten or fifteen percent in a span of two or three minutes. I thanked my dad multiple times for buying me a new phone, but he didn't seem to mind the expense.

After our family was done waiting for our phones, we all went out to eat at One Star, a Texan-themed restaurant. There was nothing particularly special about this visit besides a joke my dad made halfway through our meal. He looked over at a single star hanging on the wall, leaned over to me, and said, "I wonder if they pride themselves on being a one star restaurant." For some reason, I found this joke hilarious and I could hardly stop laughing.

Finally, my dad took us out to play mini-golf. This was the greatest part of my day, mainly due to letting loose and enjoying myself for once. It was glorious, and the clouds above my head seemed to subside for a moment. Watching my sister play was the best part of mini-golf, honestly. My brother hit one of his balls into the water, and my sister immediately criticized him. Then, for the remainder of the day, she teased him about it in her cute, singsong voice.

"Yeah, good thing you didn't hit it in the water this time," she would say.

"Shut up!"

Days like this make me grateful that I'm still alive.

AUGUST 9, 2016

My friend recently told me he is excited for the day he gets his new car. His excitement reminded me how much I hate cars, specifically my own car. What is so special about a car? The ability to drive anywhere doesn't seem as pleasant if you remember that you have to pay for your own gas. I don't even always pay for my own gas and I am still cautious about how much gas I use. My mom and dad give me gas money, or chore money, every other month or so. Getting a car isn't all it's cracked up to be.

The only reason I like having my car is the small amount of independence I feel every time I drive myself to school. I enjoy not having to take the bus anymore, which I had to do for years and years before I got my license. I should mention that my car is a hand-me-down from my mom. It's a Chrysler 2007 Town and Country Minivan. I know, I know, it's embarrassing for a teenage boy to drive a minivan. Honestly, I'm more embarrassed about driving a Chrysler. If you want to talk about car trouble, let's talk Chrysler. It seems every other day I'm running into a new problem, whether minor or major, with my car. I shudder at the thought of any enjoyment gained from owning a car.

I'm not sure how I managed to get my license. I barely passed behind the wheel because I was such a nervous wreck. Get it, nervous wreck? It's true, though. I couldn't stop shaking while I was driving with my teacher. It didn't help that I had one of my acquaintances from school sitting in the back of the car, undoubtedly judging my every move. That class was torture, but I somehow managed to pass. I received my license shortly after, which was anticlimactic. But sometimes I think I'm too unstable to even own a license. If anyone ever tempted me, I would not hesitate to drive myself into an oblivion. I hear smashing a telephone pole is an efficient way to kill yourself while driving a motor vehicle. Is that true? Let's try it out, shall we?

Listen, I'm happy that my friend is excited about getting his license. I'm just a parasitic person who constantly talks about bad thoughts and experiences. I just can't relate to how my friend feels because I despise cars. It wasn't always that way, though. I used to love cars until my dad sold his shop. My mom threw away my Matchbox and Hot Wheels cars. That's when I started to hate cars. Now, cars mean traveling, and traveling means going somewhere, and going somewhere means a destination, and a destination means trouble. I've spent so much time in cars and I fucking hate it. I've been on numerous road trips out to New York to visit my grandparents, and I hated every single one of those cold, winter drives. How much more miserable does it get? Our family only goes out there to appease my dad, who wants to see his parents. Honestly, I'm not even sure I love my grandparents anymore. They're too fucking toxic, stubborn, religious, and unwilling to change.

One time, when we were driving back home from New York, the wire on my braces came loose. It started poking my gums until they went completely raw. The chafing caused my mouth to bleed, and I sat there for half an hour holding onto the wire to prevent further damage. I could feel the saliva and blood as it stuck to my dirty fingers. Then, as I started crying about the pain, my dad managed to pull over at a restaurant. He took out his handy set of tools, grabbed a giant pair of rusty pliers, and shoved them in my mouth. He snipped the wire and it fell out of my mouth—the pain stopped immediately. Oh, you have no idea how much I love my dad for doing that. It is from times like those that he gained the nickname Superman Dad.

Another time, my mom crashed her van trying to pull into a different restaurant back at home. I must have been no older than six or seven because I remember my brother was still a baby or toddler. When we crashed, I slammed into my seat belt, which injured my neck. I got to sit inside the ambulance upon its arrival, but I never got to take a ride to the hospital. While I enjoyed being in an ambulance, I couldn't help but marvel at the destruction that my mom had done to our car. It was totaled, although I didn't realize it at the time. My mom was crying, but she called my dad to come and pick us up. It was quite the scene, if I do say so myself. But I hate vehicles, and that is just one instance of many that proves my hatred is genuine and fortified. Even the joy of a new car cannot satisfy my uncompromising hatred.

In eighth grade, I took an industrial technology class. That class was particularly difficult for me because I am not much of a hands-on person. I prefer to sit back and analyze things as opposed to tinkering with tools. I do not possess that ability, but, apparently, this is a problem. I remember how I got paired up with a kid named Andrew, and he was a mechanical workaholic. He decided we should go to a station, one of many situated around the room, and work on an engine for a week. Do you have any idea how embarrassing that week was for me? Any idea at all? My dad was a mechanic and I could barely use a screwdriver. I had no idea which wrench to use, or what part to use it on, or how to even properly use the wrench itself. My dad was never fucking home to teach me how to do anything. When he was home, we had to rush to finish things before he had to go back to work the next day. Due to this rush for time, I never managed to learn anything. There was no learning process for me to follow. How pathetic and embarrassing is that? I couldn't build that fucking engine if I tried a million times. I particularly despised myself after attending that class every day for a week. That class was a fucking nightmare.

I hate driving. I just want to drive home from school and hit Bambi, and I want Bambi to come flying through my windshield and smash my skull. That's what I want, but people will be upset with me for killing the poor, defenseless deer. I can't even win in death. I swear, I'm going to die and it's going to be a disaster. My own obituary is going to slander me. That's how pathetic I am. I could die of a stroke in the middle of reading children's books to orphans and yet, somehow, everyone would find a way to shit on me.

I want to crash my car so hard that my body is unrecognizable by even an autopsy. I want my brains to scatter over the entire road, and

I want every driver to run over those microscopic pieces. I want to get back into that ambulance because I didn't get to ride to the hospital. The paramedics told me that I was okay, but they were fucking wrong. I want to drop an anvil on everyone's head and claim it was a horrible accident, like a car accident. I want to point my middle finger at everyone and ramble on like this until they feel so bad that they start crying on the spot. Yes, and maybe someone will play with my sister so she isn't left crying in the corner. That's where I found her today. My brother kicked her out of his room, as usual, and she started crying. How fucking sad is that?

I hate myself more than I hate cars.

AUGUST 15, 2016

Today was the first day of school. The realization that I'm in eleventh grade hasn't quite set in yet, and I'm grateful for that. Also, today was either exceptionally hilarious or a formidable nightmare. The pessimist in me wants to refer to today as an utter failure, but the optimist in me wants today to be a glorious first day. As you may or may not know, I've struggled with first days of anything for my entire life. School is the worst in regard to first days. Anxiety, fear, and dread are three words that accurately describe the first day of school. But even those three words cannot explain my first day of second grade. Let's take a dive into the past.

It was my first day of second grade, and I was excited to be a part of my new school, the intermediate school. Honestly, my day was incredible. I thought my teacher was a nice, sweet lady. I thought I liked my classmates. I thought I was finally going to be happy. My little mind was wrong, wrong, and wrong.

Throughout the day, kids were looking out the windows and watching the storm clouds accumulate. There had been talk that the first day would be postponed due to the ominous forecast. We live in the tornado alley, and there was concern that we would have tornado warnings at school. The teachers were concerned, but the kids were excited because they wanted to go home early. What kid doesn't want to go home early? Probably me, but I can't remember what I was thinking. I didn't worry too much about the storms, though. Why should I be worried about what is outside? I wanted to learn.

In the middle of P.E. class, the power to the school went out. The gym was completely dark and we couldn't see anything, which made it lucky that we were all sitting down at the time. Some girls screamed, and maybe even a few of the boys. At this point, my small head started to get worried. What was happening? Were the storms coming for us? Was there a tornado outside? My questions were asked in vain. The emergency lights kicked on, as if they had grown weary listening to the questions that echoed in my thoughts.

All of the little children, including myself, lined up for the buses at the scheduled times. Everything was going according to procedure, but something seemed off kilter. What happened to the storms? How come everyone had stopped worrying? Only an hour before there was no power, and now everyone seemed to be fine. Where was the concern? I didn't know, but I got on the bus without answers to my thoughts.

I'll sum up this next section because it would be too complicated to explain without doing so. I'd probably even get confused trying to explain it. Basically, I got on the right bus, the one that I had taken in the morning, but our bus stopped and some people got off. Thinking I was supposed to get off with them, I followed them and transferred to a different bus. That was my mistake, and I paid dearly for it. I got on the wrong bus, and it traveled far from where I was supposed to be going. I was terrified because I thought I was going to be stuck out in the middle of the country forever. I decided to wait until everybody else had gotten off the bus, and then I would ask the bus driver to drive me to my house. That seemed like the safest option, as opposed to admitting I had stumbled onto the wrong bus. I already knew that.

When the last person, other than myself, had stepped off the bus, I approached the bus driver. She asked me where I lived, and I told her. She gave me a look of surprise and calmly told me that I must have gotten on the wrong bus. She told me she would drive me back to the school so someone could call my parents. She said my parents would be able to pick me up there and bring me home.

Well, that didn't exactly go as planned because, as it turns out, the power at our house had gone out during the storm. My parents didn't have power, which meant they couldn't receive phone calls from the school. I think my dad had to use a landline telephone in the garage to communicate with the school. That's how he knew to come pick me up. I was practically in tears, but I knew my parents were even more worried than I was. I had really caused them a lot of trouble and worry. They had no idea what had happened to me. It was almost as if I had disappeared, and maybe I did. Maybe I never truly got off that bus. Maybe it was only the ghost of me that got off that bus, roaming around in a delirious state, acting as if it was an individual.

As you can tell, first days are a struggle for me. That day terrifies me even in a memory. But it doesn't matter anymore because I want to talk about today. Today, let's talk about today. Forget about second grade.

Everything was normal until I went to drop off my brother, the notorious fat bastard who isn't nearly as funny as the fat bastard from Austin Powers. There were two cars ahead of me. One car dropped a kid off quickly, then pulled away. That's when I heard a continuous car honking noise, as if someone was slamming down on the horn. I looked at my brother before he got out of the car.

"Who's honking?" I asked. He shrugged his shoulders and got out of the car.

As the other cars drove away, I realized it was my car that was honking. What the fuck? Why was my horn going off like that? I wasn't even touching the horn. What was happening? At first, I was terrified because I was afraid I wouldn't be able to shut it off. One of the teachers from the middle school walked out of the building and stood next to my car, looking in through the window at me. I gave him a 'what-the-fuck-do-you-want-me-to-do-about-it?' face as I kept both hands as far away from the horn as possible. I drove away, horn still going off as I raced out of the middle school parking lot.

The honking stopped as I pulled up to a stop sign. When I flipped my right turn signal on and braked to a stop, the honking started up again. Wonderful. The honking showed no signs of stopping, and there was nothing I could do about it. I turned right onto the school street and drove down the street, embarrassed beyond comprehension, with my horn bellowing at full capacity.

As I slowed to a stop, turning into the parking lot for my school, the honking stopped. But there was a kid walking in front of me, and I hit the brakes. Suddenly, my horn started up again. I scared the shit out of that kid and he jumped backwards, scared as fuck. If I wasn't so terrified myself, I might have laughed at that poor kid. Not today, no. I was worried that my horn wouldn't stop even if I turned my car off. But all of my doubts were erased as I pulled into my parking spot, put my car into park, and turned my car off. The horn stopped, thankfully. That disastrous episode of embarrassment was finally over.

My day was fine up until lunch, the last lunch hour of the day, of course. I didn't recognize anybody in my entire lunch hour; that's just my luck. I found a familiar face, a sophomore from my P.E. class last year, and I decided to sit by him. He was a strange individual, but I didn't mind talking to him for half an hour. Except he got up and left as soon as I sat down. I was left to spend the rest of the lunch hour sitting by people whose names I didn't even know, and I felt decisively horrible. Do I really deserve to live like this? Do I deserve to be the epitome of embarrassment? Do I deserve to be the loser of the lunchroom, unable to find a table? I thought that kind of stuff only existed in Hollywood movies, but there I was, plain as printer paper, hurriedly attempting to find a table to sit at. After that, I gave up on my day.

My ultimate goal for today was to get my schedule changed, but that didn't happen, either. I went to see the guidance counselors after school ended, and there was a giant pack of people waiting outside the door. How inefficient are these stupid fucking guidance counselors? They had six fucking months to make our schedules and they still managed to find a way to completely fuck every single one of them up. That's not an exaggeration, either. I guarantee nearly every student had a problem with his or her schedule.

By the time I finally walked into their office, after a brief period of waiting, I had my schedule in my hand and ready to shove under one of those guidance counselor's big, ugly, Wicked Witch of the West noses. I was ready to throw a bucket of water on one of those crooked witches, but I decided that would be deemed unnecessary or outright dangerous.

But that's not what stopped me. Before I even had a moment to say a word, one of the guidance counselors looked over at me. I held up my schedule, and she started smiling.

"Well, you're just going to have to sign the sheet like the other people," she said. She kept smiling her devilishly sly grin, and pointed over toward a table where a conglomeration of people gathered to sign away their lives to these evil witches. By this point in my day, I couldn't care if that's what actually happened.

I went over to their stupid fucking table and I signed their dumb fucking slip of paper, which was worded with the most despicable phrases and utterly meaningless words. It didn't even make sense to me, but I signed the damn sheet anyway because I desperately needed to change my classes. I hated that Computer Aided Design (CAD) class. CAD was a pre-engineering course, and I wasn't about to pursue engineering. I wanted to pursue business. That's what I really wanted, but nobody was going to let it happen. Nobody ever allows Justin to do what he wants because Justin is truly a creature to be despised.

I was scared that my car would start honking on the way home, but, much to my surprise and excitement, nothing happened. I say excitement, but I was merely impressed by its abysmal performance. I was surprised the damn thing even started, honestly. Every time I turn that key, I fear that my car will be gone forever. How would I explain that one to my dad?

"Dad? My car died. It wanted to be like me. Now it's dead."

Is that how I should explain things from now on? Death resembles me, not the other way around. Is that how I should live my life? Or is that how I should die in death? I'm confused. Would someone please explain these things to me? Would someone please explain the hole where my brain is supposed to be? Why not? Are these things unexplainable, implausible coincidences coincidentally envisioned?

For every first day, there is a time when the last day will arrive.

AUGUST 16, 2016

Today was the second day of school. Luckily for me, today was not a repeat of yesterday. My dad took the horn fuse out of my car so my horn would stop honking every time I hit the brakes. According to him, the wiring in the steering column must have gotten tangled up. I was glad that problem was resolved without too many issues, other than my own embarrassment, of course. That made my day flow a lot smoother than yesterday.

Besides lunch, my day was normal. At lunch today, I found a table with a few recognizable faces from my own grade, a couple of acquaintances. They let me sit by them, and I think that's where I'm going to stay for the rest of the year. It was nice of them to let me stay, and I was truly thankful, although I didn't do much to show it other than tell them that it was nice to be sitting at a table where the people don't leave.

For the first time, I noticed a new kid sitting at the end of the table, far away from both myself and my peers. Judging from his size, short and skinny, I assumed he was a freshman, which would also explain why he couldn't find anybody to sit next to. I got up from where I was sitting and walked over to his end of the table. I sat down, facing him.

"Hey, what's going on?" I asked. He looked up from his food and stared at me, albeit timidly. He was even shorter than I originally thought. His arms were even skinnier than mine, which was surprising.

This gave me a small amount of courage and confidence, and I came to the decision that I would help situate this freshman on his second day of school.

"Hi, my name is Alex," he said.

"Hey, Alex. So, you're a freshman, right?" He nodded, and I felt a surge of confidence. I was right, which made me feel great. I felt extremely confident in myself, the strongest positive feeling I would feel all day.

I kept asking him questions because I wanted to find out more about him. I asked him if he liked his teachers, and he told me they were nice to him. I asked him about his classes, if he enjoyed this school, and if he had any friends to talk to. I was surprised to find out that he had just moved here from Colorado. Who the fuck wants to move to this tiny town? Never mind, never mind. Anyway, it turns out he is the newest kid of all, and he doesn't have any friends because of this.

"You know," I said, "if you want to make some friends, you should join a club or team. What about Trivia Team? It's really fun."

"Yeah, that sounds good," he said, shrinking away from me. I must have seemed scary to him, being two years older and talking to him on his second day. I can only imagine how terrifying that must have been, and I say imagine because nobody likes to talk to me unless they're trying to pick on me.

I told him that he could sit by us if he couldn't find any friends by tomorrow, and then the bell rang. I left him sitting there, fumbling with his folders. I felt a little bad about leaving him, but I guess he can manage. He said our school was so much smaller than his old school, so he shouldn't have any trouble navigating the hallways. I was still paranoid, though. I'll have to check up on that freshman kid tomorrow.

AUGUST 17, 2016

Today was the third day of school. My morning started out terribly, which immediately told me that I was going to have a shitty day. I ate breakfast while my diaphragm mocked me, throwing fake punches. I felt like I was going to throw up. I was hungry, but whenever I tried to eat I felt like I wouldn't be able to stomach my food. I ended up throwing out half of my breakfast.

In P.E. today, I felt a complete emptiness ripping at my entire being. Participating in class was the least of my concerns. I barely wanted to stay alive, yet I had to stand around and catch kickballs for forty minutes. Why was I being subjected to that torture? My mind was prepared to tear itself to pieces, and my body was prepared for the next kick. What the fuck is wrong with me?

At lunch, I sat down at the same table as yesterday. I looked around, wondering where that freshman kid was. After a few minutes, I figured he had already found another table to sit at, and I was happy for him, although slightly sad that he had ditched me so quickly. But no, he didn't find a new table. I spotted him in the lunch line, in no hurry to get his food. He started walking toward our table, and for a moment I thought he might actually come and sit by us. But no, he kept walking past our table without even a sideways glance in my direction. He didn't even look at me. He didn't even care.

He sat down next to some other people, a bunch of freshmen that I had never seen or talked to before. I was a little disappointed, but I still felt happy for him. I was glad he had found some new people to spend his lunch hour with, but I couldn't help feeling a little depressed for myself. How did he make it look so easy? I decided that I would visit him at his new table after I was done eating.

Near the end of lunch, I went and sat down at his table. I wanted to check up on my new acquaintance and ask him how he was doing. I sat next to him, and I felt the resentment of every other person at the table. They were staring at me. No, wait, they were glaring at me. They were glaring at me, trying to peer straight into the depths of my soul. Their laser vision was piercing my heart, and I almost felt like leaving right then and there. But I stayed, hoping to strike a conversation with Alex. I felt alienated, but I didn't allow that to stop me. I asked him how he was doing.

"Good."

Kid doesn't talk much, obviously. I don't blame him. If I was going to a new school, I probably wouldn't want to talk much, either. But then, as I was beginning to talk with Alex, some girl walked over to our table. She looked at me, glared, and sat down on the other side.

"You stole her spot." I turned around, and one of the girls was staring straight at me, not blinking at all. She was pissed that I had accidentally sat where her friend had been sitting. I had unknowingly stolen her seat.

I got up and returned to my table, murmuring my apologies to myself. I just wanted to be a little helpful, but I ended up being an inconvenience. I fucking despise people. That freshman wasn't even glad that I came over to his table. He didn't fucking care about me. I can tell because he didn't bat a single eyelash walking by my table. I was just a bigger, older kid in his eyes. I wasn't even fucking helpful. He didn't say, "Hey, Justin, thanks for talking to me," or anything resembling that remark. Nothing. The only things I received were an accusation, an insult, and eternal resentment.

Also, I should mention that I couldn't even eat correctly today. I thought my food was sliding off my fork, but I was wrong. My hands were shaking so much that I couldn't hold my fork steady. That's how fucking pathetic I am. I can't even eat like a normal person. Why am

I like this? Why can't I eat properly? I can't fucking do anything right. You know, this isn't the first time this has happened, either. My hands have always been a problem for me.

I was in eighth grade, once again in my industrial technology class. We were making tic-tac-toe boards before we had to leave for winter break. Obviously, this was a difficult project for me to complete. In fact, I almost ruined my project when I went to drill the holes for my marbles. I drilled through the back of the wood, but, thankfully, the hole wasn't big enough for the marbles to fall through. I felt pathetic and worthless every day in that class.

One of the worst moments was when I went to engrave my initials in the tic-tac-toe board. We were using metal cylinders with letters carved into the bottom in order to smash them into the wood, thus engraving the initials. We used a hammer to hit the cylinders. Anyway, I was trying to accomplish this seemingly simple and unnoteworthy task when my teacher walked by and stood right behind me. My hands started shaking uncontrollably, and my mind seemed to shut down. Head to the bomb shelters! Head to the bomb shelters! Incoming missiles! Get down! My world fell apart, and suddenly I felt a hand on my shoulder. It was my teacher, standing even closer than before. Close enough to reach out and grab the tools from my hands. A couple taps later and my initials were in the wood. My teacher engraved my initials, then walked away, moving on to help some other unfortunate, anxious person. But I didn't view him as a hero. All I could think about was how pathetic I was for not being able to even wield a hammer. How despicable could I possibly be? Why did I even bother waking up in the morning and coming to that stupid class? Was the class even stupid? Was I the stupid one for being incompetent and incapable of handling even the simplest tasks? My mind frantically searched for these answers and more, but, despite these crucial efforts, I was left to ponder with my shameful thinking.

I felt inadequate, irrelevant, and mediocre. That memory reminds me of every time I have ever tried to help my dad with something. Always, always, that nervous little boy feeling washes over me. I always felt young and helpless whenever I tried to help. I was always scared that I would mess up, and this terror typically fueled my inadequacies. I never wanted my dad to see that I had messed up because I knew he would be disappointed.

"Are you kidding me? How can you not do this?"

The other day, I thought it would be nice if I got my car ready for my dad to look at. You know, after my horn started going off? My dad used to be a mechanic, so I knew he would be able to resolve my predicament. I latched the hood up so my dad didn't have to do it when he got outside. Everything was normal until we were done and my dad had pulled out the horn fuse. He went to unlatch the hood, and he stopped.

"Uh, hey, this actually goes here," he said, and pointed to the correct spot to latch the hood. Apparently, I had latched the hood in the wrong spot, and I felt terrible about it even though it was a minor mistake. It would have been a disastrous mistake, but, fortunately, wherever I latched it had actually worked.

Today, when I told my friends that I helped my dad fix my car, they laughed at me. I asked them why they were laughing at me, and what was so funny about it.

"You didn't help anything. You didn't do shit—your dad fixed it."

They were right, and I knew it. There was nothing I could say to counter their laughter. They had me beat, and they knew it, too. I felt fucking awful. I can't do anything right. I don't even want to wake up in the morning. I hope I die in my sleep so I don't have to wake up, honestly. I never want to feel stupid ever again. I never want to see another car ever again. I never want to see that stupid fucking freshman kid ever again. I never want to do anything ever again.

Later in the day, I was sitting at my desk on the computer, minding my own business, when I heard a commotion. I heard my sister start crying, and then I saw my brother shove her out of his bedroom. He yelled at her for playing with her toy school bus.

My sister came over to me, crying, lost in a state of disrepair. I managed to soothe and calm her until she stopped crying, then I told her that I wanted to play. I ended up going into her bedroom and playing My Little Pony for over half an hour with my little sister. The act of being a nice person felt wrong and empty to me. All consumable energy drained from my body until I was left with nothing but a persistent numbness.

Why was I, a sixteen-year-old boy supposedly on the path to being an adult, playing with a bunch of girl toys with a kindergartener? I played ponies and Barbies with my little sister, and it made me feel terrible. I was a little happy that I had helped my sister, but my depression seemed to drag the happiness into its own solitary abyss. I don't know. I guess I just see too much of myself in my sister, and I don't want her to become like me, a warrior battling both himself and the outside world. That's when I really got upset.

Why was I the only person trying to save my sister? In that moment, I felt like Holden Caulfield trying to catch kids as they fall off cliffs. Why was Holden the only person trying to save those kids? I'm the only person trying to save my sister because I'm the only one that notices she has problems. She has problems that are rooted deeper than the flesh. She has problems that only I can see, and only I am trying to stop these problems from manifesting themselves as a monster, like me. While I was busy trying to save my sister, I forgot to save myself. Now I'm falling, falling, falling deeper into the abyss with every waking moment. I might never climb out of it this time. Usually, I find a way to pull myself out of this depressing state. But this time I don't think I'll have the strength to drag my lifeless body away from the darkness. This time, I think I've finally lost the battle.

I feel like I'm trying to paint a picture in the rain. I can keep painting and painting, but the picture is ruined. I'm trying to be happy and live, but it's not working. I'm that ruined picture. You can keep trying to make me happy, but it will never work.

I'll never be happy.

AUGUST 20, 2016

We started reading a new book today in English class. It's called *The Glass Castle*, written by Jeannette Walls. It's a memoir of her dysfunctional life and her equally dysfunctional family. We're reading a book about someone else's life. Do you have any idea how much that depresses me? That's my dream. We're reading my dream. I want to write a story detailing my life, and I want other people to devour the content. I'm going to write the greatest fucking story ever. I'm ready to chuck a hammer at that glass castle, honestly.

Another thing that bothers me about this book is how Jeannette Walls goes about life. It is quite obvious that her life is littered with stress and struggle, but she handles it too damn well. She's too good at life for her story to be of any true significance. Where is the true struggle? It seems as if she is cheating by always finding a solution to her problems in a timely and efficient manner, I might add. Is it really a struggle then? Did she ever truly struggle? Also, it's important to note that her problems are entirely physical. Her mental strength is an unprecedented force, unrivaled in its capacity. She never wakes up and battles herself every morning, day, and evening. She has no idea what that feels like. How could she? How could anybody possibly know what it is like to live my life? It's irrational to think that anyone possesses the ability to experience my feelings.

I don't know how my life is going. I feel stuck. I'm caught between having a family and not having a family. I can't tell if I love my family or if they are the cause of my problems. I can't tell if my friends like me or if they tolerate me. I can't tell if I like my friends or if I want to slit their throats. I can't tell if I'm any good at writing, but I keep writing despite my own grievances. I've been trying to get these answers my entire life.

The Glass Castle starts off with Jeannette describing a memory from when she was three years old. She was boiling hot dogs on the stove and her apron caught fire. Her parents took her to the hospital, where her burns were treated. Her delusional and idiotic parents decided they were justified in breaking her out of the hospital. Afterwards, Jeannette becomes obsessed with fire. She utilizes every free moment to stare at flames, lost in awe, consumed by the continuous flickering motion. Instead of being scared of fire, like me, she tries to get closer to fire. She's my polar opposite.

I think it's time that I relive one of my most potent memories. Finally, I must complete the horrendous task of transcribing perhaps my most powerful memory. Personally, this memory is the bane of my existence, but I suppose it is not that way for others. For others, this is just another page to read. For me, this is a heart-wrenching, soul-sucking, demeanor-smashing memory.

When I was four years old, I slept in the room upstairs, which is currently my sister's room. The basement was just a slab of concrete at the time, and the stairs weren't in the same spot they are at now, either. There were no rooms in the basement. Our basement consisted of cold concrete, a few support poles strewn about almost randomly, and a few other miscellaneous items that will come into play later.

Our family didn't have any money. I remember my dad said he used to eat three slices for lunch every day: two slices of bread and a slice of cheese; he called it a cheese sandwich. We lived paycheck to paycheck, although I was oblivious to the concept of money at only four years old. My dad struggled to pay bills while simultaneously supplying for the family, and my mom stayed at home to take care of me.

Well, there was one thing that my dad always pooled money for every year, along with his buddies and family members. That one thing was fireworks. Imagine our tiny house, without a furnished basement, only a ground floor, shitty furniture, a tiny kitchen, and only one bathroom. Now imagine throwing giant Fourth of July parties at our house. That's how we used to spend that dreadful holiday, apparently. I was too young to remember many details from the parties.

My dad and uncle really got into their fireworks. They were known in our family for throwing these lavish Fourth of July parties. Everybody loved those parties. They loved spending a few thousand dollars on fireworks, lighting them up, and sitting back and enjoying a couple pitiful sparks in the sky. At least, that's what I think of fireworks. Anyone else in my family would probably describe fireworks as large, booming, majestic spectacles. That's not me, though.

Anyway, they started to get more sophisticated with their firework techniques, specifically the launching of the fireworks. It took a long time to launch fireworks individually by hand. So, what did they do? They put the fireworks on boards and connected them to switches so they could flip the switches and launch the fireworks. At least, I am pretty sure that is what they did. Remember, I was only four years old. If it wasn't that, it was something similar.

On this particular Fourth of July, my dad and uncle wanted to finish gluing the fireworks to the boards early. It was super hot outside and they were worried the hot glue gun would accidentally combine with the heat and potentially launch the fireworks while they were gluing the boards. They decided to bring their fireworking scheme into the cool, chilly basement. Boards, fireworks, and a hot glue gun made up their stack of materials. Being a bored four-year-old, I spent most of the day in the basement watching them work on the fireworks. You know, because fireworks are cool to a four-year-old. Also, I loved my dad and uncle.

According to my dad and uncle, this is what happened:

Gluing the *last* firework on the *last* board, a spark from the hot glue gun landed on a fuse. The lighting of that fuse set off a chain reaction, and fireworks started going off left and right. Now, this is before we had a laundry room, so there was a laundry basket next to where they were working. Apparently, a board of fireworks, or maybe a couple of fireworks, fell into the basket and started going off beside my dad and uncle. They didn't even notice this at first because the scene was so chaotic. Oh, and I should also mention that my mom wasn't home at the time. My brother and sister weren't born yet. It was only my dad, my uncle, and myself in the house.

And where was I, you might ask? Me, four-year-old me, was enjoying a fun day in the basement when, all of a sudden, fireworks started going off. One second I was busy playing by myself. In the next second, smoke started filling the room. All I could see was gray smoke. I couldn't see anything else. I could hardly breathe through the nasty smoke. I couldn't talk for fear of choking on the putrid smoke, in addition to not being able to talk due to fear itself. I thought I was going to die—four-year-old me thought that. The only thing that I could hear was my dad calling for me. He kept calling my name over and over. I knew he was looking for me, but I couldn't see him. I couldn't answer. I couldn't say anything. The smoke filled my lungs, choking me slowly. I was dying.

It felt like an eternity, but my dad eventually found me. I was pinned against the wall, terrified. He pulled me out of the darkness, picked me up, and carried me upstairs. I remember him and my uncle hurrying around the house, opening all the windows, trying to filter the smoke out of the house. Smoke was pouring out the windows, billowing out into the fresh, clean air. I yearned for that air, but I stayed inside. I still couldn't move because I was left petrified by the smoke. It was too late. I had been consumed by the darkness.

It's the worst memory of all my memories. I almost killed myself and still my worst memory is that fucking smoke. Sometimes I feel like all I see is smoke. Sometimes I look around and I can't see or feel or hear or speak, and I feel lost in the smoke. There's no escape. My back is pinned against the wall, and the idea of walking into the smoke terrifies me even more. I hear people calling for me, but I can't answer. I can't move. I can't do anything. I'm trapped by the smoke. I wait for my dad to come and rescue me, but he doesn't show up. You know what? The smoke left the windows, but it didn't leave me. It's still inside me, suffocating me from the inside. Every waking moment is spent in pain from the suffocation. Some days are worse than others, but I always see the smoke. I can reach out and grab the smoke with my fingers, and I can feel its wispy tail pulling on my hand, urging me to follow.

"Come with me," it says, "I won't hurt you. I love you, Justin. We love you, Justin. We support you, Justin. We'll always be here for you, Justin. We would never hurt you, Justin. Come with us, Justin."

The smoke penetrates my thoughts, attacking me with its subtle gracefulness. How can an inanimate object be so powerful? How can my thoughts be so transformed and transfixed by one entity? Is the smoke one entity, or a collective group of entities? I don't know. I don't know what to believe anymore. The only thing I know is that the smoke is inside me forever. The smoke will never leave me, no matter how persuasive I am in urging it to grace the presence of someone or something other than myself. The smoke's eternal presence terrifies me beyond comprehension. I am always baffled by how intimately the smoke is tied into my life. Perhaps even the neurons in my brain are tied together by strands of smoke. That's a terrifying thought, but I am a terrified person. Who could possibly be more scared than me? Haunted houses are supposed to be scary, but not for me. Nothing can compare to being filled with the disgusting essence of smoke. That nasty aroma lingers in the air, sucking gratefully into my healthy lungs. I'm choking, suffocating, dying, falling prey to the air I breathe.

I'm terrified of everything. Everything. Smoke touches everything.

AUGUST 22, 2016

I got home from school today and had a bit of a surprise waiting for me. My mom told me she needed help in the garden, so I followed her outside. It was a trick, and I was completely susceptible to whatever she felt like saying. Once again, the subject of work was being used as burning fuel against me. I felt deceived, but I listened to my mom.

She talked to me about how she wasn't snooping around—she was just cleaning. See, I keep my journals on my desk for ease of access when I want to write. While she was cleaning off my desk, she found the blue, misshapen folder that I use to store my journals. She thought I forgot my English folder because she saw "English" written at the top. Well, she opened it up and saw a peculiar looking blue journal, as well as a red one. She started reading, and she was left in awe at what she had found. She never found my completed journal, though. Thank goodness for that. The content alone would have made my mom cry until her tear ducts overflowed.

She put her arm around me, hugged me, and started bawling. I had never seen my mom cry like that before. I'm not sure how much she read, but she started babbling about how she doesn't want me to be depressed or sad or anything like that. I hugged her and rubbed her back, trying to calm her down. My face was blank of expression.

She told me she knows she isn't the best parent and that she's sorry and she doesn't try to say anything mean to me. Apparently, she read something about how I hate being skinny and how my mom teases me about it.

She said she loves me and that she wouldn't be alive without us kids and my dad. She loves all of us more than anything in the world.

She said she knows what it's like to be feeling depressed and that she currently feels depressed herself. She's upset that she hasn't maintained her weight loss regimen. She used to be under two hundred pounds, but now she's slowly ballooning back up. She said she doesn't feel motivated to exercise.

She said it's okay to have bad feelings, but she doesn't want me to be depressed or anything. She also said that I'm too young to be feeling like that. It's not normal to feel super depressed or suicidal.

She said it's okay to be a guy and be sensitive. My dad may not be as sensitive as me, but he is the type of person to hide his emotions. He thinks emotions are a sign of weakness. My mom said that's not true, and that I am justified in expressing my emotions.

"That's total bullshit. Emotions aren't a sign of weakness, and don't let anybody tell you that they are."

I kept hugging her and we kept saying that we love each other. She kept telling me to stop trying to calm her down. She was worried about me, not the other way around. Yet, she was the one reduced to tears. I didn't cry, and I'm not sure why. How could someone as sensitive as me not cry? I thought I was going to, and I could feel the tears rimming my eyes, but I didn't cry.

My mom asked if I would be interested in seeing a therapist, and I immediately told her yes. I guess that means I want to improve my condition. What's wrong with me, though? That's the unanswered question that I need an answer to. What the fuck is wrong with me? Why do I act this way? Why do I behave in the fashion that I do? Why am I this diseased person? It's a question that has bothered me my entire life, and I may never have an answer for it. The future seems bleak in that aspect, but I have hope. That's why I want to see a therapist. My mom said she would be more than happy to take me to a therapist, which is amazing.

She also told me her worst fear, which is something bad happening to my dad. My mom, who barely has a high school diploma, said she would hardly be able to support us by herself. She said dad took her under his wing. She said she would only be capable of getting an eight dollar an hour job. I can't even describe how she said that. I can't think of any words to describe how much pain was in her voice when she told me that. It's true. What would she do, go back to working at the mall in the bra department? That's what she did before I was born. She hated it. Without my dad, she would easily be one of those poor single moms, and we would live in some rotten apartment somewhere. I know because that's how our aunt, my dad's sister, lives. She's divorced. She can barely take care of herself or her kids. That's how my mom would live without my dad. That's how we would live.

We picked tomatoes and green beans in the garden and then went back inside. I went and grabbed my completed journal to show my mom. I opened it up and flipped my thumb through all two hundred pages, but she didn't seem fazed. I was a little disappointed, but I assumed she was still in shock from the other journals. It's a good thing she didn't read my completed journal, honestly. She probably would have had a fucking stroke. I feel atrocious, though, because I wrote a lot of bad things about my parents in my journal, but I really love them a lot.

My mom said I'll have to tell my dad sometime later, perhaps in the next few days. How am I going to begin explaining to my dad that I have problems? That's a dilemma I'd rather not associate myself with. I think I'll burn that bridge before I have to cross it, instead of crossing the inferno and being burned alive. I never want to tell my dad that I have problems. How will he take those words into account? Will he be upset? I'm scared. I'm really, truly scared.

Deep down, that's all I've ever been. Scared.

AUGUST 26, 2016

My physics teacher is confusing as fuck. I give up in that class. I tried to give her the benefit of the doubt for the first week and a half due to her recovery from a recent knee surgery, but she's simply a confusing person whose teaching methods involve spewing out incoherent strings of thought and hoping a handful of students learn something useful.

Today, a girl did a problem on the board and got an answer of 0.4. Our teacher checked her answer and then proceeded to insist that it was the right answer.

"Yes, that is correct," she said. She said she figured it out a different way. So, she started explaining how she did the problem, completely oblivious to our blank and unknowledgeable faces. Finally, she reached the end of her less than riveting spiel.

"And I got an answer of 0.25, which rounds up to 0.3," she said. What the fuck? We told her that the girl got 0.4, which is most certainly not 0.3. Do you know what she said?

"Close enough."

Are you fucking kidding me? She marked off two problems on my homework because I had two significant figures instead of one, even though I had the correct answer. She also marked off one of my problems where I included an outlier in a set of data. However, she never told us to exclude outliers from the data. But when she fucks up it's close enough? That's my motto now. Close enough. Fuck that class. If that's how she ends up teaching for the rest of the year, I give up in that class.

In P.E., we went outside to play softball because it was the perfect temperature for a game. What was the problem, you ask? We played on the football practice field, which was soaking wet, muddy, and torn to shreds. Halfway through the game, a girl on the other team tripped and fell in the mud. When I was up to bat, I didn't want to take any chances. After I cracked the ball into the outfield, I walked to first base; I had no intention of going to second because the field was a fucking mess. Guess what? My teacher told me I needed to run, so she took off two of my ten participation points for the day because I didn't run to first. Are you kidding me? I hit the ball perfectly, got on base, and I had points taken off because I'm not busting my ass trying to faceplant into a pile of shit. Fuck that. Fuck my teachers. Fuck this school.

I could barely control myself after physics and P.E. today. I was so pissed at everybody. I was ready to throw something at the wall, or a bunch of shit. When my French teacher wasn't looking, I picked up a chair as if I was preparing to do just that. I wanted to chuck it at the wall, but I didn't. I set it back down. That pissed me off even more than before. Life is too fucking stressful.

Oh, and I should mention that it's my parents' anniversary tomorrow. My dad is nowhere to be found at home. He's been working for the past twenty fucking hours, slaving away like a robotic creation. He's been working since five in the morning, and now it is nearly midnight. That doesn't even include his commute. That's fucking inhumane. How can the demoralizing strings pulled by large corporations descend upon my dad so easily?

I'm worried he's going to fall asleep driving home. I'm talking about a guy that falls asleep sitting upright on the couch reading a book or watching television. Either way, he's going to be absolutely exhausted by the time he gets home.

AUGUST 27, 2016

I sat down on the couch and started talking to my dad today. He worked roughly twenty hours yesterday, but, for whatever reason, he was in a talkative mood today. He was barely awake for the conversation. Still, the conversation managed to be intriguing and engaging.

We talked about mostly science and history, and my dad told me some things he had never told me before. We talked about religion and I told him I am an atheist. Surprisingly, he understood my position and even agreed with me. He still believes in a higher being, but he doesn't necessarily endorse religion. We talked about science and astral projection, which my dad is extremely interested in. He told me he has attempted to project himself multiple times. Although his success varied dramatically, he was happy with his attempts. We also talked about history and my history class, but that wasn't as important.

But the most influential piece of the conversation came when my dad went on a rant. If he started narrating right now, you wouldn't be able to tell the difference. He started swearing and telling me how unfair life is. He told me how angry he used to get as a teenager. He said the concept of money bothers him ceaselessly. After maybe a half hour of ranting, he said the biggest regret of his childhood was not keeping a journal or diary.

Around this time, I made an excuse to dash downstairs and grab my journals. I brought them back upstairs, anticipating the worst, and held them out in my hands for my dad to see. He looked at the journals and knew instantly.

"Yeah, your mom said we needed to talk about that," he said.

We started talking about my journals and my depression. He told me he would also be willing to send me to a therapist if that's what it takes to make me healthy. My health and safety is his number one priority, as a child's health should be the priority of all parents. Also, he told me that he keeps pictures of my brother, sister, and I in his wallet. He said it reminds him what he is working for: three wonderful children.

Finally, after our conversation was over, he got up to go to bed. When he got up, he told me to get up, too. I got up, and he moved over and hugged me. We hugged for over fifteen seconds, and I know this because I was secretly counting in my head. I couldn't remember the last time I had hugged my dad, so that moment felt special to me.

Overall, today was incredible. I couldn't have asked for a better ending. My dad went to bed, and he left me swirling in the darkness of our living room, alone. Except this time I knew I wasn't really alone. I was simply waiting for my next companion to arrive. I'm getting the help that I need.

With that thought swimming in my head, I knew my night was at an end.

AUGUST 28, 2016

I had to write about my glass castle, which is a place where I go to escape from the world, for English class. I heavily debated turning mine in due to its personal nature. Apparently, these are supposed to be hung up in the hallway for anybody to read. I don't want that to happen. Anyway, here it is:

"Where do I go to escape from the world? In other terms, what is my glass castle? Honestly, I think a glass castle sounds delicate and easily breakable, which is not a pleasing combination for a person's dreams and aspirations. Glass castles are an escape from the strife and stress of normal life. My glass castle is nothing more or less than a blank piece of paper. It may not seem as grandiose as other, slightly more suitable castles, but its creativity is seemingly unlimited. Whenever my emotions or thoughts are deemed worthy of entrance to my glass castle, I gladly invite them and treat them as exotic guests. Writing is an escape for me, which is why nine months ago I decided to begin a journal to collect and record my thoughts, emotions, and memories. Although I imagined the outcomes of such a prestigious challenge, I couldn't have possibly predicted the reality. Nine months and two hundred pages later, I completed my egregiously constructed journal. For me, it is a revolutionary novel that serves as a testament to my determination and sheer will to accomplish any task. Plagued by suicidal thoughts and

234

urgencies, and a shockingly scary attempt at forfeiting my life, my glass castle was originally supposed to be an elaborate suicide note. I figured if I were to be an abomination of life, I should at least exit in style and fashion. However, much to my surprise, I found my journal served a different purpose. My journal was a survivor of mental and physical conflict, as am I. My glass castle proves I am capable of overcoming obstacles. After completion of my first glass castle, I have plans to build a second glass castle. Perhaps this castle will stand even stronger than the first. For now, I am contempt with an upcoming appointment with a therapist, who I envision as an engineer to aid in the construction of my next glass castle."

And on the back I left a note:

"I was debating whether or not to actually complete this narrative assignment, seeing as this piece of writing is extremely personal and honest. In doing so, I would greatly appreciate my glass castle being exempt from the display. Thank you."

I am hoping my English teacher pities me and heeds my advice. I'm tired of lying. Originally, I was going to lie about my glass castle. With this assignment, I wanted to be perfectly clear, concise, and honest. I even had my mom read over it to make sure it was appropriate for my teacher to read. That's how worried I am about this project. I'll turn it in tomorrow and hope for the best.

AUGUST 30, 2016

People piss me off to the most extreme extents. I could find a reason to be pissed at a terminally ill cancer patient, and then build upon that reasoning until I've unleashed a steady array of insults and grievances. So, who's upsetting Justin today? Why is Justin so uptight and angry all the time? Everyone, and fuck you.

I tried texting four people, and I only received one response. Sure, I could be lucky to have received at least one response. While you'd usually be correct in assuming I would appreciate a kindhearted response after multiple dismissed attempts, today that one response only strengthened my grip of irritability. See, I needed a response half an hour before I got one. Basically, that response was pointless and irrelevant. I was dumbfounded with the disappearance of nearly all my friends, and a delayed reaction by another. Why are people either constantly pestering me with their petty problems or disappearing on their own Hobbit-like adventures? Are you fucking kidding me? How can all my friends possibly be busy at the same time? Yet, they still manage to inconvenience and annoy me at times when I am contributing to my own personal image. Every interruption is a loose brush stroke that crudely paints a thick, nasty blob over an already existing patch of the completed portrait. I brush briskly to finish a painting, and the people in my life drown the canvas in putrid maroon and ebony, demonstrating a pitifully faded slice of my meager existence.

I noticed I develop and alter my personality based upon my immediate surroundings. For example, in English class I am jittery, timid, and nervous, as evidenced by a pair of shaking hands and tapping feet. In physics, I utter swear words under my breath, mumble aimlessly about the stupid nature and goal of the class, and voice my confusion, which is practically every five minutes. In gym class, I receive a jolt of static energy that floods my veins and catapults my decaying corpse into action. I also use this sudden increase of energy in an attempt to humor my classmates. In French class I act similarly to gym, except my energy is confined to a painful chair that causes my back to ache and groan as I press against the rusted bolts and screws. How do I define myself as a person, and where do I begin to decipher such a complex code of thought?

Once again, I must reiterate how much I despise people because I often forget and it returns the favor by shoving a pointy stick of "I-told-you-so" up my compost dispenser, also known as my asshole. The other day in gym class, I tried to make a girl laugh because I hadn't seen her smile before. My curiosity proved to be a burden, seeing as she promptly said to "never fucking touch me again" because I nudged her with my elbow. She's a bitch. What the fuck did I do to her? Oh, but it gets worse, trust me.

The next day, I saw that dumb bitch lurking in the lunch line. She was in front of me, but I decided to keep my mouth shut this time. When she was next to order, she was busy texting, not paying any attention to the movement of the line. I had to tap her on the shoulder (which means I touched her again, funnily enough) to snatch her dull and limited attention span. After she ordered and took her tray, she scooted her fat, floppy, Jell-O-pudding ass further down the line. I started to order and, right as I started talking, the bitch came back and told the kind lunch lady that she didn't want the food. I wanted to knock that girl's fucking teeth out. How fucking inconsiderate is this disgrace of a person? She held up the line, snobbishly ordered her food, interrupted my order, and proceeds to complain about how she ordered the wrong lunch because she's a fucking idiot. That's the type of shit I deal with every single day, and that's one example of why I hate people.

Today, I had two more experiences of meeting bad people. The first one occurred after running half a mile on the track because it was a fitness day. Well, after I finished, I spread my arms wide and acted like an airplane, moving toward a freshman girl. She fucking punched me in the stomach as I went by her. After running half a mile, that punch winded me more than it would have ordinarily, and I was upset. I asked her why she punched me.

"You ran at me."

"Yeah, well I wasn't threatening you or anything."

She ignored me and appeared to be completely indifferent toward me. On the flip side, I felt terrible. I got punched in the stomach, a girl overreacted and thought I was trying to attack her, and she didn't even apologize for punching me. What if I had punched her? I bet she would have made a huge ordeal out of that. Double standards are fucking dumb, and they piss me off. She's an entitled emo brat who could use a couple punches to the stomach, honestly.

Later in that same hour, a football player offered to lift some weights with me. Now, honestly, I was terrified. My brain was racing for a way out before I had to lift weights with a kid who weighs more than a hundred pounds than me, lifts every day, and is in peak physical condition. I looked at my puny arms and I wanted the class to be over. No, the class had just started.

I ended up lifting with him for half of the class period, and he insulted me in a roundabout sort of way. He would put unreasonably high amounts of weight on the bar, lift them easily, then offer me a turn. I'd tell him there's no way I can lift it, but he kept encouraging me. He knew I couldn't lift as much as he could, and so he used this knowledge to embarrass me. He's an annoying prick on a conceited football team that somehow hasn't won a single game in two seasons.

As if that wasn't bad enough, my teacher kept threatening to take points off of my grade if I didn't work constantly. Once, after sweating furiously as I did push-ups in a room lacking air conditioning, I took a quick break to catch my breath. She took one look at me, ignored my red face and dripping sweat, and told me to do something productive. She's a skinny fitness freak who has no problem seizing any available moment as a chance for physical activity.

I should also mention that I think my physics teacher is bonkers.

If there was an equation to solve for the missing gears in her head, I'd know the answer instantly: she's nuts. She taught us how to read the calipers wrong, which made our entire lab's data obsolete. I had to reevaluate my measurements, and I barely finished before the end of the period. I was supposed to write a lab report, too, but I don't know what I'm supposed to write because she never passed out the instructions. I swear, these people are insane.

I think people are rotten piles of trash that should extinguish themselves from this planet. I don't know, sometimes I think that. Why am I so fucking helpful and nice? Those people are luckier than Lucky Charms that I have an ounce of morality, otherwise I'd utilize every opportunity as a chance to beat the shit out of their empty heads. I hate people.

SEPTEMBER 1, 2016

So, what do I have to say about today? When I saw the slightly less moronic guidance counselor lurking in the corner of my English class, I knew my ass was in a heap of trouble. If shit hits the fan, my feet went through the roof.

She gave us one of those supposedly encouraging pep talks, but she might as well have conversed with a mirror because her words were as empty as a stereotypical black family's fried chicken bucket. You know, because they supposedly enjoy eating chicken, which isn't too bad of a stereotype. Chicken is rather satisfying and tasty. Ah, who am I kidding? Chicken is fucking amazing.

Anyway, my guidance counselor wrapped our class in a blanket of radioactive shit, put us through the wringer, and expected the blanket to not be radioactive when it came out. Basically, she's not fooling anyone, especially not me. So, what happened? She gave us an informational packet regarding ACT testing, which is not mandatory because our school switched over to the SAT.

"Although the ACT test is not required, I highly recommend you take it," she said.

Highly recommended is a horrible expression. Instead of saying highly recommended, people might as well say: "If you don't do this you are a terrible person who will fail miserably at life, and, in the event you already fail miserably, your asshole will be figuratively and forcibly probed by a consistently steady pair of hags with colorful hair, also known as guidance counselors."

According to the shitty pamphlet she gave us, the first ACT test prep night is September 7th. Each session is from 6:30 to 8:00, and that doesn't leave much room for free time. Also, do you have any fucking idea how stressful these tests are? My future may or may not depend on how well I score on these tests. Add that mixture of stress into my current bowl of stress and anxiety, and I can guarantee the recipe for my life is tasting hot and spicy. How the fuck can I concentrate on studying for a life determining test? Honestly, I'm doubtful if I'll be able to. That's not being pessimistic, either. I'm being realistic, and completely honest. I have no idea if I can handle this responsibility.

After walking out of English today, I had a sudden desire to stroll out one of the school's side doors, trudge over to my car, and drive away. I thought I could go home and tell my mom I didn't feel like finishing the school day. Or, I could drive until I lose my sense of direction, park my car, open the door, breathe an intake of fresh country air, and sit on the ground in peace and harmony for the remainder of the day. I seriously debated acting upon these thoughts, but I ultimately decided it wasn't worth it. I had a quiz seventh hour, and I don't like to miss quizzes or tests, so I stuck around.

Have you ever stirred a batter while baking? My emotions throughout the day consisted of a rearranging batter of emptiness, loneliness, depression, and anger. Is emptiness even an emotion? I think I'd consider it the lack of emotion, meaning there were more than a few moments where I lost my emotions.

Physics was infuriating, as usual. My teacher is now a certified dumbass, seeing as her answer key for the study guide was scattered with wrong or inaccurate answers. Frustrating as it was, she marked points off of my homework assignments for making the same errors. Not only that, but she often failed to acknowledge her own mistakes.

"What's wrong?" she asked.

"Uh, your answer is wrong. You should have moved the decimal over two places and rounded up instead of down."

"Oh, I see. Well, I'm going to have to disagree with you," she said to one of my classmates who challenged her answer.

Fuck that class. We learn about absolute and relative uncertainties, but with every lesson I grow more uncertain of my class choice. Ha, speaking as if I had a choice in picking my classes. Physics is, as far as I'm concerned, and based on the limited knowledge presented by the dingbats that run my school, a required course. I'm certain of one thing: my physics teacher is one of the worst teachers I've ever had. I'd say she places bottom three, and it's only the third week of school. After our class complained about her answers, she mistook our whining as a plea for easier work.

"We haven't even started yet..."

Then, in study hall, Michael kept bugging me to play a game with him. I got sick of his ploy, and I caved to his request. That fucking idiot made me forget about the homework I was trying to do, and I ended up taking a late grade for my French assignment. He can be so narrow-minded and insensitive at times, and I hate when he acts like a bratty toddler.

Now I have to deal with this abundance of stress. I still haven't heard my mom try to schedule an appointment with a therapist, either. I really need someone to talk to. My life seems dandy, but I'm walking an invisible tightrope, and some tricksters enjoy swaying the rope back and forth, hoping I'll fall to my inevitable doom.

SEPTEMBER 4, 2016

Today was rather disappointing. I met up with a friend I've known since kindergarten, but he moved away in fourth grade. His name is Joey. I don't hang out with him as often as I should, so today should have been exciting. It turned out to be the complete opposite of what I was expecting.

He needed to return a movie to his friend, Zach, and so I hopped in his car and buckled up. When Joey started driving, I thought of unbuckling my seatbelt and jumping out of the car before something bad happened. My friend sped up to seventy, flying through the neighborhood and practically blowing past stop signs. As if that wasn't bad enough, he turned the radio up to maximum volume and rolled the windows down. Rap music poured out of the windows like steak sauce rushes out of its bottle. I'm pretty sure the entire world could hear his music. I was completely embarrassed by Joey's inconsiderate and dangerous display of friendship. I didn't say anything, though.

By the time we got to Zach's house, I thanked pure luck as my survival mechanism. It's amazing that Joey didn't wreck his car during the drive over. I expected us both to die in a fiery inferno, but, thankfully, we survived. Does Joey really think he's a good driver? I decided not to ask him. I didn't want to spoil his arrogance, which is, according to him, his driving skill.

We ended up staying at Zach's house for a little more than an hour.

He was a stereotypical "white-person-trying-to-live-in-a-black-ghetto" type of guy. When we pulled up to his house, his garage door was open. We walked inside, and he greeted us. He wasn't wearing a shirt, and his shorts were pulled low to expose the top of his boxer briefs. I'd also like to mention that he was as skinny as I am, which made viewing his half-naked body unpleasant.

During this time, I listened intently to Joey and Zach's conversation. I didn't even feel included as a part of their conversation because they were talking about events that occurred at their school, which I am not involved in. Also, I felt an extreme disconnection from reality. I felt surreal, as if I wasn't truly in Zach's garage. I felt like I was with a group of strangers, and, in a sense, I was. They were talking about drugs, alcohol, hot girls, and things that I wasn't familiar with. Joey is a lot more social than I am, apparently. It's a wonder that we were ever friends in the first place.

Zach had to mow his lawn, so we left. Joey drove me around and we went inside a store, browsed in there for half an hour, and left. We just drove around and talked about stuff, but I had lost my appetite for conversation. I felt dull and out of place. I felt like I shouldn't have been with him. Why was he hanging out with toxic people like Zach? Are those his real friends? Am I his real friend? I was confused.

Joey was my first friend ever. He wrote me a note in kindergarten asking if I could come over and play with him at his house. Now I feel like he's slipping away from me. I want to be his friend still, but I can't be. If he wrote me a note today, I probably wouldn't be able to recognize or read the handwriting. That doesn't mean he has bad handwriting. I'm just saying that I feel as if our friendship is dwindling.

Maybe I never had any friends to begin with.

SEPTEMBER 7, 2016

I had a stressful day. I guess it turned out decent. Decency is rather subjective, though. I could say a television show is decent, but if I showed you the same show you might tell me how much you hated it. That's how my day was, in a way.

So, I should mention that my English teacher read my glass castle narrative. This happened about a week ago. She told me to stay after class. I watched as everyone else filed out of the room, giving me glances as they left. I knew my teacher had read my glass castle narrative, and I was ready to hear her response.

She told me that, first of all, she enjoyed my writing. Second, she will most certainly not display my narrative under any circumstances. I told her I appreciated that. Well, she retaliated with a "just-between-us" statement, saying she had to tell the assistant principal about the content of my essay. She was slightly worried about me. I said thank you, then proceeded to walk out of the classroom.

Here was her response on paper, by the way:

"Justin—

I would lie if I told you this piece didn't give me chills and brought tears to my eyes. I will absolutely <u>not</u> display this. Thank you for being so honest and candid. I really hope that you know how extremely intelligent and important that you are. In the short time that I've known you and your writing, I've grown to look forward to reading what you have to say. I may not be someone that you believe you can confide in, but just in case your other options have run out, my door is always open.

—Miss G."

Today, halfway through English class, I heard one of the snobby office ladies come on the intercom.

"Can you send Justin to the office?"

I knew I probably wouldn't be coming back, so I took all of my folders with me to Mr. Johnson's office. My classmates were all staring at me as I left, but, honestly, I didn't care. Let those assholes stare at me. I was more concerned with talking to Mr. Johnson.

I walked down to the office and went inside. I nervously sat down in one of the chairs, and Mr. Johnson welcomed me and started making small talk. Being the observer I am, I noticed he had my schedule pulled up on his computer. Also being a bit of a dumbass, I realized I wasn't noticing anything unusual because Mr. Johnson wanted to talk about my classes. So that's what we talked about. Now, I could give a detailed analysis of our conversation, but that's boring and uneventful. I told him about a couple of my classes, and eventually we bullshitted over to the topic of interest.

Being a former English teacher himself, Mr. Johnson first congratulated me on my piece of writing. He said that when my English teacher showed him the essay she was giddy with excitement. Giving the cliché "in my twenty years" spiel, he told me he has never seen a teacher so excited to share a student's work.

I nodded my head as he glorified my writing. I'm not sure what I expected. Was he trying to make me feel better? Or did he honestly express how starstruck he was with my supposed talent? Either way, I decided to let him gush the paper until its contents seemed impractical and exaggerated. I smiled respectfully throughout. Truthfully, his words merely grazed the hollow shell of tender emotions I've forcefully swallowed. Compliments are empty praise, and criticisms are an amplified creature of mass destruction.

We talked about possibly publishing my journal. He told me about a friend of his that published a book, but he said that the book only sold six or seven copies. What the fuck? Why would I publish my book if I were only to sell six or seven copies? I sure hope I know more than six or seven people willing to purchase the most integral story of my life. Mr. Johnson told me publishing my story is a feasible option, but only if I am willing. I am not going to publish my story if I am not certain it will succeed. That's my personal proposition with myself. If my story is not going to be as successful as possible, then I will not publish it. I want my story to be the best it can possibly be before it is published. A good story is written for one person, but a great story is written for many people. Why would I write a story that I don't think is worthy of selling more than six or seven copies? Why would I bother? That's my dilemma with the situation.

Anyway, the rest of the conversation was decent. As I've said before, decency is subjective. Maybe I thought our conversation was decent, but Mr. Johnson might be shaking his head at my simplistic replies and dimwitted comments. I'll never know because I'll never ask him. He'll never tell me because I'll never ask him. I don't care what he thinks about me. But I do care about one thing, and that's my story.

I've got a book to write.

SEPTEMBER 16, 2016

How am I going to talk to a therapist at this rate? Am I even worse than I was then? Am I worse than back in January and February when I almost killed myself? What about April, when I almost collapsed from the agony of life? I'm nowhere near as sad as I was back then, but I still feel low. I feel low and angry, a deceitful blend of emotions. Sometimes I just want to throw or break something, flip a table over, chuck a chair at a wall, anything.

My dad said he was angry as a teenager. He turned out fine, didn't he? Why can't I pick up the pace? Why the fuck am I struggling so much? Gosh, I can't do shit. I swear, I helped my dad put a table together last weekend and it took me five minutes to screw one bolt because I kept dropping the wrench. I was fucking terrified he was going to start yelling at me, but he didn't. Maybe he knows better now. Maybe he thinks that the yelling affected me and so he stopped. Well, it's too fucking late. Damn, I can't even eat anymore without my hands shaking. If I lift my elbow off the table at lunch when raising a spoon or fork to my mouth, I nearly drop my food because I shake so much.

I have to put on a fake smile all day. I try to distract myself from myself. My mind is my worst enemy, and my greatest asset. How is that even possible? It doesn't matter. My happiness is short-lived. Happy thoughts are momentary benefits for my weary head.

Today I scored higher on my trigonometry test than all of my friends.

I felt happy for maybe two seconds, but then the happiness ceased to exist. It died out like a cooling ember shunned from a roaring fire. As I've said before, compliments are empty praise. My trigonometry test was one of many empty and meaningless tests placed before my tired eyes and struggling hand. I simply perform at the highest capacity, and that is why I aced my test. Yes, I aced it. That doesn't even bring me happiness.

How do I discern the truth? Are my English teacher and assistant principal telling me that I'm an outstanding writer because they honestly believe that, or are they just trying to give me some motivation? My assistant principal said he'd be interested in looking at some of the stuff I've written in my journals. Right, like that'll happen. What am I supposed to tell him? Should I tell him that when I'm really pissed at my classmates I get so angry that I wish they would all die? I have no fucking sympathy for them. I become a monster, devoid of empathy and sympathy. When I'm flustered, my happy emotions are murdered by hatred and anger. That'll make for a great conversation.

I can't speak fast enough to keep up with my thoughts. When I try to talk, my words come out as an incoherent, jumbled mess instead of the beautifully flowing words in this journal. I hope my therapist understands that when I try to talk to her. I found out my therapist is a woman, which doesn't really matter to me because I don't care either way. Also, sometimes words don't do justice to how quick and furious my thoughts are. My thoughts are faster than any reader or writer.

I've got too much shit to do. I have tests and more tests and ACTs and homework and physics fiasco bullshit and my physics teacher's hieroglyphic jigsaw puzzle instructions and appointments and meetings and visits to family and relatives and friends and then movie nights and game nights and then more homework and then I finally get my alone time and I'm so fucking stressed and tired I can't even pick up my pencil, so I stare at a blank computer screen until the cycle repeats itself. That's real fucking productive, isn't it? On top of all of that, Trivia Team starts up next month. So, then I have to try and have fun and laugh and smile when inside I just want to tear myself apart and unleash my anger and hatred on everybody until they all feel my pain and the playing field is leveled with an influx of suffering.

Why don't you try and put a time limit on my mind? I had to write a history essay yesterday in forty minutes. Do you have any idea how much time bothers me? It drives me insane. Last year in chemistry class I would look at the clock so much that my teacher finally noticed. She called me out and embarrassed me in front of the entire class. I felt terrible for looking at the clock, checking how much time was left until class was over. Do you know what else is on a timer? Bombs. I'm a bomb, and I don't know when I'm going to explode. If I crash my car, does that mean I'm a car bomb?

I'm so sick. I feel so fucking brittle. I just want to hit the restart button on my life, or at least rewind it to a point where I felt happy. But this isn't a fucking video game. That's what I love about video games. You can fail as many times as you want, but you can still keep going. Life doesn't work that way. I have no choice but to keep pushing forward, even when I fail.

Do you want an example of how my mind works? Light a match and stick it so far up your asshole that the match gets lodged in your appendix and then you get appendicitis and you have to go to the hospital before your appendix bursts, and so the doctors rush to cut you open and then the match explodes and your guts fly all over the operating room and you fly away on a carpet and rub a lamp and a genie pops out and then the market boy sings a love song while he tries to get in a girl's pants because she's a princess and he's a poor little fuck with no hope but an apple and a monkey as companions. I'm so tired.

SEPTEMBER 18, 2016

Today was Thousand Dollar Sunday. Why is it called Thousand Dollar Sunday? Well, I'm glad you asked, mysterious reader. It's called Thousand Dollar Sunday because my dad spent over one thousand dollars today. That's a lot of money. Let's find out how that happened, shall we?

My dad planned to go to the store this morning to order a new bathroom door. He fucking hates this particular store because the employees who work there are completely clueless. That's why he wanted to take me along for the journey. Well, he decided to take me and my car up to where the store is located. We ended up ordering a 26" door, which dented my dad's pocket by $300; we had to order it specially because they didn't have any 26" doors in stock. My dad was pissed, but his furious emotions remained passive, thankfully.

After that fiasco was over, we went to Less-Than-Better Buy to purchase a new television. My dad wanted a television that could connect to the internet. He picked one out pretty quick for $600. Bam, $600 down. That's a $900 total so far.

We stopped at an auto shop on the way home because the oil light came on in my car. We needed motor oil and oil filters. That costs more money. I think my dad also bought a couple of other miscellaneous items, but I can't remember. That's another $100. That's a $1,000 total, hence the term Thousand Dollar Sunday. But it's not over yet. We're still counting.

By the time we finally got home, my dad noticed something dripping off the front of my car. He walked around to the front and peeked underneath to get a better look.

"Yep, radiator is cracked," he said.

I couldn't fucking believe it. His reward for spending money was a cracked radiator, a costly repair. Naturally, we drove to a different auto shop and purchased a new radiator, antifreeze, and some hope. All of those items put my dad another $200 deeper in the hole he was digging for himself. I should just refer to him as Gravedigger Dad from now until the end of time. It has a nice ring to it, doesn't it? That comes to a grand total of $1,200, roughly.

I felt terrible, though. I had a lab report to write, which meant I couldn't help my dad. It's not like I didn't want to help. I wanted to help, but I also knew I wouldn't be of any use because I'm practically helpless. My dad suggested I just go inside and finish my lab report. So that's what I did. I went inside and completed my stupid lab report while my dad slaved over my car, changing out the broken radiator with a new one.

With that, Thousand Dollar Sunday closes up shop, forever sealing the imminent struggle of money that always finds a way to slash at our family's collective throat.

SEPTEMBER 20, 2016

My mom drove me up to the orthodontist today. My appointment was scheduled after school. Everything was going fine and dandy until I got in the orthodontist's office and sat down. Almost immediately, the leading orthodontist, a sweet woman, looked at my teeth.

"See you in another five weeks," she said.

Well, as it turns out, she had a bit to add to that statement. Apparently, my bottom front teeth are not straightening correctly with my retainers. They're still crooked. She can't figure out why my teeth keep getting pushed out of line so she just tightens my retainers and sends me off.

My mom and I were about to schedule my next appointment date and time with the front desk lady when the orthodontist came back to us. My mom and the orthodontist started discussing the topic of my teeth. After some discussing, they came to a bold conclusion. My teeth are crooked because I can't swallow correctly. I've had so many metal contraptions in my mouth for the past ten years that I had to alter how I swallow because my tongue couldn't reach the roof of my mouth. As of now, I guess I swallow by pushing my tongue off my front teeth. That's why my teeth became crooked. The orthodontist lady called me a freak of nature, jokingly, saying she was so confused about my teeth. Hilarious. Absolutely hysterical.

I really felt like shit on the way home from the orthodontist. I can't even fucking swallow correctly. I can't even perform autonomous functions properly. My teeth are messed up, my breathing is weird, and my heart beats at a faster or slower rate than other people. I fucking hate people almost as much as I hate myself. I hope the roof of the world caves in and implodes this planet. You people are so fucking ridiculous. Everyone is fucking ridiculous.

I've had metal in my mouth since second grade. My teeth are almost as unfixable as my acne problems. I spend fifteen minutes a night staring at my face in the mirror, usually popping a pimple or two or three. I drain the blood with a tissue so I don't look ridiculous for school the next day. That's depressing. At this point, I'm just fed up with everything. I try so fucking hard to be as perfect as possible. What do I get in return? What do I have? A bloody face, a crooked jaw, a skinny body, and a couple of words on some pieces of paper. That's all I am. What am I to you? What do you think of me? What the fuck kind of creature am I? Gosh, how I'd kill to have someone stab me right now. I bet I wouldn't even bleed out correctly. The blood would miraculously clot itself, and I'd survive by a miracle. Go ahead, get pissed at me for saying these things. I don't fucking care. I'm done.

I can hardly bring myself to write today. I've been waiting all day to say these words, to unleash my anger upon an innocent victim, my paper. Now I can't. That pisses me off even more than before. I wanted to write about how much I hate people and how I want them all to suffer. I want everyone to keel over and die. People are fucking monsters. I hope all of the assholes at my school get into car crashes. I hope they all survive the crashes, then go into urgent surgery and hopelessly die in the middle of a life-or-death operation. I have no shame in saying that. They most likely deserve it. Who is going to tell me that I'm wrong? How could you possibly insult or degrade me any further? I'm practically a fucking corpse myself. Do you know the expression beating a dead horse? I'm a dead horse, and people keep beating me. They whack away, smacking at me with a tack hammer. Hit Justin, he doesn't mind.

I don't ask for much. I'm fairly generous. Can I at least ask for a little bit of help? Why do I bother doing this shit? Why do I bother waking up in the morning, no doubt facing a new onslaught of conceited hatred called my peers? How do you wage war against a world that has the advantage? I can't get over how I can't swallow right. You know, when I was little, my mom used to tell me that my teeth would be perfect.

"It hurts now, but just imagine when your teeth will be perfect," she would say.

Well, guess what? It's later, and my teeth are far from perfect. My mom tried to encourage me, but it didn't work. It still fucking hurts me, and it never stops. The pain doesn't fucking end. It's not like I can tell anyone that I feel like shit. They'd just downplay my emotions as whining or complaining. I've been dealing with this pain for my entire life. I'm getting real sick of it, honestly. My head hurts, I can't think straight, and my emotions are constantly dragging me down. Why am I still required to do physical things? Am I not burdened enough already? How is anyone going to help me? Help is way past the expiration date.

How in the fuck have I not snapped yet? I don't fucking care about this world. I'm capable of great things, but I have weights anchoring me down. I'm trying to fly to the end of the universe, but I'm trapped inside a measly birdhouse. I just want to unleash my anger and suffering upon everyone. I want to watch them struggle. Maybe they wouldn't be as quick to insult me if they realized what I have to deal with every second of every day.

I want to wake up and I want all of my problems to be solved. I'm sick of solving everyone else's problems. But I can't solve my own problems. How fucking tragic is that? Is that my fatal flaw, my hamartia? You know, I have to learn to swallow differently. Why don't you try breathing differently for the rest of your life and tell me how that goes? In fact, why don't you try not breathing at all?

I really am a freak of nature.

SEPTEMBER 26, 2016

A friend, Jackson, texted me today during my ACT prep class. He wanted to know if I was interested in going to homecoming with Ashley, a girl in my French class. I didn't really want to go to homecoming, and that's what I told him. Still he persisted, insisting that I go with Ashley. Once again, I told him I wasn't interested in going to a homecoming dance because I despise homecoming and dancing. Although, I will admit that I have a small crush on Ashley, and that was quite tempting to pursue. I guess I'll go to homecoming to appease both Jackson and Ashley.

Today is Monday. Wednesday I have another ACT prep session, Thursday I have my first therapy appointment, and Saturday is the homecoming dance, if I decide to go. That's a long week. I'm not sure I'm prepared to deal with that sequence of events in a manageable span of time. How am I going to live through this next week?

I'm not sure how I'm supposed to go about this homecoming dance. Should I be excited? Should I treat Ashley as a friend? Should I ask her out? I don't want to ask her out. I'm not ready for a committed relationship. Not yet. I'm not capable of maintaining my emotions, and I'm worried that I'll scare her off. What if she already likes me? What if she doesn't like me? Gosh, I'm so worried about Saturday. The rest of my week is going to be awful.

I've only been to one dance before. I went to my eighth-grade dance, and I'm more than willing to admit that I did less dancing than is optimal. Honestly, I didn't mind it at all because I still had fun, but I know that this time I'll have to dance. How could I go out with a girl and not dance? I don't know. I'm so scared.

SEPTEMBER 29, 2016

I knew today was heading into an irreversible downward spiral before class even started. I was getting my Intro to Business book out of my locker and I was talking to one of my friends, Brad. I told Brad I had to go to my teacher's dumb class. Then, I got tapped on the shoulder. Guess who was behind me? My teacher was right behind me, listening to every word of our conversation. He heard what I said about him, so that's fucking wonderful. I felt bummed out after that. I actually like him as a teacher, and I like the class. I'm not sure why I said he had a dumb class, I think I was just frustrated with bringing in a book every day because we rarely used the book in class.

It's homecoming week, by the way. I fucking despise homecoming. Do you want to know why I hate homecoming so much? Take a guess. Is it because I'm an insufferable piece of shit who hates everything? Or is it because I can hardly socialize with anyone? Maybe, and maybe. My reason for despising homecoming is based upon how the rest of the kids at our school act. Let me explain why I hate homecoming so you have some considerable background knowledge.

Last year, during homecoming week, I packed a red t-shirt in my backpack before going to school. I was planning on wearing the shirt for our class color day, which is red for our grade level. I didn't want to wear it for the entire day, though. Walking into school that morning, when I wasn't wearing a red shirt, a dozen and a half of my classmates berated me down the hallway.

"Why aren't you wearing red? Where's your red? Do you have red? What are you doing? Are you going to wear red?"

After that red fiasco, and after constantly being gossiped about by my peers, I decided homecoming was a sham. Honestly, I did try to participate. I brought the red shirt, but they didn't even give me a chance to show them. That's why I hate homecoming. Homecoming is an event for selfish bastards who are too popular for their own good.

Well, nothing is different this year. In fact, I have participated every single day so far this week. Guess what? I wore a red shirt today for class color day. Guess again. I had a blue jacket covering my shirt when I walked in the building. Before I even got to my locker I had three people ask me if I was wearing red. Luckily, I was smart enough to slightly unzip my jacket to reveal my red shirt for their petty eyes. They're the real insufferable ones, not me. How can they possibly care this much about such a silly and frivolous event like homecoming?

Later in the day, I overheard two girls talking about me. They were amazed that even Justin dressed up today. They were implying that I never participate in their silly, irrelevant games and competitions. At that point in the day, I gave up with homecoming. Fuck homecoming. What the fuck is the point of homecoming anyway? It's nothing except a bunch of colored lunatics screaming and running around with huge flags waving behind them as they stampede up and down the hallways. What are they celebrating? Our football team hasn't won a game in two years, and these idiots are jumping around like we just won the state championship game. Why is this so important to them? I couldn't care any less.

Toward the end of the day we had an assembly in the gym. It was a two-hour assembly in which I was crammed and smashed together with five hundred obnoxious brats. Wonderful. So, what was the assembly about? Well, it was for the homecoming games: a human pyramid, hula hoops, limbo, and basketball. It took two hours to perform four boring events.

The pyramid is what infuriated me. It was the first event in this entire assembly, so that means I was thrown into a hellfire mood at the beginning of the assembly. So, what happened? Each class had to send out boys and girls respectively to form a human pyramid and then hold it for ten seconds. Well, I didn't want to participate. First of all, I didn't want to be the center of attention for the entire school. Second of all, I didn't want to fall off and be blamed for the loss. Third, I didn't want to even participate in the first place because I hate homecoming. That's too damn bad, apparently.

I didn't want to be part of the class pyramid because it sounded intimidating. Plus, I was extremely nervous, and my anxiety skyrocketed during this entire affair. I kept telling my friends I wasn't about to go down and join in the pyramid when it was our turn. Soon enough our turn rolled around, and I stayed seated. I was sitting down when a bunch of guys grabbed under my arms and lifted me to my feet. They pulled and pushed me forward. I had no choice but to be a part of their stupid pyramid.

It wasn't too bad, honestly, but it could have been. When I was on the pyramid, I silently threatened to fall off and destroy any chance at winning the competition, but I decided against it. I had the repeated thought of purposely pushing someone over and then falling onto other people so our grade would lose. That's how fucking disgusted I was with the whole ordeal. But I decided not to do that because it would have made my situation even worse than it already was. Funnily enough, someone accidentally fell off, effectively carrying out my own thoughts. By the time we got back in the bleachers, the only thing people were conversing about was The Fall.

"Who fell? What happened? What the fuck is going on? How the hell did someone fall? Who fell off? Who fell off?"

My classmates sounded like confused owls as they frantically searched and prodded for their answers. *Who fell off the pyramid and gave our class a horrific last place finish in the pyramid competition? Who would have dared to perform such an atrocity? What kind of sick minded individual would ruin our homecoming pyramid?* Those are questions that likely surfaced among my classmates. How fucking selfish do these people get? They were upset with someone who fell, which is understandable, but they never stopped asking questions. They were furious that they didn't win. What a bunch of spoiled and inconsiderate assholes!

They cared so much about a pointless fucking assembly. A kid named Tyler and a couple other douchebags were standing in front of me, ceaselessly yelling and chanting their own wicked incantations. I had to restrain myself from shoving them off the bleachers. They were standing up, easily exposed, and it would have been so easy to shove them down the mountainous sea of villains, my peers. My furious rage almost propelled me to fulfill this action, but I ruthlessly resisted it.

And then my thoughts transformed. Why should I stop at pushing a couple of school-spirited twats? I wanted everyone in our school to die. I didn't fucking care. I thought of the perfect way to maximize the death toll, too. I would place explosives under the bleachers. You know, the part you can stick your feet under when the seating areas are accessible? I would line that with explosives for every row. Then, when everyone is standing up, I would blast the explosives. Their limbs and blood and intestines would rain down upon the center of the gym, drenching the dancing cheerleaders. That's what I wanted. Me. How in the fuck does anyone make me that angry?

That's the point where I wished every single one of those assholes a painful death. I wanted their deaths to be slow and torturous with an additional emphasis on suffering. How can people be allowed to act in that manner? Every fiber of my being wriggled in hatred and anger. I'm not joking. I really wanted my classmates to perish, turned into stardust for the stars to breathe.

Luckily, today was a Thursday, and it was my first therapy appointment. Anxiety was at a ten, depression ten, and anger ten thousand. Perfect. But guess what? I didn't even bother telling my new therapist any of this information about my day. I didn't want to scare her off like I've scared off countless other humans because I'm different than anything they have ever experienced. At least, that's what I thought.

My therapy session was actually quite boring and uneventful. Most of the time was spent filling out paperwork, introducing myself, and discussing what my therapy sessions would be like. I think my therapist was very nice. I think my therapy will help me a lot, and I have a lot of hope for the future. That's hardly ever happened before. Anyway, that was my day. It was rather eventful, if I do say so myself. I almost snapped and killed one of my classmates, and I had my first therapy session.

It's been a hectic day.

OCTOBER 1, 2016

Today is Saturday, the first of October, the date of the homecoming dance. Now, I could sit here and recite my night event by event, place by place, time by time, but I figured that would be boring and repetitive. Also, the dance itself was rather boring. I didn't end up dancing with Ashley, my date. Neither of us are good at dancing, which made our decision to not dance a valid one. Honestly, there was only one moment that truly stuck out to me tonight. That's what I'm going to write about.

At one point when we were driving, I looked over at Ashley and I just started staring at her. She had her eyes focused on the road, of course, and she was oblivious to my eyes pointed directly at her. I started observing her, as I observe all people. That's how I fell in love with her. I looked at her pretty blue eyes until I had forgotten that her eyes were blue, then decided to look again to convince myself that they were indeed blue. I watched how the sides of her lips curled into a smile as she laughed at her younger sister, who was acting silly in the back of the car. I watched as Ashley's mouth opened in laughter, forgetting its proper and formal code of staying closed. I observed how she bent forward when she laughed, undoubtedly enjoying and savoring each moment of happiness. I listened to her laugh echo softly in my ears, a beautifully encompassing sound that surrounded me in warmth and rays of sunshine. It was completely pitch-black outside, but I felt like I was swimming in happiness and light. I gazed at her white skin bouncing off the moonlight, illuminating her body in a pale glow. I watched her shoulders slump once more in laughter, almost struggling to stay upright. I observed her body, knowing instantly that she was beautiful. I wanted to make her feel happy and warm. I wanted her to always be happy, always laughing like she was in the car. I witnessed her singsong voice fall and rise, dispersed by the sound of laughter, telling her sister to quit dabbing in the back of the car because she needed to be able to see out of the rearview mirror. The only thing I heard was the sweet sound of her voice. The words dissolved into nothing, but the sound lingered in my ears. I smiled at Ashley, but she didn't notice me. It didn't matter. In that moment, I knew I was going to ask her out, and I knew she would say yes.

By this time, I figured she had a pretty large crush on me. Actually, I had evidence of that because her friends told me that very thing during the dance. When Ashley went off somewhere for a minute, a couple of her friends stopped by and told me that Ashley talks about me constantly, saying how much she adores me. I could hardly believe it. Me? Ashley likes me? How could anyone like me? But, somewhere deep in the darkness, a fire kindled into existence. My passion for love and romance grew once more, and I suddenly remembered my last few relationships. They all had turned out so terribly. A fear began to swallow me, but I swallowed it back down my throat. I'm such a failed romantic. I need to share my love, but I have an allergic reaction when somebody loves me. How is this relationship going to work? What am I going to do?

I'm going to ask her out.

OCTOBER 7, 2016

I had my first date with Ashley today. I asked my mom if it was fine if I went over to Ashley's house after school, and she answered with a resounding yes. I think she was just excited that I was getting out more instead of being locked up in the basement, chiseling away at my story. Sometimes you have to leave the shelter of your sanctuary in order to get the content you need to tell your story.

I drove over to Ashley's house and parked in the driveway, unaware that I could park in the front yard. That was just a mistake, but I didn't worry about it too much. Why should I worry about it? It's not like I knew any better.

I met Ashley's parents for the second time. I think they are awesome, honestly. I talked to them for over an hour, and I laughed a lot during this time. But after the laughter started dying down, I asked if I could take Ashley to the local park. It was a beautiful day outside, probably one of the last warm days of the year. I wanted to make the most of it. I had a plan, unbeknownst to anyone else at the time. I was going to get Ashley alone and ask her out. It was essential to my plan that she be alone when I ask her. I didn't want to make her feel uncomfortable by asking her out in the proximity of other people. That's a lot of pressure to say yes.

That's not to say that I wasn't prepared for rejection. I was very prepared, and I mentally barricaded myself. Ashley's objection, or acceptance, of me had no way to render me helpless. Finally, it was time.

I drove Ashley to the park, and we talked about the homecoming dance during the drive. She laughed a lot, and I smiled back at her as I drove. By the time we got to the park, I wasn't even sure what we were going to do. I offered to walk with her, and she said yes.

I started easing into the conversation, but I poked and prodded her until I got an answer. She wanted to date me, and I immediately jumped on the moment by asking her out. She said yes! I could hardly believe it. I was so excited, and I could barely think straight. I knew our relationship was going to be incredible. Finally, I had a moment of happiness. I'm still ecstatic, honestly.

I'm so happy.

OCTOBER 23, 2016

This life is slowly tearing me apart. I'm trying to grow wings in the hope that I can fly, but people tell me that my feet are crooked and I can't walk correctly. Little do they know, I'm close to flying over the competition like a seagull taking a shit over the entirety of a city. Where do my thoughts take me now? Should I shoot higher than the clouds beyond? Do these wings hold the power to lift me up above the life I had that was focused on the ground? Even my dreams seek escape from reality. Somehow, a sudden gust of wind always forces me back down to ground zero, where my past was drowned.

Why glide when you know that you can fly? People tell me to look at the ground, but I'm too busy staring at the monster in the sky. The king of darkness rests high in the stratosphere, barring access to those people below the clouds. His castle home is the paradise where I seek relief from the burrows that hide my life. This is my reprieve, but it's more of an eternal expedition where I hope to relieve my constant competition.

Before I seek hope in the light of day, I often find I've lost the words that I used to say. Canary birds chirp as I fly above, but the sadness that I seek seems to drag me lower than the lows of my deepest woes. Hummingbirds mock the speed of my wings, telling me that I'm missing an integral piece of an airborne cruise: a motivation. Where is the hope for a better life? What happened to being the hero of your own story? How can you be a hero if you don't even believe in yourself? And what kind of bird doesn't know how to fly? Penguins have a better grasp of aerodynamics than I do, which is really saying something because I've grown a pair of feathery wings. What kind of bird am I? Am I a mockingbird that doesn't sing? Am I a parrot that fails to mimic? Am I a hummingbird that cannot hover?

I tell myself to fly, but the free fall calculations from gravity tell me to die. Physics and acceleration slowly drag me down, throwing chains around my feet and pulling down. History lectures me about how this has happened before. How did I not learn from humanity's past mistakes? English spreads the word of my inevitable defeat, and French earnestly deciphers my surreal plunge. Businesses and corporations voraciously market my descent as I fall sporadically. Mathematics greedily adds the explosive profits from my humiliating failure. Finally, I decide that I'd rather fall back to the ground. Letting loose a feather from my diseased body, I allow it to flutter to the ground in order to appease the chains and shackles that aid in the abrupt cancellation of my plans. Each feather marks my accumulated failures over the years. At this point, I might as well try to fail. If I try to fail, perhaps I will succeed. A failed failure is a success, and a completed failure is a successful failure. Either way, I am benefited with the thought of success.

Now, as another of my feathers is plucked from the sky and thrown into the heaping ashes that lay in a tumultuous ruin across the ground, I sulk in anticipation of my next attempt at flight. I await the day where I fly higher than the jurisdiction of chains and shackles, higher than labels and titles, and higher than the ground I once called my home. I'm sick of being just another human being. I'm ready to be me, but I'm the only one who is ready. One day they will let go of these chains, and I will ascend into the clouds. There will be no feathers left to pluck from my irritated body by the time I take the throne as a bird among skies.

Why glide down when you know that you can fly?

NOVEMBER 10, 2016

Today was, at the very least, interesting. At most, it was a near cataclysmic disaster. Now, I say it was a near disaster, but, in reality, it was more than a simple disaster. Today was not, "Oh, I seemed to have misplaced my homework and now I will receive a bad grade," or any other trivial inconvenience. If anything, today was a series of trivial inconveniences strewn hectically throughout the day before and after my mental and physical collapse. What's wrong with me?

My day started out as normal as any other human being, if a day in my life is considered normal. Spoiler alert: normality is a particularly sinister fallacy of humans. At this point, the concept of humanity is estranged to me in the way that an estranged wife or husband is resented, hated, and brutally criticized by both families. After today, I am more than ashamed to call myself a human. A concentration camp filled to the brim with visitors could be placed before my eyes and their tempered gaze would not falter in the slightest. Imagine being unable to muster empathy for the infinitely suffering men, women, and children as they await their merciless deaths by execution, starvation, and genocide. Today, my accusing lens placed every human, whether the victims, oppressors, or bystanders, under scrutiny and assault. I eagerly wished to grant them the mocking bite of death, as opposed to a gentle, soothing kiss. But allow me to explain my predicament before prejudices are accumulated against me.

I woke up this morning with little rest or determination, as seems to be my creature of habit. This habit is further perpetuated by the fact that I barely feel the need to continue life. Somehow, I managed to find the strength to make it to school in an efficient fashion, as I do every successful morning. Honestly, that is an accomplishment in and of itself. It's a shame that my accomplishments are ridiculed and diminished to the point that happiness appears as meaningless as a window built into the floor.

By the time first hour had started, I was prepared for my entire day. I printed out an outside source for my in-class history essay third hour, and I finished my physics homework for fourth hour. Now, what happened next can only be explained in its proper context through a complete analysis of my first hour class, which sparked my frustration and forced my blood to bubble beneath my skin.

After printing out my history papers, twenty-five pages thick, I looked for a stapler. My friend, Michael, beat me to the teacher's desk and grabbed the stapler before I could react. He tried to staple his papers and failed because the stapler's inventory was lacking. One brief intermission later, the Great Stapler War raged on as our teacher provided a fresh round of ammunition.

By this time, we had both taken our seats as I watched a bitter feud unfold. My friend smashed down on the stapler to test its new contents only to find that the staple formation was spread too wide to be effective. I started laughing because it was quite amusing to witness his obsession with stapling his papers; I had put mine away as soon as he retrieved the stapler.

He fixed this crucial error and excitedly performed another test. The staple satisfied him, and he decided to finally staple all twenty-five papers together. The War would soon be over, and a truce was nearly settled. Well, he stapled his papers, but the staple got stuck halfway through the papers. As if that wasn't bad enough, the staple fucking snapped in half as he tried to pluck it out! Oh, damn, my laughter was extremely contagious at this point. It was a wonderful beginning to my day. I felt a little rude for laughing at him, but it was rather amusing. Or so I thought.

Apparently, my friend didn't take too kindly to my laughter. He took my history papers and crudely stapled them together to frustrate me, but he ultimately failed. I removed the staples and ignored his belittling insults. See, his most powerful attribute is his relentlessness, and he never ceases to utilize it as an opportunity for insults. But something else happened that threw my day into the wastebasket.

My business teacher started talking about an incident involving his friend's son. Apparently, the kid went to get pizza with his cousin, but the cousin made an unexpected stop en route to the pizza place. As it turns out, the cousin was dealing cocaine, and both the cousin and the kid were booked with felonies. The poor kid has a criminal record because he was in the wrong place at the wrong time.

This story sparked a debate between my friend and I. I told him that drugs should be, at the very minimum, decriminalized. It also wouldn't hurt to legalize drugs. I provided my stance on the issue, vouching for the decriminalization and legalization of all drugs, and he countered me fiercely. I should mention that it is rather demeaning to argue with someone of such a conceited stature. For one thing, his argument consisted of one or two thoughts continuously thrown back at every new thought I conceived. Another item that bothered me was his inability to view my side of the argument. I always try my best to offer insight and judgement for his argument, but my efforts are rarely reciprocated. Today, a fiery passion united my thoughts, and our debate raged on. We were both equally unyielding to the opinions of the other, but his remarks and accusations quickly surmounted my mental defenses. We argued for the rest of the class, and the argument carried into our second hour, English.

By the time we reached the computer lab in English, my friend further provoked me by talking to our other friends about our debate. He heavily favored his side of the argument, which is reasonable due to him being biased, but he neglected to share the necessity of my argument. Instead, he chose to nitpick my words in order to manipulate my friends into agreeing with him. Almost instantly, the argument went from being between my friend and I to being between three friends and myself.

As the pressure piled on, my emotions began to control my thoughts. I began to have trouble speaking as I attempted to persuade my friends into viewing my side of the debate. My speech was slurred and almost drunken, and a slight stutter most likely prohibited me from attracting a necessary audience. Seizing this to his advantage, my friend laughed at my failures and mocked my opinion based solely upon my speaking patterns. Of course, the other two supposed friends shared in the laughter and mockery.

The embers of our debate glowed hot and red, but school was still in session. The librarian was teaching our class about how to use a database to search for academic journals and articles for our upcoming essay. I was having trouble, not to mention I was furious with my friends, and she came over to investigate my progress.

I don't remember exactly what happened next, but I have a rough idea as to how the situation unfolded. Due to my struggles, the librarian attempted to help me (I probably wouldn't have struggled as much if she didn't talk so damn fast). She guided me through our school's website, made me click on multiple links, and told me to log in to my school account. After typing in my username and password, the website kicked me out. My friends continued to laugh at me.

At this point, I was exasperated by the petty concerns of reality. My legs shook nervously, but my arms were universally linked by the strongest material in existence: my emotions. A clotted rage shook my arms, silently prodding at the temptation to strangulate. My murderous gaze vivaciously peered into the back of ignorant heads, humans unknown to the barbaric cruelty that fiercely dominates my being. Homicidal thoughts blanketed my mind with a comforting reassurance. Severe pain and a tormented death awaited as rewarded consequences bestowed upon any who dared to challenge me. Undeniable hatred constructed a perpetrating offense. I planned to attack.

"Your website sucks ass."

The words left my mouth with a snarl. My lips eagerly spat the words, curling them into a ball of targeted frustration. But my body shook twice as vigorously once those spiteful words exited my demeanor.

I wanted the librarian to punish me for insulting her livelihood, but I was instead greeted by silence. She ignored my comment. Oh, sweet, tender joy. Luckily for me, my friends noticed my painful remark. They thought it was funny.

"Oh my gosh, Justin! You swore at a teacher!"

Yes. Thank you for pointing out this fact that I must have surely been unaware. They continued to laugh. Their laughter allowed hasty fuel for my anger. Two of my classmates were sitting in front of me in the computer lab and, at one point, they turned around to look at me. Suddenly, they turned back around, started whispering, and giggled like schoolgirls. I had to restrain myself from leaping over the desk and punching one of them. I truly wanted to punch Michael, who instigated my overwhelming anger. Or perhaps one of my other friends, who quickly pointed out how upset I was becoming, and continued to snicker at me for the next five minutes.

Somehow, I managed to survive for the next twenty minutes without murdering anyone. But I wanted to. It would have brought me immense gratification to witness the death of anyone in that room. My pleasure would have tripled if I were the one to commit a murder. Alas, I was denied this privilege. I didn't even manage to throw a single punch. How was I so thoroughly denied? I don't know. All emotions, spare anger, grew cold and lifeless during English class. The agonizing deaths of my contemporaries would have offered me an insurmountable satisfaction. The empathy the remaining survivors would feel for their fellow classmates would be null and void because they, too, would quickly be consumed by my next homicidal hunger. Sympathy and empathy were nonexistent to me at the time. The concept of emotion was devoid of meaning. I felt numb, cold, and sadistic on the inside; on the outside, my ears blazed and my body continuously shook. The veil of darkness descended upon my weary eyes.

I wanted to get into a fight with someone. I wanted to fight all of my friends. I didn't care. I didn't just want to fight them, either. I wanted them to suffer and die. I wanted their entire demeanor to crush beneath my fist. I wanted them to perish in agonizing pain. That's how fucking angry I was with them. They made me so angry that I had homicidal thoughts.

When I finally cooled down after study hall, I became very depressed and had to go through the rest of the day holding back tears. Me. How can people do that to me? How can those people wake up in the morning knowing they reduced me to that? I was shaking so bad. The worst part was when they laughed at me. They thought it was absolutely hilarious that I was upset. Not a single word of empathy or sympathy was uttered from the large, wasted oxygen pumps they call lungs. They did not offer a single reassuring or comforting phrase for me in my desperate time of need. No. They laughed at me.

The remainder of my day was sliced into depression and anguish. I almost started crying during French class. I was doing my homework and I wrote down the wrong verb. Naturally, I went to fix it. I tried to erase the word, but I ended up crumpling my paper. It might as well have been my heart that had crumpled. That tiny mistake crushed me. I had to fight back tears for the rest of the class period, and the emotions lingered into my next class.

The only people today that I didn't hate were Jason, Roger, and Ashley. My friend Jason kept silent about me in English, which didn't help much, but it was better than being laughed at or openly insulted. Roger helped me in physics when I was working by myself. He also offered me some food at lunch. I quietly declined, but I appreciated his kind gesture. As for the rest of this despicable planet, I would have received great satisfaction in their disposal or immediate removal.

NOVEMBER 13, 2016

I am adamant to the act of belligerence actively casted as a blacklisted spell for carnivorous animals I call my friends. Where is the peace treaty I seek among the domestic securities I feel insecure about? The anxiety unleashed is hardly sheathed before the sword becomes a weapon of murderous intent. Blast an atom through my skull before the atoms arranged in my abdomen absorb the universe in a black hole anomaly called the breath of death. Who dares deny my entreating entrance to the house of the dead? The mausoleum chambers must be rectified, but my actions seem as hopeless as a boneless wish. Does it concern you that my mind works faster than the speed of light? I am, in fact, the unappreciated act of actual impoverishment forced upon this fractured civilization. My tomb remains intact, but the mummy inside is barely dead.

It may be time to face facts: certain doom awaits the crest of mortality, but my impending resurgence reverses the crude act of cruelty I call the dubious human community. What was that? I heard a thought explode at the sight of a pernicious valley carved from the knife of the bold and brave. The valley is a testimony to my lowly demise, but I peak like a mountain when I find a reason to release all lies. I relinquish my fury, but I refuse to testify as a witness to the supernova death of animosity. Animosity is a raucous ruckus for the raunchy. I must apologize for my attractive syllables, but this equal dispersion of intelligence is barely permitted. Who would dare read my thoughts? The extended fear of being eternally sucked into the repressive vortex is as spacious as the asshole of a naked ass. Does that make sense in the context I have created? Are my words simply a concept for the common illness I suffer from called insanity? Psychopathic tendencies seem to mine my mind for the worst of its enemies. Am I a psychopath for searching sneakily for the path to darkness? The road to suicide is full of wariness, but I nevertheless approach it intently.

NOVEMBER 24, 2016

I'm writing this fifteen minutes before midnight, so it seems unfair to label the date as Thursday, November 24th. But I'll do it anyway because fairness is not applicable with reality.

Today was Thanksgiving. I could spew my thoughts on family, food, religion, emotions, or even a seemingly wasted and unproductive day. I'm not going to do that, though. Nothing of significance happened today. When I woke up this morning, a courageous act by my standards, I felt pressure and anxiety about life. By the time the day was over, I felt the same. Why should I write about today?

It's been a year since I began my first journal. It's over. It's been a hectic year, twelve hectic months since the beginning of my first journal.

I started my journal on November 24th, 2015. I don't know why I started it. I don't know where I found the motivation to begin my story. At first, my journal was designed with the purpose of being read by someone else. Later on, I realized that the language I used was idiotic; the only person reading the journal was myself. My journal lacked a purpose.

I found a purpose within the first twenty pages. As severe depression imposes upon its innocent victims, I kindly uphold its brutish condition. Eventually, I concluded that my journal would be part of a masterful plan. This plan quickly became an intricately detailed and incredibly heartfelt suicide mission. I had glorious ambitions for my suicide, and my journal became my most powerful asset. Its demented pages became my only friends. I openly sought their advice in times of hardship. They enticed me with their deadly propositions, and I openly accepted their offer: death.

I decided that my journal would serve as a suicide note. Constantly, I toyed with this fanatical idea. Even in school, as I roamed the meager institution destined to be a contributing source to my downfall, I thought of my journal. My journal became the representation of my thoughts, and my thoughts subsequently became a manifestation of death. Suicide seemed to be the only ending fit for my miraculous demise.

Slowly, my thoughts shifted from extreme sadness to anger and hatred. My anxiety developed into an excuse for carrying out angry intentions. The combined efforts of sadness, anger, and anxiety created a new, overwhelming monstrosity called numbness. Being numb is the absence of emotion; it's a lack of identity, sympathy, or empathy. Attempting to kill yourself is an act of numbness. Personally, I may attest to this action. The dangers of being numb rested idly inside my distorted mind.

For some reason, I became infatuated with the glorification of completing my journal. I felt that completing my journal would lead to a sense of accomplishment, and possibly acknowledgement for its literary prowess. Neither of these feelings seemed to manifest, as it turned out.

After completing my journal, I only felt relief and a premature onset of worry. That journal had been the pinnacle of my existence. When it was completed, I lost the motivation to live once again. Oddly enough, this thought spurred me into a direction of prosperity, including a renewed sense of hope for the future. I wanted to live again, which counteracted the entire purpose of my journal. But did I really want to continue living? That question, and the falsities it provoked, such as hope for the future, determined the remainder of my summer.

Now, in the present tense, I am adrift in a world of lackluster accommodations called problems. I feel as if I am subjected to the torturous rituals of life despite my original intention to cleanse my body from the definition of existence. Where do I find the motivation to rip asunder the chains that shackle me to the bowels of creation?

Where must I purge my formally proclaimed abnormalities? What am I supposed to live for?

I seek answers to these questions on this vicarious voyage. As of now, I am only alive for a few specific reasons. The first reason: I am too much of a perfectionist to commit suicide. My suicide must be perfect, and its reception by friends, family, and strangers must follow suit. This seems improbable at best, which is probably why I'm still alive. The second reason: I do not want my parents, sister, or girlfriend to be upset at their perceived loss. Say what you will about this reason. As for me, perhaps I think too much. If I didn't think this much, there is no doubt that I would be dead by now. Finally, the third, and most important, reason: my writing. I do not seek to perish from this planet without first bestowing upon it my greatest attribute. I want to be renowned for my words, remembered by my storytelling, and admired for my stories.

With these hopes in mind, I cling to the bosom of life. Forever destined and bound by pressure, I shatter the expectations placed before me. Companions abound, this warrior emerges from the tyranny of depression, leaving in his path the bristled bites of fatal opportunities unachieved.

NOVEMBER 28, 2016

How vile and low does the ship of my self-esteem seem to sink? It only takes three hours of being by myself to convert my mind into a self-destructive, indestructible force. The correlation between myself and my emotions is a direct association between betrayal and backstabbing techniques. Where do I even begin to process this tyrannical influx of depression? Should I attack this foul and untamed beast at its source, myself? What is the matter with my mind?

Throughout the day, an oppressive void of numbness circulated through my respiratory system with every breath I took. The only emotions I presently feel are anger and sadness. All other emotions have been nullified by the darkness inside my head, forever blackened by the harsh cruelty known as reality. My dangerous imagination taints the secluded illusion of isolation. Today I felt drawn and receded from my peers, and this recession aided in my untimely demise.

By the time I started my homework, I had to resist the urge to secede from humanity. I wanted to exterminate myself. How could I possibly struggle with such a simple ordeal? I couldn't even read a book properly. Undoubtedly, my peers do not share my voiceless complaints. They do not have problems performing normal actions. Apparently, I am the only person capable of descending to the role of admirable failure. If you were wondering, I am admirable due to the untapped potential peacefully retained in my broken brain.

But as I stared hopelessly into the deceptive depths of my book, I began thinking. How could I dare to be such a lonely entity? At that point, tears softly rolled down my cheeks, but I bade them no notice. Instead, I focused upon the sheer and insurmountable loneliness portrayed in the past, present, and future forms of my life. When my mom went to bed and my phone stopped buzzing, I realized how truly alone I am in this world. It is amazing that I have survived this long without constant supervision or surveillance. Again, why am I this lonely beast doomed to fervently wander aimlessly in search of happiness and passion?

And so, with those kind words singing irresistible lullabies in tune with my melancholy, I stood in front of the mirror. I held an immense staring contest with the sadistic monster that calmly smiled back at me. He gave me a few words to ponder, as well.

"Justin does not deserve to be happy. Why would he deserve such a memorable emotion? No, Justin only deserves the wrath of his foes and oppressors. Not only that, but he also deserves to be deserted by his companions and shunned by his friends. Subsequently, the consequences addressed to Justin consist of absolute loneliness. This is the eternal punishment for being Justin."

And so, standing in front of the bathroom mirror this time, as opposed to the mirror in my bedroom, I continued to cry. I allowed my bloodshot eyes to mingle with the puffy redness of deceitful tears. I am, by mass definition and example, a pathetic scuff of a person.

I had an argument with myself in the mirror about whether or not it'd be considered murder if I killed myself. Those are the types of thoughts that make regular life seem like an annoyance, a nuisance so profoundly misguided. I also thought of just getting in my car and driving, driving with no particular destination, unless death is an appropriate stop. I want everything to dissolve and fade into black nothingness. I'm tired, and I need more time for this. I need more time for everything. But, as always, time is my most notorious enemy and my strongest ally.

DECEMBER 1, 2016

Where do I begin discussing my day? Should I start this woeful experience at the very beginning, or should I skip straight to the dilemma and avoid the exposition altogether? Am I going to spin this depressing day into a creative masterpiece for my journal? Or, quite the opposite, will I simply record my day event following event, meticulously recording my issues? Perhaps this will be a combination of everything I have stipulated above. There is only one way to find out: I have to write it.

If it seems reasonable, I'd like to address that my day flowed smoothly until the final bell echoed around in my eardrums like a drumbeat bounces off the band room walls. Flowed smoothly is an understatement; I was motivated and ecstatic earlier today. But, as I have kindly witnessed my entire life, even the brightest days can be followed by the darkest storms.

My happiness abruptly halted sometime past three o'clock. Placing a specific moment as the instigator of my troubles is difficult, and for that reason I will choose not to pinpoint a specific reason for the surfacing of my depression. If I had to take a guess, I would assume my happiness faded when I became part of a group photo for Trivia Team. We were required to take a photo together, and this produced a new wave of anxiety for me. During the photo, my brain eagerly reminded me that I despise having my photo taken. As if to complicate matters worse, we had to take multiple photographs. My troubled mind raced, and it proposed the idea that I had looked so disgustingly ugly and ridiculous that I ruined the first photograph, thus prompting a second, third, and fourth. Unlikely, but the thought was still present in my head.

After the group photo, I stood close to my girlfriend and her friend. I was excited for the first Trivia Team match of the year. However, my hope deteriorated as Jackson came up to me and started discussing last year's Trivia Team. He confidently claimed that he was the captain last year, not me. That is false. If he had to take a lie detector test, I would have zapped him right then and there.

Last year, I was nearly unanimously chosen by my peers to be captain, not Jackson. Originally, I didn't even want to be captain. I thought I would be incapable of handling the role and adjusting to the responsibility it presented. I proved myself wrong, however, and I surprised both myself and my team with my cunning wit and repeated ability to consistently provide answers. Those moments were rare treasure troves of happiness that I savored during a time when I barely had the energy to successfully get out of bed in the morning. Being the (mostly) successful captain of a team seemed like an impossibly unachievable dream, and yet I achieved. Yet, Jackson attempted to discredit me for one of the few feats I take pride in. I do not deny that he was the strongest nerd, if that is a suitable term for him. Most matches he answered either more questions than me or the same amount of questions as me. I never had the upper edge in the trivia department, but it didn't matter. For every question I lacked in competition, I surpassed Jackson with my leadership, humor, and listening skills. Even Michael, known for his constant complaining and berating, complimented me multiple times about my performance as captain.

When Jackson left my conversation, I began to feel the first wave of depression. I almost immediately doubted myself. My heart lurched, begging for the warmth of achievement, accomplishment, and confidence. I felt the physical shift as my heart quickened its pace, then suddenly jumped downwards. This wave of depression eagerly formed, attacking me while my defense mechanisms were not available. I had no idea this wave would ultimately develop into the destructive force of a Japanese tsunami.

A shallow numbness dissolved my emotions in the same manner sugar dissolves in water, separating itself into a larger group. My emotions became numb and unmoving. Typically, I feel happy when my girlfriend laughs or smiles, but at that moment I watched her laugh hysterically with her friend and I felt nothing. Not a twinge, not an urge, not a single muscle moved. I wondered how I could possibly fail to laugh or process happy emotions, but it was to no avail.

By the time we were on the road to our match, I was determined to find my motivation and spirit once more. I was close to salvaging my evening before the proximity of unknown people and their behaviors punished me. I felt personally attacked and isolated, and these emotions appeared to go unnoticed. Specifically, I felt this way when Allan, our team captain, or someone else would talk and then ask me a question. They could see I wasn't capable of answering, but they asked me their questions anyway. It's quite demeaning to be proven inadequate at something as simple as answering a question.

A certain sadness loomed over me the entire bus ride, and it increased in intensity upon the arrival of our destination. Oh, and I almost forgot to mention this, but I felt incredibly lonely during the bus ride. I sat in between my girlfriend and Jackson, and amidst a throng of people, yet I felt the inescapable clutch of loneliness. When I went to talk to my girlfriend, her head would be turned in the opposite direction, facing her friend or her sister. She was either lost in the lull of conversation or entertained by their humor for the duration of the bus ride. Jackson was reading a book. Allan was making me feel uncomfortable by taking pictures of me and asking personally demeaning questions. Amanda, my girlfriend's sister, made poorly tasted jokes the entire ride. So, I sat there, concentrated in thought as I so often am.

But back to the topic of the match. By the time we arrived in the school's library, I felt irritable and numb—a deadly combination. My concept of self was approaching an unbreakable turning point. Soon, my wrath would be unleashed upon the next person unfortunate enough to come into my vicinity.

I figured I would be starting in the match, seeing as I have proven time and time again that I can consistently answer questions. But no, I was denied this privilege with little to no consideration. When it was decided that I would be sitting out, I knew we were going to lose. I wanted us to lose. That's what our team deserves to be: a collective group of losers. And there were no doubts to my feelings. As harsh as I may be to others at times, it is nothing to how harsh I am to myself.

As if not starting was bad enough, I was separated from my girlfriend. First, we were separated on the bus, and again during the match. That was the nail in the coffin, in my opinion. It wasn't so much the separation that made me upset than it was the manner in which we were separated. We were separated on the bus because of a new rule this year that states males and females cannot sit together. We were separated during the match because Allan, our glorious captain, decided that "two lovers" were not fit to sit next to each other. Beyond that point, the night was a series of disappointments. It's a damn shame, too, because I was truly looking forward to this day. I thought today was going to be relaxing and happy, and, once again, I was rejected. But I wasn't rejected. It was more than being simply rejected. I was disgraced and discredited, assaulted and battered, abused and branded, and carelessly disposed. Then rejected. After all of those, I faced an unfaltering rejection statement. I was rejected by other people in addition to being rejected by the cruel outcome of this horrific night.

I contemplated and wrestled these thoughts throughout the match. I watched my girlfriend at times, and even her joyous laughter couldn't make me feel happy. My lips did not budge at the sound or sight of her. The numbness resonating within my body was not at all budged. Honestly, watching her laugh only made me feel worse. I wanted to be happy with her. I wanted to be making her laugh, too. I couldn't do any of those things tonight. My self-esteem was nonexistent, my confidence was shattered, and my dignity was melted. When Ashley's laughter made me feel worse, that's when I realized how serious my emotions were tonight.

I was placed into the match after the first half, twelve questions after I should have been put into the match. Too late, too late, too late. That was my only thought. The time for apologizing had passed. If I was not welcome at the beginning of the match, I certainly would not be a hero for such a poor group of disgruntled misfits in their time of desperation. That's what it felt like. I felt like a fucking pawn in their sweet little game.

The person playing my piece was particularly aggressive and abusive, and he or she had absolutely no remorse moving me into unavoidable peril. Too late.

I missed the first question that I buzzed in on. It was about Harry Truman's Vice President, and I missed it. That was the end of me. Allan leaned over to say something to me after I messed up.

"1945 isn't an election year," he said. Those few words fueled my depression.

Later in the match, I forcibly broke the tip of my pencil. A girl on our team handed me her pencil, and, without hesitation, I broke that pencil as well. I didn't fucking care. I wanted it to be over.

They should have put me in at the start. Ask my friend Roger and he'll tell you that I could have answered quite a few questions in the beginning. I sat there on the sidelines for the first twelve questions, hissing answers under my breath. The pain it caused me was agonizing. I could have answered half of those questions in the first round. But it doesn't matter. That wasn't my primary concern. My concern was my thoughts and emotions, or lack of emotions. I felt numb and agitated, ready to strike at any moment.

After the match, which we horribly lost, I returned to the bus in silence. I took my seat by the window, staring out into the darkness, wondering if the darkness inside my head is blacker than the night's.

By the time the bus stopped for food, the worst of my night was approaching swiftly. I figured I would get off of the bus for no reason other than moving about, and I did. I followed my girlfriend and her friends into some stupid restaurant. Meanwhile, I was still lacking emotion. I waited patiently as each person placed an order. It almost turned out to be a decent distraction from the prior events of the evening, but, as seemed to be the common denominator today, I was wrong.

A girl in our group selfishly wanted to buy something with approximately ten dollars. She felt so strongly in this conviction that she admitted there was no room for compromise. Now, this is where I felt immensely hurt. At this despicable point in my day, I would have gratefully watched the world burn and perish. I wanted that, I craved it, and I yearned for it to hold truthful. Despite these thoughts, I waited for the cash number to pop up on the register. When I saw the total was over ten dollars, and I looked over at this girl's plain ten-dollar bill, I immediately pulled out my wallet. I slipped a dollar bill onto the counter and returned to waiting patiently. The change, twenty-eight cents, came and I gingerly placed a quarter and three pennies into a donation slot for children suffering from cancer. What is wrong with me?

My parents taught me to be a generous person, and apparently this is true. My dad told me I should always offer money to those in need, and I do. I guess it is supposed to bring a sense of pride or happiness for helping someone less fortunate, but tonight it did nothing for me. I actually felt worse after I gave up my dollar. I was starving, but I told myself I wouldn't spend any money on food. Yet, I contradicted my thoughts in order to help someone through my generosity. I felt absolutely awful. How could I do something like that? How could I so easily persuade my previous thoughts into helping someone, a despicable, selfish person who should have ordered something that she could afford? How could I allow my mind to slip so atrociously? How could this lapse in thought be perceived as the destruction of the rest of my evening? Was my evening already destroyed before this ten-dollar fiasco? Ten dollars, happiness costs ten dollars… relapse, relapse, relapse, collapse.

This next part is going to be the hardest to write, and probably the most difficult to read. Be prepared, sweet, innocent reader of these words. Of course, you're not innocent. You are a guilty savage for reading these words under the perception that you are just and good. You are equally at fault for the events that transpired this evening.

When we got back on the bus, I returned to my seat in silence. Except this time was different. This time, my numbness subsided in favor of debilitating depression. Again, I peered out the window, into the darkness. It felt different. The darkness didn't feel separated from the light. Honestly, I could hardly see the light. All the items in my view felt dim and dull, devoid of white and its friendly shades. I had become an entire creation of darkness, cradled and soothed by the black of the night. I was a helpless infant of the night, created with the sole purpose of spreading destruction. Staring out that damn window reminded me of seventh grade, and a collage of memories assaulted me.

Throughout middle school, I spent an hour on the bus ride home after school. Every day, five days a week, I rode the bus to and from school. I always sat by myself, mostly for my own isolation. I could never sleep on the bus, but I found out I could pass the time by looking out the window and grasping the scenery with my mind. I loved attempting to memorize the colors of bushes and the shapes of flowers. I used to gaze into the individual leaves of each tree, watching them fly off in the fall, disappear in the winter, and flutter up from the remnants of the ground in the spring. I would stare into the lines on the sides of the road, watching as the white stripes weaved and swayed because they weren't painted in perfectly straight lines. I enjoyed all of these things and more on those tedious bus rides. I developed a system, and I embraced it. When I wasn't embracing the scenery, I was lost in thought, constantly thinking.

Anyway, back to the present. I started thinking about those days and how lonely I felt, how much time I spent doing absolutely nothing, being unproductive and useless, how worthless I am, and how sad I felt. The numbness dissipated, but it was replaced by an overwhelming sadness.

The bus started moving. I felt the darkness moving with me, and I knew it was mine. It was going to consume me, and I was going to let it consume me. I put my black hood up so nobody could see my charred and black face, forever tainted by the shadows. But my head rocked against the bumping window, and it spawned an idea in my demented head. I wanted to fly out of the side of the bus. I wanted to kill myself right then and there. At first, I weakly tapped my head against the glass in worthless attempts. But then I started smashing my head harder and harder until I could feel a throbbing sensation of pain and exertion pounding thoroughly through my brain. I heard my girlfriend yell "Stop!" and I stopped.

I started to cry lightly, allowing a few stray tears to rush down my wounded cheeks. I hid my face from my girlfriend after that because I didn't want her to see me. How would I have looked at her like that? I was crying and shaking like a damn baby. I hated myself for it. I really did. So, I smashed my head against the window even more forcibly than before, and this time it only took one or two bashes to feel the sting in my forehead. Once again, I heard her tell me to stop, and I obeyed the voice. I didn't listen because I felt that she was concerned. No, I listened because I didn't want her to be upset with me. I wouldn't have been able to handle it. After all I had been through, it would have completely crushed me if she had yelled at me.

And so this cycle of hatred and sadness continued. I felt uncomfortable, and I decided to lie down. Her gentle hand was a pleasant surprise, but it didn't offer much. I was still crying, perhaps even more than before, under my hood. I kept my hood closed, and I was terrified that someone would pry it open. I knew exactly what they would say with a look of pure and utter shock upon their disgusting face.

"Are you crying? What? Why are you crying? What's wrong? Hey, everybody, Justin's crying!"

Skipping ahead a little, after we got to the parking lot and my girlfriend told me to be safe driving home, I knew it was bad. You see, when I met with my psychiatrist yesterday for the first time, he made me promise something at the end of the visit. He made me promise that I wouldn't hurt myself before my next appointment, which is Saturday, two days away. At the time of the appointment, I thought it was dumb because I was given such a short span of time. But driving home was a struggle for me today.

When I started driving, it rushed back all of those memories from February 3rd, 2016, the day I almost killed myself after math team. Today was Trivia Team. In February, I struggled during the competition. Today I didn't answer a single question, same as that February match. In February, I sat alone on the bus and nobody talked to me. Today, same as in February. I hardly uttered a word during both bus rides. I cried both days. I felt alone both days. People were singing during both bus rides, and it made me feel sad because I could not join in their singing. I felt out of place both days. And, of course, both days featured long, freezing walks to my car. Luckily, this time I had my girlfriend. I wasn't alone today, and my car wasn't the only one in the parking lot.

As I was driving, it took nearly all of my self-control to drive safely. It strained me, but I managed to get home safely. Safe enough, anyway. Safe physically, but crashed mentally. With that in mind, I started thinking about the darkness again. I came up with a phrase that perfectly describes me. I don't know why, but I guess I needed that phrase to bolster my confidence, even if the phrase itself is a manifestation of the darkness both inside and outside my head. Fuck today. I'm done with today.

I am the Descendant of Darkness.

DECEMBER 3, 2016

I went to see my psychiatrist for the second time. I didn't write about my first visit because it was rather boring and uneventful. I had to sign a bunch of paperwork, and then my psychiatrist asked me questions for about an hour. Boring, right? Well, this second visit wasn't boring at all. In fact, I would consider it to be the most important moment in my entire life. What happened? Let's discover together, shall we?

I didn't know what I was getting myself into when I sat down in that damn chair. I wasn't expecting much from this new visit to the psychiatrist, although I was incredibly anxious. For some reason, being observed by a psychiatrist brought out my best friend: anxiety. My psychiatrist writes on a piece of paper every single time I talk or answer a question. That's very unnerving, and I was scared. I didn't know what he was writing. How could I have known?

He told me I have bipolar disorder. That was his diagnosis. There was no time for a reaction. I'm bipolar. The thought hung heavy in my head like a rain cloud sags lower than all of the other clouds, being dragged down by the immense weight of itself. That's how I felt. I couldn't even register the thought. What? I'm bipolar. It's not my brother who is bipolar, as I have thought for years. Isn't that ironic? I had been diagnosed, and there was no turning back. I was speechless. For once in my life, I was at a loss for words. I had been wondering what was wrong with me for years, and now I know. Why didn't I feel better? I should have been happy. I should have started crying and begging my psychiatrist for more of his vast knowledge on bipolar disorder. I should have wanted to know everything about being bipolar. But why would I do that? Shouldn't I know better than anybody? After all, I'm the one that is bipolar, not my psychiatrist.

He prescribed me a mood stabilizer, Abilify, to suspend my emotions. I had been waiting my entire life to hear those words, and yet nothing registered inside of me. I still felt empty. What was wrong with me? I can't say those words anymore because I already know the answer. I'm bipolar. What does that even mean? Are these mood stabilizers going to actually help me? I don't know. I'm not sure what to think. I'm bipolar. That thought kept circling inside my head, impressing me with its vigorous strength. I couldn't think about anything else. I'm bipolar. My cousin also happens to be bipolar, but he has managed to live a healthy life on his medication. Is that going to be my future? Am I finally going to be happy? I don't know. I'm bipolar. I don't know what to think about this new revelation. The disclosure of this information is paramount to my survival, and yet I feel nothing. I'm bipolar.

Now I know what's wrong with me.

DECEMBER 13, 2016

I've been fishing only a few times in my life and I can assure you that it is one of the most boring acts of fun or relaxation I've ever participated in. First of all, it is time consuming. Who the hell has time to go fishing? Second of all, the equipment needed is extremely expensive. If you somehow manage to get out to the water you'll be lucky to catch a nibble, let alone a fish. While you're busy waiting for a fish, your only option is to sit (or stand) in silence and listen to the supposedly soothing sounds of nature. Seems like a waste of time and effort, honestly.

In my opinion, fishing is absolutely boring. When you catch a fish, you either throw it back (if you're fishing for sport) or you kill it and save it for supper. What kind of demented fun is that? I don't know, perhaps I am overreacting. I think I'm being realistic, but that's debatable.

I think my dad sums up fishing best.

"Fishing? Fishing is boring," he says. "But catching, that's where the fun is at. Nobody wants to go fishing. They want to go catching."

See, our neighbor who lives across the street has a decently sized pond in his front yard. I don't know much about fish or aquatic life or anything, but I do know you can catch a good-looking catfish in his pond, big enough to tell a fisher's lie. I could say I caught a catfish as long as I am tall and it wouldn't be a lie because of how deep and menacing that pond looks, and on account of how many damn catfish live in it. There's some truth to that last statement, too, because I used to fish in that pond with my uncle. We used to call my uncle Captain Kirk, and I used to imagine he was a real captain and the neighbor's pond was an ocean and I was a sailor on Captain Kirk's crew. But we never had a boat to use, not to mention we didn't need one, so we always stayed on the dock and fished from there.

I must have been no older than seven or eight when I went fishing for the first time. I took my little fishing rod and reel, happily ran across that treacherous road separating our house from our neighbor's house, and followed my uncle. He seemed to be an expert about fishing and types of bait and hooks and rods and reels and fish. I could hardly wrap my head around using worms as bait. I always thought worms were nothing but nasty little critters that slithered across the ground when it rained and you had to try not to step on one, almost like a children's game. Apparently, worms could be beneficial, too. And so I started fishing, casting out my first line with some help from the Captain.

It probably took some maneuvering, but I ended up catching a giant catfish that was, as I said before, as long as I was tall at the ripe old age of seven or eight years, of course. I was probably excited about it, but for some reason the joy of catching that monstrous beast never stuck with me. I didn't really enjoy fishing like I should have. Why couldn't I find anything fun about fishing? I could never figure it out at that age, and I still couldn't figure it out ten years later. Until today. Today, I figured out why I hate fishing. But first I'll do a quick rundown of my morning and afternoon.

My day started on a tipsy moment as I was getting ready for school. Last night I doubled my Abilify dosage due to my psychiatrist's orders, and I felt the side effects of it this morning. I was dizzy and disoriented throughout the morning, and, to be honest, the feeling lingered for the rest of the day.

I first realized my day would be awful during English class. We just finished reading Ken Kesey's *One Flew Over the Cuckoo's Nest* and now we're beginning a project. We were assigned into groups of four or five to complete the project. Our objective was to effectively diagnose and give treatment options for the mental illnesses of four characters: Chief Bromden, Harding, McMurphy, and Nurse Ratched. One of the possible diagnoses for McMurphy was bipolar disorder. When I heard my group discussing bipolar disorder, I felt entirely surreal. How could my fellow classmates so easily discuss the bane of my existence? I started to feel like McMurphy, and I wondered how he felt sitting inside that damn ward room.

But my thoughts shifted until I started to look past McMurphy. Why should I limit myself to one character? See, I started to feel like a character in a story. If truth comes to truth, I am a character in a story. These words are my story, and I am the character behind these words. I may even be part of the words themselves. How are you going to prove it, though? Are you going to sit there and try to analyze me as a character like my classmates? That's just what this world does, huh? This world is always trying to analyze and study me. How do you analyze something you know nothing about? You don't have the foggiest idea what it's like to be me. These words are simply illusions about my emotions. You aren't capable of handling the truth. I'm a dynamic character with static characteristics. How do you analyze that? Who is my character foil? What are the motifs in my life? What am I running from so damn bad that I need to sit down and write my thoughts? I dare you to propose my hamartia. I'm an increasingly interesting character displaying maximum statistics, a statistical advantage. I hold persistence at maximum capacity, highest status, hand-made quality. I have bipolar characteristics, intrinsic polar opposites comprised of opposition. I'm always at the North and South poles, but I never touch the heat of the equator. The equalizing line of equilibrium is a concept barely grasped by my mind. Analyze that, you fucking trash compactor. You're nothing but a dust collecting pest hell-bent on being the best student.

I felt like that the entire rest of the class. How could my peers so easily discuss about McMurphy as if he were bipolar? I felt that I could have taken McMurphy's place and my classmates could have been talking about me. They weren't exactly disgracing McMurphy, but it still felt odd. It felt wrong, like hysterically laughing at a funeral. Except it was worse than laughing at a funeral. It felt more like crashing your car into a funeral procession and then deciding not to take the blame because there were no deaths, other than the corpse slowly deteriorating in a box. I think that's what I felt during English class.

Physics was frustrating, as usual. Allow me to give a description of how an average day in my physics class unfolds. Physics class can be easily defined with a simple analogy, really. Physics class begins when our teacher sets up an industrial fan at the front of the classroom. She flips the switch to the on position, waits for a cold breeze to begin flowing, and then climbs up onto her desk, which rests next to the fan. Unbuckling her pants, she calmly allows her ass to moon our entire class. With her ass facing the fan, she begins to shoot diarrhea out of her asshole like a rapid-fire machine gun spurts out bullets. Taking her crutch, she begins smacking the diarrhea droplets as they fly out of her ass. The beating of her crutch forces the chocolate soup to furiously spin in a flying vortex of nastiness. As soon as it began, the plug loosens and the fan stops whirling. Her asshole turns to a steady drip, drip, drip instead of a full-blown eruption. And it's over. But that's what my physics class is like, in my opinion. Our class is repeatedly doused, day after day, by wave after wave of shit shrapnel.

By the time French class rolled around, I was practically in tears. I literally almost started crying in the middle of class. Ashley sat across from me and she could tell I was having trouble, but there was nothing she could do for me. Honestly, I think she was hurt more than I was. She really wanted to help me, but she couldn't. Nobody can help me.

Later in the evening, I had to sit through my little sister's Christmas concert in the auditorium. The only thing I could think about was those kids. I couldn't get my mind off of all the happy little kids dancing and singing on stage. It was truly sweet, innocent, and joyous. But my dark mind wondered what those kids would grow up to be. What would they be like in high school? Which kids will be the drug dealers? Which ones will be the druggies? Who is going to overdose? Where are the bullies? Which kids will be the victims of bullying? Where are the popular kids? What about the nerdy kids? Where is everyone going to be when they are older? Are they going to keep living in this small, rural town? Will they move away to a bigger and better area? What is going to happen to these tiny, happy kids?

I thought about these things because I knew that I used to be one of those kids standing on stage. It was always terrifying, honestly. I always had butterflies breaking out of cocoons inside my stomach.

They would relentlessly push upwards, flying out of my esophagus. But I had a major difference from all of those kids up on stage today. I was never happy. I was always a sad, pathetic kid with an eerie childhood. Deep down, I know I'm still like that. I'm a bipolar freak, in case you didn't know already. But, for some reason, I want all kids to know that they deserve to be happy. Even adults should know that they need to be happy sometimes. I think people forget about being happy because life is so demeaning.

I figured out why I hate fishing. I feel too much like a fish to enjoy fishing. When the sunlight reflects a certain way through the water, I know people can see my rainbow gills. I'm different from all of the other, normal fish. As I swim through the water, I try to jump in the air as a grand spectacle of entertainment. As I go up, I smack my head on a block of ice because the river has frozen over. The poor fish thought it saw an opening in the ice, went to jump, and disappointingly rebounded off of the clear, unbreakable ice. The river played a deceitful trick by tempting the innocent fish to break the surface.

The little fish spots some delicious bait, an excellent treat. He goes to grab the bait, but he ends up getting his mouth snagged on a fisherman's hook. One yank and the fish is out of the water, flopping around on someone's deck or boat. He flops around on the deck haphazardly, struggling for his life. He wants to die, but he still has enough oxygen to survive. Then, almost worse than dying, the fisherman tosses him back into the water. The fish spends every waking moment waiting for the next hook to appear. That's all that fish can do; it worries until there is nothing left to worry about. That's when the next hook descends into the icy water, churning up a miniature hurricane. The fish is never safe.

DECEMBER 18, 2016

This is a monologue of monological thoughts spewed to an audience of one, myself. I beat a horse to death then kept beating it even while it was dead. That's called beating a dead horse. I beat words like I beat my horses, until they're dead. I use words so often that they grow weary and collapse, then I pick up a stick and beat them again. My pencil attacks words, letters at a time, until the page is turned and the words are dead. The maniac has returned for a mentally induced sequence of psychotic mania. I am in a frenzy, a frenetic blend of emotions, and foaming from the mouth. Mentally, I'm as delirious as the disgruntled incubation of chickens in the Arctic Circle. Physically, I feel like Edward Scissorhands trying to wipe his ass without giving himself a raging case of hemorrhoids. I'm a natural hemophiliac trying to pass off my disease as something innocent, like necrophilia. What? That's not innocent? It's wrong to stick your dick in the eye socket of a skull and crossbones? The Jolly Roger meets Richard the Dick, a private pirate seeking to claim yer booty. I am a maniac experiencing mania in a fit of hypomania. I received a bipolar diagnosis thirteen years too late. "Hi, my name is Justin and I live in a constant comatose." Is this Alcoholics Anonymous? Sorry, I think this is the wrong meeting. I was scheduled to meet with Death. Have you seen Him by chance? No? Okay, well, have a shitty day, you damn alcoholics. I hope you all relapse and keel over like a beer can dropped on the ground, spilling out its Miller Light or Coors Light or

Bud Light or Corona Light or any other generic brands you enjoy slurping. The lingering smell of beer on your breath makes me wish that my nausea would induce a fit of vomiting. What's wrong? Did I somehow offend a compulsive drinker? Are you upset that I'm a compulsive thinker? Or does it bug you that I have the quickest wit? Does it irk you that I use multiple synonymous terms to say the same thing more than once? If you can stomach that corrosive acid you call a drink, you can stomach the piercing insults I call my words. But you should be warned about the side effects of dealing with a pragmatically inclined individual. Anger and denial, an unflinching disposition, the realization of hatred, and death are all side effects. I wish every one of you callused, old, snarling bastards would take a snap at me so I could prove how hypocritical you are. I'll grab you in the throat until you're hopelessly choking, unable to swallow the pain I have produced. I'll stab you in the abdomen until the skin where your abs ripped is dramatically thinned. Do you think I'm provoking you while I'm mindlessly choking you? Truth is, I don't care about what you think. My anxiety cares about it, but I don't. And those are the differences between you and me. And that's why I'm sitting here talking to myself through my own words. Am I provoking myself into talking more? Or am I simply a provocative person with a popular persona for causing disturbances? This is the dilemma of the frenzied maniac. My excessive thoughts become mortifying expressions of amplified destruction. I am the maniac that acts out of cordial fashion, the reintroduction of verbal whips and lashes to smack across your naked asses. I desire adequate and painful action, the fulfillment of irrational thoughts in action. I'm acting as a collective passion, which is why I see myself as never crashing or collapsing. I never completely crash or collapse because the collective whole is still out there battling the world. One part of my system may be left defenseless, but that doesn't mean the rest of me is broken or diseased. I am unreasonably perverse, and pervertedly adverse to those who seek success. What are you trying to be successful for? Don't you know there is only room for one maniac? Are you still suspicious? You know, they say people who make lists are more likely to be successful. That's a load of bull because there is no proper way to measure success. How do you determine who is successful and who is a failure? Am I successful for spinning these words off the loom before the cloth arrives at the factory? Does this make me a maniacal menace with a full force of pent-up rage to burn these pages with? Lost in the frantic fury of a furious and fiery rage, I go berserk as humans on reality television shows acting like beastly animals. I go on a manic episode like the grand finale of a popular and successful television series. I am successful if you measure success by the stature of my repertoire. If you were to read my repertoire, portfolio, or resume, you would be stunned at the repetitiveness it presents. How can one maniac be so insightful and indulgent in his thoughts and actions? How can one maniac be such an incompetent and hypocritical asshole? Those are bipolar issues, if you must know what I just stated. Black and white thinking is like an Indian skinning scalps while a doctor stitches up the Indian's severed head. How did nobody fucking notice the degeneration of countless generations? If you hadn't noticed, I'm at the end of the line of this tug-o-war known as life. I am as hated as *The Communist Manifesto* manifested for purely platonic reasoning. Why draft the creation of a principle of government if you never intended for it to be ran this way? Why give birth to a child if you never thought it would behave this way? Why am I spewing these thoughts nonstop like I spilled the letters to a Campbell's soup alphabet can? Forgive me and my thoughts, for I am quite appreciative. Here, allow me to appreciate the infestation of cosmetic surgery meant to improve your hideous facial expressions. I appreciate the fact that you would rather look like a plastic Barbie ass as opposed to a plain old ugly donkey ass. Oops! Did I somehow offend you once again? Do I need to reinstate my thought patterns, tactical maps of matter maniacally arranged by the simple thought of achieving a pattern? My mind works like a chronologically organized hoarder, stacking items in boxes labeled from the shipment date to the time received. What were you expecting, the chronicles of my life released in chronological order? My memories are dispersed in an order of appearance in direct conjunction with my own thoughts and experiences. Why should I start directly at the beginning and finish at the end? How in the fuck am I supposed to determine the end? Is suicide the end of this twisted tightrope? The rope is bent out of proportion, tangled like a silky web. The web itself is mainly a symbol for the mania that goes on inside my head. The hyperactivity of hypomania is an act I have seemingly mastered, finally plastered to this engorged brain and enforced by an entire gang of rambunctious thoughts. The master of being hyper, I seek to revoke the acquisition of accusations about me being a lazy, malfunctioning, skinny-boned particle of malnutrition. My rise to stardom becomes the North Star for those who wish to delve deeper into the mystery of an exciting sequence of events I like to call my present tense. Past participles, oblong obstacles sticking out of the pages, are a unique ending to the past. My future tense is hardly working, unimaginably unfathomable, a paradoxical problem proven false. Why is it a problem if it was proven false? Is it a problem because I created a paradox? That's why I said my present tense; that's me in the moment spawning a creative conscience unrivaled, unchallenged by fascinatingly boring rivals. I'm a spontaneous monster, suddenly popping out of a thought bubble. I'm an outdated method, a coat hanger abortion ready for action at any given moment. I'm truly a creative spectacle, a spectacular production of maniacally based manufacturing. I'm a devious dreamer of schemes, scheming endlessly. I'm a divisor of dreams, dividing and slicing up fragments of reality and cremating them. Schemes of previously unimaginably complex imagination run rampant in my avid dreams, trampling the common process of predetermined thoughts called your thought process. Your conscience wouldn't dare attempt to comprehend the animosity deployed and upholstered by the irritable infestation of imagination in my demented brain. I'm a bombastic spastic prone to excessive and over exaggerated crashes. I was built in a factory by a handful of savages who damaged my internal gears, cogs, and rhythms. I was built to withstand these few hateful handfuls. Did you miss my diagnosis, the misdiagnosis of scattered dialogue and stories? Medication couldn't eliminate the brain waves you thought could be vanquished. How do you evaporate the core of the sun? How do you control the core of my thoughts, fused together by the insatiable heat of cruelty and inhumane abuse? Aripiprazole is nothing but an intrusive chemical pending entrance into my mind, but first my bloodstream. It swims upstream until it reaches my brain. Then, the mood stabilizers hit me like a tranquilizer dart stuck in the jugular, safely tucked away and tugging at my brain like a hook caught between the gills of a salmon.

When my mood is upbeat, I'm swimming downstream. When my mood is lower than any beat can measure, I'm swimming upstream straight into the current, wondering why I'm not making any progress. Do you honestly think that medication can contain the beast within? My psychiatrist thinks that. He seems to have forgotten that the beast is already alive and thriving, peaking for its full potential. The beast has been unleashed, the chains guarding it eroded away long ago, and now there is no earthly substance strong enough to tame it. Otherworldly words couldn't feint this beast. Normal words couldn't fight this beast. I can't defeat this beast. This beast has conquered me, stomped on me dominantly like a predominantly dominant round of domination. I excitedly present the revisitation of thoroughly executed thoughts. These are the thoughts of a maniac. This soliloquy is nearly at its end, but first I must give an aside to the audience. Wait! There is no audience besides myself! How do I give an aside to the person standing on stage? With that thought, the monologue that monolithic literary dynasties greed for is finally over.

DECEMBER 21, 2016

You're lying down, staying low while I glide across the air on this high note. Did I say glide? I meant I'm really flying through the sky, doing the impossible; previously implausible dreams are now a vibrant reality. Never tell people your intentions or they'll mock you for your intelligence. Never tell people your plans or they'll tell you that the rock you're trying to climb is improbably difficult to climb, the pass you're trying to walk is impassable, and the canyon you're trying to jump is incredibly impossible. They'll tell you that you're not talented enough to do the things you love, but you have to forget the words they say in order to create your own. They'll try to tell you that you can't accomplish things, but you have to rise above their diminished expectations to demolish their supposed usurpations. They'll try to kick you off that rock, try to drive you out of that pass, and try to push you into that canyon. You have to overcome the obstacles they have placed before you. When these obstacles arise in an accumulated fashion, you must prove that you are capable of handling the stress presented. You must devour their insults and allow them to be fuel in the cylinders and pistons that drive your determination to conquer and conquest. That's how you be successful.

For every kid dreaming up supposedly unachievable dreams like me, these words are for you. This is for every obstacle you've ever faced. This is for every inspiration you've never chased. This is for every aspiration you've had to make. These words are your ticket to success. Stride and bask in the glorious feeling that is given by these words. Quit trudging through the drudgery of normal life. Grow new legs made of stilts and catapult yourself over the competition. But they say you should be a leader instead of being a follower. I say you should first gain the knowledge and wisdom needed to be a leader. What good would a leader be if he or she couldn't lead? They say you shouldn't follow in other's footsteps. I say you should follow those footsteps until the person walking in front of you gets a cramp and keels over. After that, you're free to make your own footsteps. You can determine your own path, but choose wisely. They may tell you to pick the fastest path, but I say pick the most efficient road to success. If the road is already paved, take it anyway. Don't listen to the things that others try to drag you down with. They'll try to tell you to trudge through the road not taken, but I say choose the better option. They say not to follow others, but I say stick a pilot light up someone's ass and use them as a guide. Allow their words to be your goad. Allow these words to be your inspiration. Now, set out with a purpose to achieve the most given your newfound determination.

DECEMBER 23, 2016

I'm the commander of a ship flipping shit, spewing loose fuses at the deckhands and making a mess of the deck. Swab the poopdeck, swab the poopdeck! Who the fuck is going to clean up this mess? I called my deckhands, but nobody answered. My first mate deceived and deserted me, leaving me with nothing but the high seas to call my own. Where are my deckhands? I yell across the deck and hear nothing in response. Where did they go? Why am I alone? I'm a commander in peril, facing perilous obstacles never before conquered. I'm an explorer who has never set foot on new land. Come out, deckhands! I know you're on this ship! Did they commit a mutiny? Did they think I would be this pissed and livid? Did you think I would assume the role of a psychopath? What is this monstrosity I call my ship? Why is the wood warped and splintering? Why is the mast bowed and ready to collapse? Why is the steering wheel teetering on its edge? Wait a second, circles don't have edges! What the fuck is wrong with my mind? How dare I notice geometry at a time like this! My mind is warped like the boards of the ship, out of proper proportion. That's a statement blown out of the water. Now, as I sit here and crumble, I feel seasick. Is that a sea breeze I see floating in the mist? Misty water in my eyes, and I pissed off every whale and otter floating around in the muggy water. What? Once again, where are my deckhands? Did someone throw them in the mist? Did they throw themselves overboard like they were walking the plank? Maybe they forced each other to walk the plank until one member remained, and he decided to jump overboard and join the rest of his crew. Report for duty, crew! My crew was filled with the worst pirates a captain could ask for. Am I a captain or a commander? Help, I am in danger of being paralyzed by peril! SMS, SMS! Save my ship! What are you looking at? Why are you not responding to my message? How come you won't save me? Where did my deckhands go? Perhaps my deckhands are merely under the top deck, enjoying a cozy round of beer and rum while they gamble conceitedly. Who can spit the farthest? Who can break the most pieces of wood in under ten seconds? Who can spit a line of words made from fire faster than the ass of a gazelle running away from a hungry lion? It's a hopeless chase because the lion is in haste, fast-paced, and traveling at a faster rate. Once again, I must reinstate that I am the commander of this ship, and I ask of you to sail away on a journey with me. Retrieve the troves of treasure that await those who seek discovery! Sail this ship, worthy deckhand. Guide us to safer waters, where the sea does not nip at our heels and snap at our bow. Bring us to the light of passage, where the salty spit of this icy sea would not dare to be thrown against our stern. Watch our starboard side as we sail away!

I'm the commander of this adventure, and I say you should venture elsewhere. This is a warning. Turn back now before the ship is sunk, the treasure forgotten, and hope is lost.

DECEMBER 25, 2016

It's Christmas day. In my younger years, Christmas was an exciting time because it was something to look forward to. Now I'm lucky to possess the strength to wake up in the morning to open presents, assuming I am worthy of receiving presents from my parents after all the stress I cause them. I feel as if Christmas and the festive spirit is only present as a facade for people to conceal their troubles, burying their worries until the holidays are over. How can people be excited for something as silly and frivolous as exchanging gifts? This time of year depresses me, and I know I'm not the only person who becomes depressed during the holidays.

I guess I should start by saying that I am thankful for my parents and my family. I appreciate everything they have done for me. I am grateful that they support and care about me. It's just a shame that their efforts and sentiments are almost entirely worthless. I feel as if the weight of this mortal world is crushing my skull, pushing my body into the ground, and sucking me into the vortex below. I'm not talking about Hell because I don't believe in any of that far-fetched, hocus-pocus, God and Satan, fake, phony, implausible, Heaven and Hell bullshit. I'm talking about dying. I feel like this world is pulling me into the altruistic void of death. I'm receding, falling faster with every waking moment, and tumbling in limitless space if I somehow manage to sleep. I couldn't sleep last night.

I used to not be able to sleep before holidays because I was so excited to wake up. Once, I stayed up all night before Easter, sitting in bed reading Magic Tree House books until I saw sunlight wrap its delicate fingers around the windowsill. That's when I knew I wouldn't get in trouble if I woke my parents up and asked if I could start looking for hidden eggs. Of course, I never had a problem finding eggs. In our small house, I had practically memorized the locations of each egg. That was a long time ago.

Have you ever wondered what one of my thoughts looks like? I wondered that this morning as I sat there in the living room, gingerly unwrapping my presents as if I was afraid they would run away from me when I opened them up and they saw who they belonged to. I would run away from myself, given the opportunity. But, I started thinking about what my thoughts would physically feel and look like. My mind began this process by imagining the extraction of a thought from my disturbed brain, my tortured consciousness, and my lack of a reliable conscience. The extracted thought was grimy and black. It sloshed and splashed and oozed and wiggled, splattering tar throughout the room. I pressed my hand down upon its center to reduce its struggle. During this time, I further analyzed my thought's appearance. It resembled a peculiar combination of motor oil and dried, black paint lazily stirred together. It was dark, black, and grotesque in every aspect. With a thought like that, it's no wonder I question my own sanity. I hold my thoughts in the highest sanctity, which is why I was stunned to find how depressing my thought appeared. I felt disgruntled with the results of my examination. I carefully picked up my thought and shoved it back into my ear, pushing until I could no longer feel its rough texture against my smooth skin. Maybe that's why my ears always appear greasy. Perhaps my thoughts attempt to sneak out of my ears. Or, maybe they simply poke their tiny heads out for a quick look around. Either way, despite being illogical, it would make sense. Does that make sense?

Merry Christmas to me.

DECEMBER 31, 2016

'd turn a golden path laced with roses into a moldy patch of rotting dandelion seeds. That's called spreading my seed, my attitude, and turning everything in my way into weeds. I'll turn around and spray a crime scene with Simple Green and Clorox bleach. How do you investigate a clean and blank slate? Is there anything incriminating about cleanliness? I was simply scrubbing the nastiness of the crime down the drain. Out, damned spot! Out, you fucking corpse! Oops! I didn't mean to get rid of that body without first consulting with an investigator. Detective? You call yourself a detective? I only speak to Sherlock Holmes and his partner, Watson. Who the fuck are you? Who do you think you are, parading around the crime scene acting like you're confident enough to solve the crime itself? I'll stab a piece of furnished copper wire with a metal rod and proceed to ask who started the electric fire. Why is my hair frizzing with static electricity? I'm too dynamic and constantly changing to be involved with your static sense of self. I'm going off the wire, straight off the fax machine and the telegraph. I'm a relic of the past coincidentally trapped in my own past. Is there a prerequisite for that? Or am I the precedent? Did I set the bar higher than the precedents I previously set? Truth is, I surpass my own precedents to provide enough evidence to prove that I am the greatest. I'm a king of kings, and I'm still built sturdier than the Colossus of Rhodes. You defile my presence with your eyes twitching, bewitching witches with your evil grins. Meanwhile, while you're busy scratching your ass and patting your crack, I've got other shit to deal with. A tower of shooting flames is telling me to bring the heat. I see faces in the flesh, stuck between the threshold of life and death. I smell their rotting corpses burning in the heat. I taste their ashes on my tongue like flakes of melted snow. I hear their screams echoing in my ears. I feel their heat, specifically searing me and making my eyes water. I speak these words with no filter, no edit, no rewind, no censor, and no bullshit. You're so full of shit, if I called a septic tank cleaner I bet he wouldn't know where to begin. Repeated harassment is apparently an appropriate action for someone who acts like an asshole, like you. I'd suffocate you by taking a clothespin and clipping your nose, putting my hand over your mouth, and then sitting back and watching you struggle to gasp for air. You're a disgrace for reading my words with a dismissive and abysmal attitude. As punishment for your negativity, I should piss all over your initials carved into the toilet bowl. You carved your initials there because you're a conceited prick that likes seeing your own name even when you piss. Can't you take a fucking break from loving yourself for one second?

I'm ridiculously meticulous, checking my clock for the accuracy down to the nanosecond. I hear the tick tick ticking every fucking moment inside my head. I check the seconds, but I never come in second. I'm a first prize, first place, first served, first came, self-made man. I ride on top of my confidence, too much confidence. I'm confident in the regard that I am the greatest spinner of words, the winner with courageous fingers, the brave hero of fantasies and fables morphed into reality. It's no longer confidential that I have the most confidence of anybody ever born. How could I be that type of person and get away with it? How can I be so mischievous? How can I do things so evil that villains get encouraged by it? I'm as radioactive as setting off live grenades in a microwave cooking nuclear waste. If you ask about my accolades, I'll just tell you anything about myself. Everything I do is an immediate success. I'm immensely successful, with strong pectorals to boot. One time, this guy tried to tell me that balls are heavier than thoughts. I told him that I think he thought wrong. Some say I think outside the box. I say I was always outside the box, trying to sneak a peek inside. But I'll throw that fucking box in the ash pit and burn that shit. I want the smoke to rise up and pollute the entire atmosphere. The simple thought of thinking burns up the crinkled box called your cerebral membrane. How well does cardboard stand a chance in defending the amped entrance of the commander in thought? I am the commander in thought, commandeering the creative boundaries stipulated by the immolation of your brain. I stand and breathe deeply on the precipice of deep thinking. You silently retreat to the tumultuous caverns of opinionated thought that you so kindly rupture constantly. You're a scrambled opinion, a synchronized act of misunderstanding acted upon outside forces. From the Diddy to the Donkey to the Kong, I'm the greatest king. I'm the king of a Vietnamese and Agent Orange infested jungle. Constantly attacking and being attacked by the Vietcong, I wield my royal scepter. I'll run through your house and perturb your suburban residence like an airplane experiencing turbulence. I'm turbulent, an uncontrolled substance tried to be turned into a controllable object controlled by the press of a remote control. I splashed canola oil and acid into the engine of the plane, and now it's corroding the metal of the blades. I'm about to fly and crash this plane like a terrorist gone insane, an Arabic man screaming gibberish and shit. I'm splashing these oils and fumes all over the place; the scene of the crash became a memorial to rejoice my name. They say you can only take one path in life, but how can that be true? I'm a sociopath and a psychopath. How am I supposed to choose between two synonymous terms used to describe the same person? Fuck the mirage that I claim as my attitude. I'm bursting out, snapping off these chains and going insane. The abortion doctor forgot to latch my straitjacket before I hopped out of the womb and consumed him and his family. Is that animal enough to be called a part of the animal kingdom? This attitude is crazed, maniacal in every aptitude. In a manic mood, even serotonin and dopamine are slowly choking me through strangulation and suffocation. Even on the brink of suicide, the rush of my creative thinking was a spectacle to behold. My wind warps like it's going hypersonic, blowing the sound out of a barrier of water. That means I'm blowing this backwater town out of the water. Maniacal hope is like an open wound, festering with pus still flowing from the cut. I'm a medical anomaly, an animal claimed to be a clinical psycho. The meditation medicine won't allow me to meditate. I'm trapped in this eternally mixed state of being. This medication seems to boost my impatience like a rocket booster tank propelling a rocket into space. I'm launching into orbit, warping space and time in my wake. I'm a galactic astronaut, the entire aspiration of humankind. You're all miniature humanoids to me, microscopic ants of mankind. Childhood and boyhood were foreign concepts to me, but now I'm soaring through the galaxy on a quest to save the universe. You can worship a baby rocking in its manger. Meanwhile, I'll be rocking off in my spaceship. Blasting off for the stars, I take my past and snap its throat and slice its jugular. I'm an intergalactic warrior, a true space warlord. I'm on a mission to pass and surpass, and this is the starting line. My train of thought goes off on a tangent and still manages to stray back on track.

That's how my mind exploits a single thought and churns it into a melting pot of fantastical imagery for your mind to wrap itself around.

JANUARY 1, 2017

The past year has been, for lack of a better word, insane. Yet, somehow, the passing of the New Year seems anticlimactic, as if it shouldn't even be happening. In all honesty, I couldn't care less. It doesn't even feel real to me. Did this past year actually happen? Am I imagining this? Is all of this, the journals and the therapist and the psychiatrist and the parents and the school and the girlfriend and the depression and the bipolarity, a figment of my vast imagination? Did any of these things happen? That's what I'd like to know, but nobody is going to let me know.

Last year, I hardly wrote at all in January. I hope I can manage to write more during this month, but you never know until it happens. January was the height of my depressive slump. Does that make any sense to you? It doesn't make any sense to me, but I said it anyway. How can there be a height in a slump? In all honesty, I think January was one of the worst months for me, personally. I wrote a meager amount of entries in January, as compared to the productivity of other months.

I see a flash and a spark fly in the darkness. I still tap into the dark, the black hole that has consumed my entire life. I use its massive mass and knowledge to my advantage, spitting out its thought as if I planned it. I used to try and read the map of my life in the dark, but now I sit and wonder what will become of my path. There's the snap of a flint and steel and I see the spark again, and my hands reach out to grab it. My fingers burn at its touch, but I firmly grasp it. My palms are sweaty, hot-blooded meat ready to serve. But I swerve, and my car goes maniacal and berserk, dodging telephone poles and cars alike. I still see the same gray clouds I saw when I was four years old. Except now the sky darkens, preparing for the apocalypse I call my rise to stardom.

JANUARY 5, 2017

I almost crashed my car today. I apologize for not building up any suspense, but I couldn't possibly hold back this torrential influx of words. These words are eager to be devoured by your awaiting eyes. Your eyes strike the page like coiled vipers, hissing in anger as you quickly glance over the words. You must devour these words. Eat them, digest them, and use them. Become these horrifying words. What happened today? Well, let me tell you a story.

I was driving over to Ashley's house after school. I approached a T-bone intersection. In front of me there was a highway, the very same road that I live on. Anyway, I looked to my left, checking for cars. I didn't see anything. I looked to my right, and I saw a bus coming. I wanted to get out in front of the bus.

How much time had passed? I thought it was only a split second, but it must have been more than that. What other explanation could there be? My medication had a warning label on the bottle. My medication impaired my driving abilities. No! I had forgotten.

I turned left out into the intersection, trying to get ahead of the bus. When I did this, I was checking to my right, looking at the bus. Then, I heard a horn blaring against my eardrum. I whipped around and looked to my left. There was a different bus barreling toward me, about to crash into my car. I barely got out of the way. I missed that bus, the one coming from my left, by approximately ten feet.

By the time I got to Ashley's house, I was shaking and crying. She held me in her arms until I stopped crying, but the damage was irreparable. It was my fault. I pulled out in front of that bus without looking, and it nearly cost me my life. I almost died today. See, it's strange. I've been wanting to die for years, but, when the opportunity presented itself, my instincts took over and I dodged the bus. What the fuck is wrong with me?

JANUARY 9, 2017

I'm strange, covered in scales with alien antennas popping out of my head. I'm a fire-breathing dragon born from the irrational myths of the past millennium. My talons come out because I'm chemically imbalanced, teetering on the edge precariously, but still breathing the hatred of my arrogance. My adrenaline rushes are like firing an entire military arsenal. My flesh and body dangle at the sight of a problem or issue. Most people say there is a delightful air outside and they'd like to go out there, but I say I'd rather stay inside and stare at my own computer glare. What's with the rhyming? The overly complicated complication of complicated thoughts is called my cerebral interior. Your inferior genes match your fake designer jeans, peasant. You're a fucking serf, and breathing the same air as you makes me gag in disgust. You're disgusting, a disgruntled man whose despicable sight gives me indigestion. You're abysmal, and I'm saying that as I sit here sipping down a bottle of Pepto-Bismol. These conversations are inferior interactions for my brain to try and rationalize. The rapture from my talent is indivisible, implausibly inconceivable, yet I still dare to dream. I aim higher than an archer pointing their bow and arrow straight into the air. That archer is trying to commit suicide, but it doesn't matter to me. I could hardly care about some random archer I happened to pass by. I broke the mold when they sculpted my mind. I'm the most hypocritically adept at being inept, plus I'm showing a knack for lacking in discrepancies. What kind of a paradox is that? It seems every time I write I create a new paradox for your mind to suffer from. You'll be thinking of this conundrum five to ten days from now, wondering how I handled these words in the span of time I managed. I utter ceaselessly as I write, but I never stutter. These words are clear as antifreeze mixed into your glass of water. My tantalizing thoughts are dripping down the wall, painting the entire room with doom and gloom. I'm a lunatic who was spoon-fed looniness for my entire childhood. They say the pen is mightier than the sword. I say I'll split the sword in half so I have double daggers. I'll dual-wield my new weapons, slashing out at those who go against my word. My pen is the penultimate weapon, lashing out at all of those who oppose my word. I'm an antagonist, an antonym for generous people, an antecedent, the fear present in your mind before a beating. I'm an alcoholic's housewarming gift, a basket of wine. I'm a savage warrior running into extravagant homes and killing all the inhabitants. I want to abolish my hair follicles until I look like a chemotherapy recipient, a cancer patient patiently waiting for their next round of treatment. The chemotherapy gives me a chemical imbalance, and now I'm imbalanced, strange, and quirky.

It's safe to assume that I am different from most people. But, in a unique way, everybody is different from one another. That's what makes us human. I know I'm not the only person that has felt different from the normal, spoken and unspoken codes of society. Who could feel any more different than me? For that reason, I feel compelled to address the different people. It's normal to feel different, if you know what I mean. That's how I feel every day of my life. I feel different, and, for me, that's normal. If you feel that way, it's safe to assume that you're different. Being different is the foundation for being a successful force in this twisted world.

JANUARY 11, 2017

I've been taking Abilify, also known as aripiprazole, to stabilize my mood for the past few weeks. However, due to upping my doses every other week or so, my body has become restless. My psychiatrist told me, through his thick, Indian accent, that this is a common side effect.

"Yes, this is a common side effect," he said. "You must take fifty milligrams of Benadryl every night to counteract the state of restlessness that your body is currently in."

He also said that the Benadryl will improve my morning routine, which has been a struggle. My antidepressant, Lexapro, gives me a drowsy, uneasy feeling. I've also been having diarrhea, headaches, a loss of appetite, dry mouth, excessive yawning, and difficulty functioning as a productive member of society.

These medications are dragging me down, but I thought they were supposed to be helping me. Why must my body be assaulted for it to flourish? Perhaps all good things were once twisted, black, and filled with darkness. I know I am filled with darkness, but maybe the darkness has slowly been seeping out of me. Maybe my medication is siphoning the darkness out of my body. That's a pleasant thought, and I openly welcome any pleasant thoughts.

Overall, my quality of life has improved tenfold since beginning Abilify, specifically. My antidepressant helps me avoid having suicidal thoughts and tendencies, but that's not as important as my mood stabilizers. These mood stabilizers give me control over my own body, which is something I never had before. I couldn't control my thoughts, actions, or emotions. Now, with the help of my therapist and psychiatrist, I can express myself in a revolutionary, new and improved form. I always wondered what was wrong with me, and now I know. The mystery is gone, and, although I am slightly disappointed at leaving behind my previous life, I can move forward.

With the aid of my medication, my past hardly haunts me anymore. My memories are obsolete objects of the past, but my future is an illustrious and grand challenge that awaits my grab. I'm pursuing an unparalleled influence, a truly distinguishable talent that sits in my grasp. Finally, I have a purpose in my life. I'm going to publish the greatest story of all time, and I'm going to sit atop the *New York Times* Bestseller List. I used to be unsure of my goal, but now I know exactly what I want to do with my life. I won't be subjected to a menial job performing physically and mentally draining tasks. I'd rather sit at my desk and craft a spellbinding story, a tale of fascination that makes a reader's imagination crave for more.

I told my dad about my plan yesterday, and he seemed to agree with me. He thought it was great that I knew what I wanted to do. But he was also a little concerned, as I expected.

"You shouldn't put all of your eggs in one basket," he said.

"Why not? Isn't that what happens on Easter?"

He got quite the chuckle out of that one. I laughed a little, too. I appreciated the moment, and I savored it for as long as it lasted. I felt genuinely happy, for once. It wasn't a manic happiness. I just felt happy, almost like a normal person. I'm happy.

JANUARY 19, 2017

What happened today? The darkness swallowed me, eagerly devouring the entirety of my being. I was scared I was going to vanish into the darkness. I didn't want to be lost forever, floundering aimlessly in a black expanse for eternity. The smoke snuck up from behind and attacked, hitting me while I was down. It suffocated me, choking me ceaselessly. It was a truly merciless and unrelenting force. I wanted it to finish its job. I wanted Death to surround me. I wanted Death to run His skeletal fingers over my shriveling skin. I wanted to rub my grimy fingers against his smooth cloak, and I wanted to embrace the warm, entrancing fabric. That's what I wanted to happen. Instead, I became engulfed in smoke.

Today, sitting in class, I felt like dying. There was no progression of events preceding this moment. It was as sudden as if somebody had promptly smacked me across the face. That's what it felt like to me. Of course, I somehow managed to continue functioning despite the obvious malfunctions taking place within the hidden compartments of my equally secretive brain. My seemingly adaptive ability to perform at a high standard while being mentally detained is a feat that I constantly achieve in efficient fashion. I must apologize for my words, but it should be known that the darkness swiftly consumed me today. My mind is simply acting accordingly to the actions that the darkness encompasses. I'm accompanied by the darkness. I am the darkness.

What was happening to me? I felt confused. My medication had ceased to stop the invasion of utterly horrifying smoke and darkness. Wasn't my medication supposed to help me? What was going on? Help me! I'm sinking into the smoke! My head bobs up and down, gasping for air. And then someone pulls me out of the darkness for a brief moment. It's a person. He's talking to me. Then he fades away, pushing me back into the smoke. I'm lost again. I reach around with my hands, frantically trying to find something to rest upon. I'm exhausted, subdued by the irreversible darkness. My arms wearily drop to their corresponding sides; they are losers in a losing battle. I feel as crestfallen as Odysseus returning from his Odyssey. This is my Odyssey.

I felt the sudden desire to ditch school and drive myself into an oblivion, a common expression utilized by my mind. I didn't want to kill myself, though. I wanted to crash my car into an innocent car carrying multiple passengers, get out of my car seemingly unscathed, lie on the ground, thrust my hands to my eyes, and sob endlessly on the cold, wet pavement. I wanted to feel the sticky blood upon my palms, rushing through the ravines that traverse my skin. I wanted to hear the paramedics arrive in confusion, wondering why I was sobbing on the ground. I wanted them to rush to my aid, but to no avail. I wanted their futile efforts to be wasted on me while the people in the other car died incredibly painful deaths, trapped beneath the wreckage of their own arrogance. That's what I wanted. But that's not what happened.

I also thought of driving until I reached a beautiful pasture. I wanted to get out of the car, sit in the middle of the grass, and wait. I wanted to wait until it was dark. I wanted to wait until people started worrying about me. I wanted to wait until people finally cared about me. I wanted to wait until this world gave a fuck about me. I wanted to wait until I fucking died from the pain of impatience, becoming fed up with waiting. I wanted to wait until they found my lifeless body. I wanted to wait until someone grieved for me. I wanted to wait for all of these things, but none of them were going to happen. I guess that's what life does to you. It builds you up, then demolishes you twice as fast as you can build yourself up, crushing you until your foundation crumbles. I guess it's time to start building again.

I want to go to a mental hospital, a place where I'd be at peace with people similar to myself. I wouldn't have to worry about how I looked or who talked or didn't talk to me or how social I was or wasn't. Doesn't that sound like a peaceful place? I wouldn't have to worry about people snapping photographs of me every single fucking second of the day. I wouldn't have to worry about people making fun of me because everyone in the facility would be in the same predicament as me. These thoughts bounced around in my head like a pinball bounces off various items in an arcade game. It's definitely better than finding the tension in a set of ropes, or trying to take a trigonometry test while you wish you were dead. That's what I did today, by the way.

I also had a Trivia Team match today. We lost, as usual. That may sound demeaning, but at this point I don't care what you worthless people think of me. If you're still reading this garbage, you must care about me slightly. But I'm the razor edge of the knife that hasn't sliced your fingers yet. It's inevitable, and you'll be less tempted to use the knife if it slices your fingers. I'm vicious, throwing tantrums with my malignant bite.

The weather corresponded to my mood. It was pouring rain for the entire evening, further developing the darkness that had spawned inside my head. I stepped in a puddle getting back on the bus when we went to leave. My shoes were soaking, and my feet were sloshing back and forth. The clouds were a metaphor for my sadness, obviously. Typical of Justin, isn't it?

I can't even take my fucking medicine right. I can't do anything right. I went to take my medicine and I ended up spilling half of it out of the bottle. How fucking pathetic can I possibly be? My one saving grace, if I may call it that, is my medicine. I can't even take my medication without causing problems. What the fuck is wrong with me? I kept spilling my medicine no matter how many times I tried to get it right. I ended up throwing my pill bottle into the cabinet, as if that would solve my inadequacies. I went downstairs and started crying into my pillow. I was alone.

My parents wanted to know what was wrong with me before I sulked downstairs. They wanted me to get it all out. Get what out? You think I always have shit to say? What the fuck is with all of you people? My girlfriend did the exact same thing. They wanted to know what was wrong. You think I fucking know what is wrong all the fucking time? I lived my life in confusion for seventeen years, and now people expect me to have the answer to everything. What the fuck is wrong with everyone? More importantly, what the fuck is wrong with me?

I could hardly live one day without my medicine. How did I do it for seventeen years? Gosh, I started sobbing twice as hard when I had that thought. How did I do it? How did I manage to live like that? At this rate, you would have thought somebody would have noticed something wrong with me a long time ago. But no, I'm too damn good at hiding my emotions around other people. That's a problem. But it's not a problem anymore. I don't have problems because I'm not a real person. I have returned to the darkness. Once again, I emphasize that I am the darkness.

This is the Resurrection of Darkness.

JANUARY 22, 2017

Last night I had a horrific manic episode. Once again, I felt like my medicine had stopped working. Why wasn't my medication working? I had just taken my medicine after dinner. A few hours later, I already felt the effects of the medicine wearing off, leaving me vulnerable and defenseless.

I started pacing around the couch in our family's living room. I circled the couch for twenty minutes, thinking absently to myself. I thought about my book that I was going to write; that's the one you're reading right now. I thought about the story I was telling. I wondered how I was going to get it published and who was going to read it. I asked myself if people were going to like and appreciate my story, no matter how vulgar or inhumane the content. As I circled the couch, my thoughts circled faster and faster around my head, spinning me into a frenzy. I became a frenetic monster with an equally monstrous appearance. I became bipolar.

I kept circling the couch with a vigorous rigor, an increased pursuit of an unobtainable goal. Where was the end? There wasn't an end. I would have kept circling that couch forever if my brother didn't come upstairs and ask me to look at a game he was playing.

"No."

The word came out of my mouth with a vulgar spit and a hateful taste. I flung the word at my brother. What did that idiot want to show me now? Couldn't he see I was busy with my thoughts? Couldn't he see I was busy pacing the entire surface area of our living room? Couldn't he see I was mentally unstable? No. That also happens to be the word I spat at my own flesh and blood, my brother.

My dad looked up from the book he was reading, then started talking to me. "Go see what he wants," he said.

I told him no, too. At that point, I would have told the whole world no to anything they could have possibly asked me. Somebody could have gone up to me and offered me a million dollars and I would have screamed in their face. That's how I felt. That's what it feels like to be irritable and manic. Fear factors and scare tactics blast in my ears, berating me with a constant dread.

Later yesterday evening, after I had started doing my homework, I felt a strange compulsion to run upstairs with my backpack. When I ran upstairs, I dumped the contents of my backpack into the middle of the living room. Folders, spiral notebooks, and papers rained down upon the living room floor like confetti during a victory celebration. Except this time I wasn't celebrating anything. I was pissed, and rightfully so. I was sick and tired of school and homework and stress and being bombarded with a parade of garbage. My mom yelled at me.

"Hey! Clean that up! What are you doing?"

She doesn't understand what it's like to be me. How could she possibly understand? I barely understand myself, honestly. How could anybody understand? These thoughts raced through my head, speeding around in a circle, whizzing and buzzing.

"No."

There it was. It was that fateful word again. No. This time, though, I didn't say it with a hateful attitude. In fact, I said it in a whining, high-pitched voice, as if I was about to cry. That's what ended up happening, by the way. I started crying, rushed into the kitchen, threw myself against a set of cabinets, slumped to the floor, and let the tears roll off of my cheeks and onto the hardwood floors of our kitchen. Everything happened so quickly, and I wasn't even sure why I was crying. Was I crying because my mom had yelled at me? Was I crying because I was experiencing the psychotic nature of a manic episode? I wasn't sure. But

I kept crying for another half an hour, wasting away what little time I have in my life.

Today, after experiencing such a horrid episode yesterday, I was cautious. I talked to my assistant principal, Mr. Johnson, again this morning. We talked about possibly publishing my book, and I got excited. I couldn't stop thinking about it for the rest of the day. It's the only thing I want right now in my life, and maybe I need it. It's the only thing that will soothe me. But, if my story doesn't sell, I fear that suicide will be an overhanging thought that will shadow any of my happy emotions.

After school let out, my dad drove me up to the psychiatrist for my appointment. The psychiatrist was disappointed when I told him that my medication had stopped working. He told me I was experiencing side effects from Lexapro, my antidepressant. I was becoming irritable and uneasy, a terrifically terrible combination. But my psychiatrist helped me. He prescribed me a different medication as an antidepressant, and he told me to stop taking Lexapro. I want to get better, but at this rate I'm not so sure that it will happen. Why won't my serotonin and dopamine just have a truce and balance themselves out?

The road to success is surveyed as having numerous obstacles.

JANUARY 26, 2017

You're trying to assess me as you stand in the middle of the room with your best friends, tapping testicles together. That means you love each other as much as you love yourself. Conceited egomaniacs run rampant like a scampering herd of animals. But you fail to realize that I'm an unsolvable mental case, truly the pinnacle of being a basket case. I'm a pile of baskets stacked at the top of the highest mountain, peaking with my own insanity. I'm dancing, slapping answers onto papers knowing that there's no chance I could possibly be right. When I get the papers back, I take a glance and wonder how I managed to salvage an unsalvageable answer. Are you ready for the next section to read and investigate as I travel at a manic pace? I'm in a panic, but the next session will spin into a general consensus of welcoming. My peers appear in succession, formally declaring a cession of the unalienable rights they call their freedom of speech. They're giving it away to me to use and alter for a higher glory. I'm talking so fast I can barely be understood. These words should be read faster than an atom flying around in the Large Hadron Collider. I'm colliding, smashing atoms within the contention of my mind. I'm just getting so exasperated with all of the hatred plaguing me daily. I'm still an alien, but I'm not that ancient or anxious. I'm bailing history references out of the mist and into the text, a successful endeavor mixed among the rest. Treat me as you will, but know that I spit fire at will. Hit me with a timer and watch the clock tick, but my fingers type as furious as any berserk and curiously leering teenager thinking up new conspiracies never thought before. Here's a suggestion for those of you who doubt my capabilities. When's the last time you had to battle your mind? Has the pain ever mentally stomped you into the manure and muck that sprinkles your mind with a despicable odor? I'm odorous, owing an ode to older folks who broke the yolk wide open when they conceived the very idea of me. I'm filling the sea with plastic bottles and wired straps of metal, electrifying the water and churning the tide. Tsunami waves ride me like Saddam Hussein bombing from the inside of a plane. What was that? I'm not supposed to mention that? Editor! How are you going to censor an uncensored mind of the delirious kind? Reader! How dare you try to claim I'm lying when I say my mind produced these thoughts teetering on its edge! I'm entering the nuthouse, clearing a clear path for clearance. Avoid altering your appearance or it'll be slightly apparent that you're attempting to enter singlehandedly. Use the medication as an excuse to lose the screws that were set loose! I don't have a screw loose, but I do have a superego bigger than the belief of a little red caboose. How dare you say I'm not allowed to rhyme? Are you trying to pick a fight with me? I'll fight like the cyclopes, gobble you up and pick the bones clean out of my teeth. How do you justify the right to lie? I don't eat nasty meat. Psych! Did you feel that burn? Do you feel these words burning into your skin? Why don't you take a little razor to your wrists? No! What am I even saying? I'm the one that's truly crazy, a maniac gone insane. They say I went off the deep end, but I'm really diving in shallow waters, floating around and stalling the depth of my life. I won't allow the tension to de-escalate, resulting in my manic states. Put me in the mental hospital with Nurse Ratched and McMurphy! That's where I belong.

One flew east, one flew west, one flew in the cuckoo's nest.

JANUARY 31, 2017

Let's discuss the topic of insomnia. I should be treated as a raging insomniac, a zombie wandering the halls at night. I'm an insomniholic, an inventor inventing words. Where does my next bout of spasms take me? Where does my next hate-induced state displace me? What's the displacement of a maniac searching for his grave? I'm ready to cage a ravine and use its darkened depths to fuel my raging pages. My writing unleashes addictive substances that crawl beneath your epidermis. I'm crawling under your skin, poking around in wonder and amazement at the disgusting evidence presented. My words get stuck in your teeth until you poke a toothpick around in there, allowing your saliva to dissolve these carbohydrates. I'm nutritious, a decent value meal for those who can't afford it. You're forever searching in earnest for the next sentence I dispense. It's an eternal handicap, but you don't mind being handicapped because you enjoy the parking privileges. You're a real selfish piece of work, but everybody hates their job. It's no wonder nobody likes you, is it not? I'm popping words out of my mouth like a Pez dispenser. Meanwhile, you morons are still practicing your oxymorons. I hurl herds of beasts of burden. I'm constantly hurting because I've been beaten down like a beast of burden. I carry the burden, the unstoppable force never before hurled. Your mind is trying to keep up with my mental drawings, but it's drawing blanks. I'm twisted like a pretzel, bent out of proportion. I'm a sadistically ballistic bullet speeding through the air, aiming for your heart. I'll smack your Aorta with a horrible noise, then splatter your blood out of the corner of your peripheral vision. As if to top it off, you stubbed your toe and now you're in pain. I'm rubbing it in, loving it. I teeter on the edge, but my life comes full circle. How can that be? I thought circles had no edges. Geometry, where the fuck are you? I thought you were supposed to be a helpful class for me to take, but I was wrong. I've seen your true colors. Your true color is brown because you're a real piece of shit. I obliterate your impervious faces until they're no longer indestructible. I'm a destructive force that will disintegrate any who get in my way. Get out of the way! What are you, stupid? Why in the fuck are you reading these words? Did you think you could take a chance at messing with the best? I'm a champion crowned victor among the grandest of champions. Can't you see me with my crown resting upon my head? It's not made of roses or thorns, despite what you may think. My crown is made of emotions, victory, and intangible objects never before grasped. How can a crown be made of a substance unknown to others? I defy the logic of conventional reasoning, still training my brain to think the same thing as me. I'm dramatic enough that I need some space on stage to release this pent-up hatred. I'm a maniacally unreliable narrator telling an unspeakable story never before spoken. I do the impossible, proving anything is possible. What's that? Was that an oxymoron for you morons to decipher? To you, I say lasso the stars. If anybody tells you that's impossible, brand them with a hot iron and hang them out to dry. They say I have to go big or go home and hit the road. That's why I'm bigger than balls and why I stand taller than most. You're awfully appalling, setting up permanent residence in a death bed. I get fulfilled by filling my stomach with a desirable will. I will spit at will, sitting in my chair, leaning back and yawning as I crush these thoughts. Are you unfamiliar with the success ratio I have ascended? The master is in attendance, in case you unsuccessful folks haven't noticed. But don't worry about not being successful. Keep your head high, your mind straight, and your brain functional. I'm still dysfunctional, but I managed to find astounding advantages in my writing. I was dealt an astronomical disadvantage, and I was pounded into the ground like a line of driving piledrivers. Yet, somehow, I came out of the pandemonium as a lonely man with a bigger conundrum. What was I to do with my screws loose and hanging, dangling off of the cliff as I drive my car beside it? I tried to live a normal life, but I came back empty-handed, demanding compensation for the scratches scratched into the waves of my brain. I realized I can warp the dimension of words into a cyclone of spinning courage. I built brick and mortar on top of the foundation until my mind became an independent store. Your words are an abundance of redundant statements repeated in haste through the form of speaking you call communication. I'm incapable of reaching my mental capacity because my thoughts fancy the act of being magically enchanting, enhancing the spectrum of thought. I feel like I keep repeating the same statements with a different arrangement of letters and words. How many times must I mention that I hate mentioning things? I'll create a conflicting paragraph of paradoxes for you parasites to engorge and dissect. I don't eat much because I'm so full of it, loving every moment my fingers flex their muscles. What was that? Does an imposter dare to posthumously postulate theorems aimed at me? I'm being smart, which is why I'm getting targeted. They say I'm too smart for my own good, but they can't decide what's good for me. I've been on more than enough drugs and medication, but I still can't resist the temptation to write at a manic rate. I'm deciding what's good for myself. I'll punch you in the face twice, but you'll get charged with the hate crime. I'll disassemble an assembly of patient faces. The grenade in my hand is wanting to be thrown again. The pencil I have created is a monstrous atrocity, constantly clinging on to me. I attract all of the atoms because I'm an attractive nucleus. I'm a group of nuclei, spinning electrons like words circling around the inside of my mind. They say to say it, not spray it. I say I'm more likely to do both of these on my quest to be a superstar among other stars. I think you underestimated the underestimation that I'm facing. People always underestimate me, the most enthusiastic disease to plague this world. The expression is hitting two birds with one stone, but I'm hurling a boulder at an entire flock. I'm Optimus Prime running on less sleep than optimal. It's an optical illusion if you ever see I'm losing. I'm really winning, remaining better than most who dare to test me. Why do you think I ace my tests with ease? Still, I'm green with envy, looking like a fucking leprechaun. It's envy that makes me this envious being, you see? I'm green and covered in scales, slithering across the ground like I've been drafted for Slytherin. I'm an envious fiend about to attack my enemies with a series of recurring entries. I'm barely human when I'm fuming, feuding with other people until the collective anger fuses. You're all a bunch of infectious pests pestering the ingenious genius. I'm a diligent paragon, but it's apparent that I'm too arrogant to be deemed a master of paragraphs. I'm just a boring and excited storyteller, telling an ongoing story.

FEBRUARY 3, 2017

Today is my special day. It's my anniversary. Now, you may be thinking about a different type of anniversary, but that's not what I was talking about. Today is the first anniversary of my suicide attempt. It's been a full year since I drove home from that math team meet with death as my intent. Do you remember that occasion? I'd jog your memory, but I'd much prefer to run it straight into the ground. I'm sorry. It's been a long year.

Is it a coincidence that I had a meeting with my psychiatrist today? Some people believe in fate or destiny, but I think it's a happy little coincidence. My life is full of moments like these. Why else do you think ten dollars is a recurring theme in my life? Everything is full of coincidences. Having a psychiatrist appointment on the anniversary of my suicide attempt is rather astonishing. Of all the days in the week, my appointment happened to fall upon today. Isn't that a crazy coincidence?

I talked to my psychiatrist today using my most abysmal attitude. I told him about the side effects of Cipla, my new antidepressant. Lexapro wasn't working for me, and I had to switch. Anyway, I told my psychiatrist about my sleep deprivation, dry mouth, and drowsiness in the morning. For reasons unknown to me, he didn't seem too concerned about these side effects. Last time, with my Lexapro, he was extremely worried. Why wasn't he worried this time? I told him about wanting to fly out of the car while driving, but he didn't seem to care. I also talked about almost smashing the window on the bus ride home from my recent Trivia Team match. He still didn't seem to notice or care. He told me those thoughts can happen to anyone.

My psychiatrist asked if I had ever thought about going into a mental hospital. I told him I thought about it sometimes, which is a lie. I think about how overwhelming things are all the time, and I hope and wish that I will end up in a mental hospital. Why didn't I just tell him that? What the fuck is wrong with me? Of course, of course, I know what you are going to say. I'm bipolar. I understand that argument. But why did I decide not to tell my psychiatrist about that?

After I was done talking to him, he sent me out of the room and invited my dad inside. They spoke alone, without me. That always bothers me. I started fuming in the waiting room, impatiently waiting for the moment they opened the door. I wanted to rip the fucking hair out of my head, and I nearly did. I didn't care if I was bald because being bald means nothing if you're dead. That's right. I wanted to die again. Rejoice! My suicidal thoughts have returned. The saga of darkness and torment continues. Where does one begin to dissect this distorted brain?

Later in the evening, when we were driving home, my dad started discussing the things my psychiatrist had said. Apparently, they are thinking about sending me to a mental hospital, but they're not sure. They're also not sure if my new antidepressant is working or not. Nobody can figure me out because I'm too complex. I'm a one-thousand-piece puzzle itching to be solved, but half of the pieces are missing or torn apart by merciless fingers. I don't know. Perhaps I am exaggerating this tale. Then again, I highly doubt I can exaggerate the facts. I'm going to end up in a mental hospital—another challenge for me to conquer. When everything has been said and done, I think I'm going to turn out as a human being.

I've never been human enough to live.

FEBRUARY 5, 2017

There is no exaggeration present in this next tale. Of course, there are two sides to this story, as remains true for all stories. But I'm here to tell my side of the story. As for the other side, I could care less about it. It doesn't mean anything to me. Why should I care about the opposing argument, which contradicts my own? I don't care.

What happened? Why am I asking you these questions, reader? I have more than enough questions to last a lifetime, if you want to know the truth. I'm not writing to ask questions, though. I'm writing because of something that happened to me, something uncontrollable and unpredictable. Most influential events seem to spawn spontaneously, almost as if they were created out of thin air, or thick air for those of you that are reading this closer to sea level. I'm writing about an event that I was completely unprepared for, which ended up costing me dearly. I paid for my sacrifice by way of tears, anguish, and rage.

I was attempting to do my homework on a Sunday night. Why did I wait until Sunday night to do my homework? Well, I don't exactly enjoy doing homework. Who would? It's an incredibly demeaning task that offers little to no reward. It also happens to be a decisively terrible commodity. Anyway, I procrastinate my homework like any other high school kid. I'm no different than my peers in that aspect. However, I do differ in the manner I procrastinate. While my peers simply procrastinate due to their staggering failures, I procrastinate for a different, better reason. I procrastinate because that's how I survive. I enjoy being behind in life because it gives me a reason to push forward. While that may seem counterintuitive, I believe this method works to my benefit.

While I was attempting, and ultimately failing, to do my homework, I nearly had a mental collapse. Why was I dueling such a disparaging opponent? Why was I being burdened by simple physics calculations? For whatever reason, my mind melted like the Wicked Witch of the West. That's how I felt as I tried to do my homework. I felt like I was having a stroke. I could practically feel half of my face sliding, slipping away from its counterpart. It would be gone forever if I didn't do something. What was I going to do? How did I save this new variant face, dramatically differing from its former self? I'm starting to look different. I'm starting to look like I did months and months ago, before anyone knew about my bipolarity, my depression, or my struggle. I feel like I'm going through metamorphosis, transforming into an impermeable monster.

My dad came downstairs. At first, I paid no attention to him. I was sitting at my computer desk, concentrating on not having a mental breakdown. I knew it was inevitable. I knew there was no turning back if I started crying. I kept telling myself not to cry. If tears started falling, I would be in a heap of irreversible trouble. I must not become a monster of demonstrative proportions. I must remain the same person or else I'll go insane. Don't cry, don't cry, don't cry! The words slapped me, beating me into a drunken stupor. I could hardly function.

There was a basket of clean laundry on the floor. It had been resting there for approximately two hours. Now, I had consciously thought about dumping out the clothes, separating them, and putting my clothes away. But I couldn't bring myself to do it. I didn't have the energy to get out of my chair. That's what depression does to you. With depression, even the simplest tasks become a nightmare. How am I supposed to live like this? How does anyone expect me to function as a proper human? I can't do this. I remember thinking that. I just can't keep doing this.

"What are you doing? Are you going to put this laundry away? It's been sitting here for two hours."

I turned and looked at my dad. I shook my head, then told him no. I wouldn't be putting away any laundry because I couldn't move. Also,

I was doing my homework, which holds priority over a pile of clothes that aren't moving anywhere. But my dad viewed my denial as an act of defiance, a challenge to his authority. He felt his superiority was lacking abundance, and he rose to the challenge.

"Put the laundry away."

Now, here, I was voiced a command. My dad told me to put the laundry away. There is no denying his commands. In this house, he is a kind, loving father, but he is also an oppressive dictator, a king among men.

I made a mistake. I told him no. I couldn't. I can't. I couldn't physically muster the energy to complete this new, overwhelming task. I was still stuck on trying to finish my homework. Mentally, I was collapsing, caving in on myself. I placed my head in my hands and started crying, the tears rolling softly down my cheeks. No! You idiot! You've made another mistake! I know. Trust me, I know. I've made more than enough mistakes in my lifetime.

My dad asked me, once again, to put the laundry away. I just kept shaking my head, completely oblivious to his impatience. My body shook with sobs, rocking itself into a fervorous uproar. I was dying, and I knew it. My dad didn't know this, though. His only thought was that I was disobeying him. I was being a disobedient child, obviously. Was I being disobedient? I think I was just helpless, lost in my fervent search for an answer to my issues.

My dad rushed up to me, grabbed me by the arms, and pulled me out of the computer chair. Now I was standing, facing him and his tremendous anger. I felt like a child. Did I misbehave? Did I step out of line? I don't think so, but my dad thought the opposite. As I've said before, there are two sides to every story. I'm here to tell mine.

We exchanged many words during this time interval, and my anger started to heat up, as well. It was a battle of raw emotion, a waging war between two unfriendly forces. I'm getting into battles over baskets of laundry. What's the point of it all? Why should I fight a pointless battle? I started swearing at my dad.

"What the fuck is your problem?" I asked him. In response, he grabbed me by the neck, pushed me into my room, and slammed me onto the bed.

"What the fuck is my problem?" he asked, probably in disbelief. "Don't swear at me, that's my problem!"

He was standing over me, yelling at me as he grasped my throat. Then, he told me he loved me. He told me he loved me as he had his hand around my neck. If that's love, then I don't want to be loved.

"I love you, but you have issues! You can't do whatever you want just because you have problems! You're not exempt from doing things! You don't have the opportunity to swear at me!"

I looked up at him and I saw a boiling, burning rage in his eyes. What kind of love is that? I guess it's a man's love for another man, a compassionate love among two similar men. Yet, he's still insisting that I am susceptible to my issues. Are you fucking kidding me? Maybe he's just another issue for me to deal with. Maybe he's the cause of most of my issues. Maybe he doesn't know what he's talking about. Maybe he's heard this before from his own father. Maybe he's repeating his father's words to me. I don't know.

As my dad was yelling and spitting all over me from the force he was exerting, my mom hurried down the stairs and barged into my room. I was amazed at how fast my mom entered the room, considering her back has been bothering her lately.

"Look at his neck! Get your hands off of him!" she yelled.

My dad let go of me and I crumpled onto my bed, smacking my head against a scattered pile of laundry. I just kept crying, putting my head into the clothes. I was sobbing uncontrollably. My grief was inconsolable. No amount of comfort or relief could alleviate the pain that I have accumulated in my lifetime. This moment, after a skirmish with my dad, was no different than the hundreds of other horrific moments in my life.

After my dad left the room, my brother, who was standing witness to this entire ordeal, started crying. My mom went to comfort him before me. I wasn't upset about this because I knew it would take much more effort to make me stop crying. The damage was already done. All of it happened so quick. My mind could hardly register what had happened. Regardless, it happened. Everything happened, and whether or not my mind comprehends this information is irrelevant. This memory is irreplaceable, forever solidified into the inferno of my mind.

Then, later in the evening, my dad came back downstairs and stared at me. He stood there for a few seconds, looking at me. How could he do such a terrible thing to me and then casually gaze at me in the same day? Did he feel no remorse for his actions? Did he feel justified in his brutality and anger? How could he beat up on a poor and defenseless soul such as I? I don't know. I just don't know anything. I should be in a mental hospital, and yet I'm being thrown around like a ragdoll because I'm an insufferable bastard who is suffering beyond compare. How do you lecture a broken mind? How do you confide your words into a tortured body such as mine? Those are questions that I'd prefer be left unanswered. The truth scars worse than lies.

We talked about sending me to a mental hospital, but it didn't matter to me. At this point, nothing matters except my girlfriend and my journal. I want everything else to disappear in a billowing cloud of smoke. Smoke touches everything.

I was having such a good relationship with my dad, but now it's been broken. Once again, I am left to fend for myself in this large, scary world. I feel like I'm having a relapse, reverting back to my old form. The disastrously depressed Justin has returned. The Descendant of Darkness seizes his worthy throne once more!

I'm so scared of my dad, once again. It's just like it was before. It's exactly how it was before my medication, before my bipolar diagnosis, before my journals, and before my depression. The world has returned to darkness. Some people might say the darkness has always been a recurring force that ceaselessly torments me. Some people think there is no darkness at all and that I'm just casually making up these words for the sake of publicity. But I know better.

The darkness never left.

FEBRUARY 9, 2017

I was admitted into a mental hospital today. Now, here is the real question. Do you want to know what happened? I'll tell you.

I'm locked without the cage, admitted into a mental hospital. Teething anger, I'm foaming from the mouth, lost in a delirious rage. I'm venting with these words, dispensing sentences from the tip of my pencil. They probably wouldn't let me have a pen in the fear that I'd stab myself again and again. When does this nightmare end? I'm an evolutionary artist, a man trapped by the illusions presented in his own paintings. I'm an ill and tempered patient, bound and gagged by my own statements. I rehearsed my audition to get the part of a mental incarceration. The hospital arrested me, testing my ability to duel with a pen. What am I even saying? I only have a pencil left, but the lead is deteriorating fast as my hand pushes faster. These nurses will need a new set of patience by the time I'm finished contemplating thoughts never before sought. Wait! Did I say pencil lead? I meant I'm dealing round after round of graphite. I'm stalling my life, brawling with my dad and acting as if nothing happened. Interjection! I must admit to the fact that something most certainly did happen. Let's take a peek into the mind of a familiar familial crime, shall we? One second, I need to sharpen my pencil. I'm ruthless, wearing apparel that tells you I'm barely bearable. I'm a mountainous bear up on a cliff, and towering over the valley like a demented monster. I frequently frequent this cliff, constantly wondering if I should dare to take the leap. It's not a leap of faith. I'm an atheist, using religion as an alias. I'm using it as a scapegoat, but I can't escape a goat with razor horns. I'm spraying Agent Orange like a can of Febreze. I feel a brief and instant breeze, but I'm somehow suffering from heat stroke. If I'm stuck in this stroke, why am I still choking? These therapists have too much arrogance to solve my proposed equation. A broken mind and confused emotions equals what? It equals me, a breathing and seemingly lifeless freak. How do you soothe the fucking heat? I possess an aura, an energy profoundly oral through the use of words. I'm thermal, blowing up in your face like an explosion. You can start the fire, but I'll steal the fucking heat. I'll be the passive action amidst a group of warring factions. You'll be the falling action, an act that most insist is left forgotten. I'm the rising, climbing, and climactic action packed into an anticlimactic crash. I say I'm a skyrocket, but is that opposed to a ground rocket? I'm stuck in the ground, laboring beneath the struggle. I don't beat around the bush. I'll beat that fucking bush until it's reduced to needles. That's raw, untamed rage sprouting up from out of the page. I'm wearing deodorant spray so you can sense my rage. It's a natural scent that confuses you as I inflict more pain. This is what it's like when you're going insane. Luckily, my paper is patiently awaiting the next words to be dumped onto the page.

I could write an entire story about my first day at a behavioral health facility, which is fancy talk for a mental hospital. I could spend the time to jot down every crucial moment of my unstable, hectic day. I could talk about how anxious I was during the one hour drive going there. I could discuss and describe the horror of sitting in the waiting room, nervously tapping my feet and hands. I could write about the kid named Tim who was admitted on the same day. I could describe how he taught me a new mindfulness exercise involving my hands. I could analyze every detail of how a man gave me a psychological evaluation. I could tell you about how the man marked me down as having experienced sexual and childhood abuse. I could share how I was sexually abused years and years ago. I could describe the walls and the flooring and the intricate scenery I was presented. I could sit here, calm and patient, and jot words about how anxious and fidgety I was during those few tense moments when my mom departed. I could tell you about how my mom left me at this forsaken place. I could write about how my anxiety skyrocketed upon my desertion in this vast, foreign wasteland. I could introduce my roommate, Elijah, as a new character in my intricate story. I could expand upon this topic and go into more detail. I could write about Antonio, the boy across the hall whose arms are covered in cuts from self-injuries. I could weave a tale examining my first group discussion. I could record all of the patients from the hospital as new characters. I could write about the doctors and nurses and how they tended to my every request. I could spend hours describing my first day. I could talk about this day forever. But I think I've done enough talking.

This story is at its end.

For I on ceaseless words hath fed, and sunk the ship of Paradise. I'm not Kubla Khan, but this is my ending. My name isn't Ozymandias, but I'm a King of Kings. I may not be as strong as a statue, but even the Colossus of Rhodes couldn't stand forever. My body, soft as Achilles' mortal heel, pales in comparison to my high and mighty words. The Library of Alexandria's knowledge burned fiercely and profusely while my knowledge slyly smiles. Athens is a city divulged in ruins, and yet my head is a bustling metro converging upon a populous expanse. Salem's witches bore illicit lives, although my own thoughts would receive my corpse is burned at the stake, for good measure. The limestone coating that covered the Great Pyramid of Giza failed the test of time, and I, a mere human occupying a hollow shell, suffer more than erosion and yet I am still held together. Spartans wouldn't be capable of living from my perspective; muscles, weapons, and physicality become meaningless in an imagination as vivid as psychedelics. Aristotle, Socrates, and Plato are hallucinating if they believe their superior teachings, whimsical words of wisdom, and collective intellect could prohibit my self-destruction. An entire system of the Paris Catacombs doesn't seem frightening when competed against my smoking-lung-tar-black thoughts. Daedalus and his labyrinth are hardly unnerving, considering my mind is an incomprehensibly vast void of series upon series of labyrinths. Stephen King's horror stories are as ridiculous as

Child's Play, and my life represents the nonfiction category of the horror and gore section. Daedalus returns with Icarus, both donned waxen wings, and threatens Icarus and I. His feeble attempt at controlling me results in failure. Despite his disapproving gaze, I slowly convince Icarus to fly higher, higher, until his palms hold the burning sun. His wings melt, he falls to his impending doom, and I remain unscathed. Daedalus may be livid with me, but I shake off his trivial, revenge-stricken, grief-stained threats and accusations. Shall I compare thee to a fucking waste? Shakespeare's iambics run rampant across a pentameter, but his sonnets still can barely grasp my attention. My mind craves hypervigilance, considering I must remain more vigilant than the seven dwarves grouped in a protective circle. Straight lunatic, call me Renfield, reversing fortunes and taking a bite out of Dracula. I'm Big and Bad, not a wolf, but I've slaughtered more than Three Little Pigs. My life is an Olympic trial, stabbing javelins up people's asses like Vlad the Impaler. You may adore people like Elvis Presley, but he died on the toilet and I still couldn't give a shit. I'd storm the Bastille only to transfer myself to the Gulag. My words are as stigmatized as Stalin and Hitler sucking one another's dicks. Even though I'm alone, I'd still fight an army of vikings. Tibetan monks could dedicate their lives to my thoughts, but they still wouldn't understand me. The Pope's royal decree is as demented as me bombing Normandy. I enjoy provoking controversy, so I'll call the reign of ISIS a holy crusade for peace. Before your thoughts turn out of whack, I'll explain myself. Define crusade, then remember Islam claims to be a religion of peace. Showing solidarity is an act of common error, you see? Twist my words and I'll snap your neck. I'll give Death my middle finger, covered in Yankee Doodle's Hershey chocolate. Cloaks don't fit my skeletal frame, but Death is still afraid of me. I asked Him if he's still thinking about taking me, and I sadly slumped at His reply.

Quoth the Raven, "Nevermore."

Here, I present the ending of my journal, and the completion of my voyage to Paradise. Do you know that feeling when you accidentally bump into an old friend you had a fallout with? Or maybe a former lover whom you hold an unbudging grudge for, even though the relationship ended healthily? If you've ever experienced that, or a similar predicament, you know how uncomfortably awkward those few, tense moments can be. That's how I feel right now as I write, closing the door on exhaustion as I near the finish line of this hectic race.

My original plan was to commit suicide upon the completion of this journal. Dramatic, right? Classic ending, too predictable to conclude such an awe-inspiring, controversy-sparking story. My life is a Greek tragedy, or any Shakespearean play, and now I'm Hercules prepared to cross the River Styx. Hades, why are you blocking me out? Truth is, I'm not going to kill myself yet, if at all. Yes, I know what you're thinking.

"Spoiler alert? Come on, Justin, why did you spoil my appetite for death?"

What are you criticizing me for? I'm not even the same person I was eight disastrous months ago. Do you want proof? Take a look at my handwriting eight months ago and compare it to now. I press down on the paper so hard that I usually end up breaking my pencil. Is that proof enough for you persistent assholes? Listen, I just broke the tip of my pencil writing that last sentence.

Why didn't I provide the date for this entry? Dates don't mean shit to you, do they? I use dates as a torture device, in case you somehow didn't know that already. I have some of these horrific dates memorized. They are seared into my brain for eternity, along with the events that went with them.

This journal was the most important piece of my life for the past year, and even a few months more. Whenever I was upset, worried, or depressed, I knew I had my journal. Actually, this journal saved my life on at least one occasion. Driving home from a math team competition in which I didn't score a single point, I nearly succumbed to suicide. Drifting into the other lane, slowly edging the last few inches of the pavement, I remembered my journal. How could I die without telling my side of the story? Quickly realizing my nearly fatal mistake, I wasted no time returning to my lane. I was three minutes from home. I'd only had my license for three months, and I knew my crash would have been labeled an accident caused by inexperience and speeding. That happened on February 3rd, 2016. That moment was among the scariest split seconds I have ever experienced. Within seconds, I made the decision to end my life, and it only took a few more seconds to save my life. You know, I drive past that same spot twice a day, coming to and from school. It easily could have been my death site if I didn't have this journal.

Being honest with myself, this journal wasn't perfect. I dislike certain entries, specifically my earlier entries, but I promised myself I wouldn't censor my writing. My main priority for this journal: accurately convey my thoughts, emotions, and memories. Would it be narcissistic to say I believe I've demolished my goal? I think I've earned the right to claim I'm proud of this journal. Personally, this journal is a masterpiece, a contemporary work of literature. Whether anyone else dislikes the content of this journal is irrelevant. Quite frankly, I might be the only person who finds serenity and solitude by reading through this journal. But, hey, maybe someone else enjoys my style. Even if nobody ever reads these words, besides myself, I'll continue to appreciate my own capabilities. I've never completed a task as mentally taxing or physically enduring as this journal. I'm never short of story ideas, but none of my stories last longer than a few egregious pages. This journal is a flawless gem among a dismal sea of repeated disappointment.

If I turn my head to look behind, I'll still be facing ahead. Seriously, think about it. Literally, if you turn your head, your body is still positioned forward. I thought that was interesting, and then I remembered what my journal is. I always have the option to skim through this intricately detailed story, or any of the memories I possess, but the presentation of this choice offers little consolation. Every time I turn that page, even if I'm reading or writing about a distant memory, I'm still moving ahead, both literally and figuratively. I may be too focused on my past, but that's behind me. Not too intent on my future, but I'm already facing that direction anyway. Future moves me forward, despite my temper tantrum urging to revive the past. Soon enough, this journal is Jurassic, my words have fossilized, and my bones are ossified. I'll be a dinosaur, drifting aimlessly until the next extinction. My neck may be as long as a Brontosaurus, and, tempting as it seems, I resist any urges to crane my neck toward the meteor-sized-crater behind me. Why retreat to certain death if I spy a glint of hope, albeit brief? Better to try and fail than fail without trying. Right? Learn from your mistakes, right? No. As I've learned, mistakes are an opportunity for ridicule at your own expense. Theme of my life, I guess.

As I've sullenly accomplished before, I translate my thoughts onto an eagerly awaiting paper. Eternal prisoner of these burdened lines, I step forward, one memory in front of the other, one foot at a time, awaiting unseen horizons. Eyes drawn and receding, hair thinning, muscles deteriorating, I hobble onward, newly created thought bubbles popping spontaneously. There, above the chasm of torment, I nod my head, provoking the monsters lurking within. Turning without a word, I sheath the graphite daggers I've been known to resemble. Indeed, it is a bold and heroic gesture for someone so untamed and unpredictable. The wounded literary warrior presents his Houdini-esque finale.

Alone, this survivor crosses the threshold of suffering, leaving in his wake the decimated ruins of his former self.

Printed in the United States
By Bookmasters